THE LOVECRAFT ANNUAL

Edited by S. T. Joshi

Contents

Abbreviations used in the text and notes:

AT	*The Ancient Track* (Hippocampus Press, 2013)
CE	*Collected Essays* (Hippocampus Press, 2004–06; 5 vols.)
CF	*Collected Fiction* (Hippocampus Press, 2015–17; 4 vols.)
IAP	*I Am Providence: The Life and Times of H. P. Lovecraft* (Hippocampus Press, 2010; 2013 [paper])
LL	*Lovecraft's Library: A Catalogue,* 4th rev. ed. (Hippocampus Press, 2017)
SL	*Selected Letters* (Arkham House, 1965–76; 5 vols.)

Cover illustration by Allen Koszowski. Hippocampus Press logo designed by Anastasia Damianakos. Cover design by Barbara Briggs Silbert.

Lovecraft Annual is published once a year, in Fall. Articles and letters should be sent to the editor, S. T. Joshi, ℅ Hippocampus Press, and must be accompanied by a self-addressed stamped envelope if return is desired. All reviews are assigned. Literary rights for articles and reviews will reside with *Lovecraft Annual* for one year after publication, whereupon they will revert to their respective authors. Payment is in contributor's copies.

ISSN 1935-6102
ISBN 978-1-61498-393-4

A Tale of Two Providences: Topographical Realism in "The Haunter of the Dark"

Dylan Henderson

Whenever H. P. Lovecraft wrote to one of his correspondents about "The Haunter of the Dark," he almost always mentioned that he had assigned his own home to the protagonist, Robert Blake. Thus, the fifth and sixth paragraphs of that story, which describe Blake's residence atop College Hill, also describe 66 College Street, where Lovecraft and his aunt Annie E. P. Gamwell had lived since 1933. If the jocular tone of these letters is any clue, Lovecraft regarded the inclusion of his own home as something of an in-joke, an Easter egg, which he thought would amuse his many friends and correspondents. In a letter to Clark Ashton Smith, for instance, written the day after Lovecraft had finished the story, he touched upon his use of setting, noting with characteristic modesty that "the abode of the victim is #66—indeed, I've described the place a bit" (*Dawnward Spire* 622). Similar passages appear in other letters, but Lovecraft never explains *why* he decided to incorporate 66 College Street into the story, nor does he discuss *how* it affects the narrative. In a letter to Robert Bloch—who is, ostensibly, Blake's real-world counterpart—Lovecraft simply wrote, "as an abode, I've lent you good old 66—as you may deduce from the description" (*Letters to Bloch* 160).

Lovecraft's nonchalance encourages readers not to pry too deeply into his use of setting, and as a result, many scholars have regarded it as little more than a curious and amusing footnote to a story that is, in turn, something of a joke between Lovecraft and Bloch, who had employed his mentor as a character in "The Shambler from the Stars." In the eyes of many, the tale belongs to the middle ranks of Lovecraft's fiction, and even S. T. Joshi, who considers it "an extremely well-executed and suspenseful tale of supernatural horror," concedes that the story "does not involve any grand philosophical principles" (*IAP* 960). I would agree, of course, that "The Haunter of the Dark" never reaches the heights achieved by, say, "The Call of Cthulhu" or "The Colour out of Space," but I would also argue that, if not impressively philosophical, the story *is* deeply personal. To understand why, we must first reexamine Lovecraft's decision in November 1935 to incorporate 66 College Street into his last original work of fiction—a decision that is far odder than it might initially seem.

After all, Lovecraft's approach to setting had changed dramatically since he completed *The Case of Charles Dexter Ward* in early 1927. That story clearly reflects the joy Lovecraft felt when, after living in New York City for two years, he returned home to Providence in the spring of 1926. His love of his hometown, which he had missed so dearly for so long, inspired him to lovingly reconstruct the city on the printed page, and some of the longest and most beautiful descriptions in his entire oeuvre appear in chapter 2. With such an auspicious start, Lovecraft could have continued in this vein—perhaps, in time, becoming a conventional regional writer like August Derleth— but instead he rejected the work, believing that his passion for the city and its colonial history had unbalanced the narrative. Writing to R. H. Barlow in March 1934, he famously dismissed the novella as a "cumbrous, creaking bit of self-conscious anti-quarianism," which he had "expunged [. . .] from my list of acknowledged writings" (*O Fortunate Floridian* 120).

Dissatisfied with his use of Providence and its history, Lovecraft started to explore other settings. Not counting the works he revised for Adolphe de Castro and Zealia Bishop, Lovecraft's next three stories all take place in rural locales he knew well, though not as well as Providence: "The Colour out of Space" in central Massachusetts, "The Dunwich Horror" in north-central

Massachusetts, and "The Whisperer in Darkness" in southeastern Vermont. The first two, of course, occur near or in imaginary places (Arkham and Dunwich), but that hardly matters: in both stories Lovecraft is describing a rural countryside that he has seen with his own eyes. After "The Whisperer in Darkness," however, which Lovecraft completed in the fall of 1930, he began to experiment with a variety of landscapes. Abandoning the real and the familiar, attributes that had defined his use of setting since he moved to New York in 1924, Lovecraft started to place his tales in either exotic or imaginary locales, places he had not been and could not go.[1] Hence *At the Mountains of Madness* takes place in Antarctica, "The Shadow over Innsmouth" in a fictional seaport, "The Dreams in the Witch House" and "The Thing on the Doorstep" in Arkham, and "The Shadow out of Time" partly in Arkham and partly in the Australian outback. From an author's perspective, Lovecraft's increasing reliance on Arkham makes sense: being completely imaginary, it released him from the restraints that reality imposes on writers and gave him free rein to invent details, whether historical or geographical, when and if he needed them. Thus, Lovecraft's decision in late 1935 to use Providence as the setting for "The Haunter of the Dark" reversed a trend in his writing nearly a decade long and presented him with a challenge—how to write about his love for the city—that he had, in his own mind, failed to overcome nine years before.

Even more curious is the actual description of 66 College Street and its environs, which introduces the reader to College Hill. Though lengthy, the first half is worth quoting in full:

> Young Blake returned to Providence in the winter of 1934–5, taking the upper floor of a venerable dwelling in a grassy court off College Street—on the crest of the great eastward hill near

---

1. Prior to 1924, HPL had occasionally used the New England landscape in his fiction—sometimes quite effectively—as in "The Picture in the House" and "The Festival." However, "The Shunned House" (completed in the fall of 1924) marks a turning point: from then on, detailed, finely drawn settings became a major component of HPL's approach to weird fiction.

the Brown University campus and behind the marble John Hay
Library. It was a cosy and fascinating place, in a little garden oasis of village-like antiquity where huge, friendly cats sunned
themselves atop a convenient shed. The square Georgian house
had a monitor roof, classic doorway with fan carving, small-
paned windows, and all the other earmarks of early nineteenth-
century workmanship. Inside were six-panelled doors, wide
floor-boards, a curving colonial staircase, white Adam-period
mantels, and a rear set of rooms three steps below the general
level. (CF 3.453)

How different this is from Lovecraft's other descriptions! With
the notable exception of *The Case of Charles Dexter Ward,* Lovecraft's other major works, specifically those that incorporate
lengthy descriptions of the landscape, use the setting to usher
the reader into a Gothic environment laden with fear. Consider,
for instance, "The Colour out of Space" or "The Dunwich Horror." Much like Edgar Allan Poe's "The Fall of the House of
Usher," which famously opens on a "dull, dark, and soundless
day in the autumn of the year" with a journey through "a singularly dreary tract of country" (317), these stories begin by placing the reader in a "lonely and curious country," thereby
establishing, from the first, a tone of unrelenting gloom (CF
2.417–18). The setting's role in these narratives, in other words,
is to contribute to Poe's unity of effect, what Lovecraft approvingly called "the maintenance of a single mood and achievement
of a single impression" (*Supernatural* 56).

And yet, the lovely description quoted above disrupts the
story's somber mood and creates a very different impression.
Much like E. F. Benson's weird fiction, which often opens with a
description of the English countryside, it introduces the reader
to a peaceful, homely world, a "cosy and fascinating place, in a
little garden oasis of village-like antiquity." This is not a world to
be feared, as the narrator of "The Colour out of Space" instinctively fears the region west of Arkham, but a world to be loved,
cherished, and protected. What is especially odd—and of crucial
importance—is that this description, this paean to 66 College
Street and the hill on which it stands, is not provided by Blake,

who lives there, but by the supposedly objective and seemingly neutral third-person narrator, who is retelling Blake's story with the help of his diary. Now, it would not be surprising if Blake were enthralled with his new home, but why does the narrator, who claims to be "dispassionately" summarizing recent events (CF 3.453), devote so much time to the appearance of the house and its surrounding neighborhood? One could argue that the narrator is merely documenting Blake's enthusiasm—if Blake showed any, but he does not: from the beginning his focus is outward, away from College Hill.

Is this description then, which has no bearing on the plot, a flaw in an otherwise carefully constructed tale? Is Lovecraft, unable to repress his enthusiasm over a house in which he had lived since 1933, indulging himself at the expense of his readers, as he did when writing *The Case of Charles Dexter Ward*? Or is Lovecraft (who, shortly after writing "The Haunter of the Dark," told E. Hoffmann Price that he would "willingly starve" before he would conform to pulpish convention) marring his own work for the sake of an unfunny joke (*Letters to E. Hoffmann Price* 214)? If not, what purpose does this setting serve? How, in other words, does it change the story or affect how readers interpret it? I would argue that, far from being an eccentric but meaningless digression that adds nothing to the story, Lovecraft's incorporation of 66 College Street encourages readers to approach "The Haunter of the Dark" biographically—as a retelling of one of the pivotal moments in Lovecraft's life. Approached in this way, "The Haunter of the Dark" is not just a minor tale or the last of Lovecraft's major works, but a poignant, insightful look back at the author's troubled life and his relationship with the two cities that played so great a role in it.

Many readers have, quite understandably, thought of Blake as Bloch—and nothing more. Bloch himself, having been told that he was the protagonist by Lovecraft, assumed that his mentor had based Blake on him, an honor he considered "the high spot of my life to date" (26). Indeed, all the external evidence supports such a reading: Lovecraft dedicated the story to Bloch; in his letters he labeled it a sequel to "The Shambler from the

Stars"; and he told everyone that he was killing off *Bloch* in the story. And yet, though intuitive, such a reading quickly runs into problems. As John D. Haefele has shown, there is surprisingly little continuity between the two stories. Aside from a single sentence in the second paragraph ("his earlier stay in the city—a visit to a strange old man as deeply given to occult and forbidden lore as he—had ended amidst death and flame, and it must have been some morbid instinct which drew him back from his home in Milwaukee" [CF 3.452]), Lovecraft makes no mention of the previous story, nor does Blake, who is an expert in the occult, resemble Bloch's protagonist, who is a novice (CF 3.452). Haefele hypothesizes that Lovecraft, having conceived of the story much earlier, passed it off as a sequel in a gentlemanly attempt to repay Bloch, whose story did not influence "The Haunter of the Dark" in any meaningful way. If that is so, I suspect the sentence quoted above is a clue. Noticeably out of place and slightly hyperbolic, it introduces a supernatural element far too soon in the narrative, a mistake Lovecraft is not known to make. In any case, Lovecraft himself admitted to Henry Kuttner, who had evidently noticed how little the two stories share, that "my "Haunter" is hardly a real sequel to Bloch's "Shambler"" (*Letters to C. L. Moore* 234).

By placing Blake in Lovecraft's own home, where he works in Lovecraft's study and sits before Lovecraft's window, the author encourages us to think of Blake, not as a stand-in for Bloch, but as the last in a long line of thinly disguised substitutes for Lovecraft. After all, despite his name (which Lovecraft has, characteristically, anglicized), Blake closely resembles his creator, a fact that has not gone unnoticed. Peter Cannon goes so far as to call him "the most Lovecraft-like of later protagonists, especially as measured by his ecstatic response to the westward view from his window" (120). As Cannon suggests, both men share a fascination—if not an obsession—with a very specific scene: an urban landscape viewed at sunset. Five years before he wrote "The Haunter of the Dark," Lovecraft told August Derleth that these scenes, which imparted to him "vague impressions of adventurous expectancy coupled with elusive memory," formed such an important part of his emotional and imaginative makeup that he considered them among his reasons for living (*Essential Solitude* 302).

Blake, it seems, feels much the same way: he has, as far as the reader knows, no friends or family, only a "few local acquaintances," and very early on in the story, his other interests (specifically his fiction and his artwork) disappear from the narrative (*CF* 3.454). He is left alone at his desk, gazing "dreamily off at the outspread west," a view that, for the reader, defines him (*CF* 3.454). Consequently, Blake's life "lies not among *people* but among *scenes*—[his] local affections," as Lovecraft might say, "are not personal, but topographical & architectural" (*Letters to Family* 583). Both men exist, first and foremost, as Emersonian eyeballs, motivated by an irrepressible desire to *see*. In that sense, Blake's determination to explore Federal Hill and locate the church he has seen through his window recalls Lovecraft's years in New York, during which he, wanting to see everything that city had to offer, systematically explored as many art museums, historic buildings, colonial neighborhoods, and neighboring towns as he could locate, in the process displaying an enthusiasm for aesthetic experiences that stunned his friends.

If these similarities were not enough, Blake's list of recently completed stories ("The Burrower Beneath," "The Stairs in the Crypt," "Shaggai," "In the Vale of Pnath," and "The Feaster from the Stars") provides another hint, for their titles invoke the Gothic and Dunsanian stories that Lovecraft himself wrote in the early 1920s, the sole exception being "The Feaster from the Stars," which obviously alludes to Bloch's tale (*CF* 3.454). And yet, if Blake is modeled on Lovecraft, which Lovecraft is he? The Lovecraft of 1924 (the year he married Sonia H. Greene and moved to New York) was not the Lovecraft of 1925, who felt like "screaming in sheer desperation & pounding the walls & floor in a frenzied clamour to be waked up out of the nightmare of 'reality,' to my own room in Providence" (*Letters to Family* 339), nor is he the Lovecraft of 1926, who, in W. Paul Cook's words, "had been tried in the fire and came out pure gold" (43). If we read Blake's experience metaphorically, then the character we meet at the beginning of the story is not just a generic avatar of Lovecraft, but a depiction of the author at a very specific point in his life: he is Lovecraft just prior to New York.

When the story begins, Blake is at a crossroads in his life, much as Lovecraft was in 1924, prior to his marriage in March. After a burst of creativity, which produces the aforementioned stories as well as seven paintings, Blake finds his work stalled: "In the spring a deep restlessness gripped Blake. He had begun his long-planned novel—based on a supposed survival of the witch-cult in Maine—but was strangely unable to make progress with it" (CF 3.455). That is actually the *last* reference to Blake's fiction—an indication that, after that point, he is all but unable to work. In 1924 Lovecraft faced a similar predicament. Two years earlier he had tried to write a novel, but he soon gave up: the fragment we have, "Azathoth," is less than 500 words (Burleson 133). A year later, in 1923, the first issue of *Weird Tales* appeared on the newsstands, its initial editor, Edwin Baird, providing Lovecraft with the most stable market for his work he would ever have, but by early 1924 it was ailing. To make matters worse, the surge of enthusiasm that had followed Lovecraft's discovery of Lord Dunsany in 1919—which Lovecraft claimed "gave an immense impetus to my writing; perhaps the greatest it has ever had" (*Dawnward Spire* 56)—had largely dissipated: not counting his collaborative work, Lovecraft completed ten stories in 1920, eight in 1921, five in 1922, and three in 1923. In 1924, he only completed two.

As an author, Lovecraft was struggling to find his niche.[2] Dunsany's later works displeased him, and yet his imitations of Dunsany's early works were equally unsatisfactory. In time, Lovecraft would see the problem: untethered from reality, his "'Dunsany' pieces," as he called them (*Letters to Elizabeth Toldridge* 38), bombard the reader with outré occurrences that

---

2. In his essay "Some Notes on a Nonentity," HPL himself dismisses much of his early work as imitative and extravagant: "My stories of the 1920 period reflect a good deal of my two chief models, Poe and Dunsany, and are in general too strongly inclined to extravagance and overcolouring to be of much serious literary value" (CE 5.210). And yet, one would not wish to be without "Dagon," "The Picture in the House," or "The Rats in the Walls."

are more random than they are weird and, as such, do not reso-
nate with the reader. As Joshi notes while discussing *The
Dream-Quest of Unknown Kadath*, the longest and most ambitious of Lovecraft's Dunsanian tales: "the various fantastic creatures Carter meets along his journey—zoogs, gugs, ghasts,
ghouls, moonbeasts—touch no chord in us: they are not meant
to. They are all very charming, in that 'Dresden-china' way
Lovecraft mistook Dunsany to be; but they amount to nothing
because they do not correspond to anything in our memories
and dreams" (*IAP* 660). By 1926, the year Lovecraft returned to
Providence and started *The Dream-Quest of Unknown Kadath*,
he understood that, and the works that followed ("The Colour
out of Space" in 1927, "The Dunwich Horror" in 1928, and
"The Whisperer in Darkness" in 1930) reach a higher level of
intensity than most of his previous works precisely because they
are anchored in a very real world. In 1924, however, Lovecraft
had no solution, no clear way forward, as his declining output
and his abortive attempts at experimentation show.3 In need of
a change, Lovecraft found himself, as he would later
acknowledge, falling under a spell, hypnotized by the new and
the unknown, by an urban landscape viewed at a distance, by
his first glimpse of New York City: "It was a mystical sight in the
gold sun of late afternoon; a dream-thing of faint grey, outlined
against a sky of faint grey smoke. City and sky were so alike that
one could hardly be sure that there was a city—that the fancied
towers and pinnacles were not the merest illusions" (*Letters to
Maurice W. Moe* 84).

In much the same way, Federal Hill beckons to Blake:

At sunset he would often sit at his desk and gaze dreamily off at
the outspread west—the dark towers of Memorial Hall just below, the Georgian court-house belfry, the lofty pinnacles of the

3. In 1925 and 1926, HPL began a series of, for him, radical experiments in
setting ("He," "The Horror at Red Hook," and "Cool Air") as well as voice
("Pickman's Model"). Other stories ("The Silver Key" and "The Strange High
House in the Mist") would continue to tinker with the model presented by
Lord Dunsany. Although none of these attempts are to be despised, in retro-
spect only one, "The Call of Cthulhu," would be wholly successful.

downtown section, and that shimmering, spire-crowned mound in the distance whose unknown streets and labyrinthine gables so potently provoked his fancy. From his few local acquaintances he learned that the far-off slope was a vast Italian quarter, though most of the houses were remnants of older Yankee and Irish days. Now and then he would train his field-glasses on that spectral, unreachable world beyond the curling smoke; picking out individual roofs and chimneys and steeples, and speculating upon the bizarre and curious mysteries they might house. Even with optical aid Federal Hill seemed somehow alien, half fabulous, and linked to the unreal, intangible marvels of Blake's own tales and pictures. (CF 3.454)

Blake, like Lovecraft in 1922, cannot be sure that the "roofs and chimneys and steeples" of Federal Hill—analogous to the "towers and pinnacles" of Manhattan—are real, are anything more substantial than the "merest illusions." Seeing the quarter as if through thick glass, his vision distorted by the smoke and the dusk, Blake thinks he sees, or convinces himself that he sees, the real-world embodiment of his own art. Onto the "unknown streets and labyrinthine gables" of Federal Hill, Blake grafts his own vision, his dreams of Pnath, Shaggai, and "profoundly alien, non-terrestrial landscapes" (CF 3.454). Of course, one could argue that, from the start of the story, the Haunter is trying to hypnotize Blake, but why is he, out of all the residents of Providence, so susceptible to its spell? Blake, it seems, suffers from a sort of hyperopia: blind to the charms of College Hill, he looks outward, to the west, past "the dark towers of Memorial Hall," past the "Georgian court-house belfry," past the "lofty pinnacles of the downtown section," to the cluster of gables, chimneys, and spires that is *nothing more than the mirror image of his own College Hill—seen from a distance, at sunset.* So convinced is Blake, who believes he has found his dreamworld in reality, that nothing can turn his eyes back to the glories of his own home, which he has so quickly forgotten: "When the delicate leaves came out on the garden boughs the world was filled with a new beauty, but Blake's restlessness was merely increased" (CF 3.455). And so, forgetting about his unfinished work and leaving behind his once-beloved home "in a little garden oasis of village-like antiquity," a place he has yet to mine for inspiration, Blake acts on a whim and sets out for a mirage. Reading this, how can we not think of Lovecraft, who in March 1924 traded Providence, the place that, as he would later realize, had shaped him from birth onwards, for New York City, a place he had seen, but did not fully understand?

And, exactly like New York, the hill Blake has seen through the evening mists is neither "unreal" nor "intangible." Indeed, as both men learn, the "dream-thing of faint grey" on which they have been projecting their fantasies is all too real:

> Plodding through the endless downtown streets and the bleak, decayed squares beyond, he came finally upon the ascending avenue of century-worn steps, sagging Doric porches, and blear-paned cupolas which he felt must lead up to the long-known, unreachable world beyond the mists. There were dingy blue-and-white street signs which meant nothing to him, and presently he noted the strange, dark faces of the drifting crowds, and the foreign signs over curious shops in brown, decade-weathered buildings. (CF 3.455)

This is not a "smoke-wreathed world of dream" (CF 3.455) or a Dunsanian fantasy, but a twentieth-century ghetto—its features "bleak," "decayed," "century-worn," "dingy," "strange," and "foreign." At this moment, as Blake wanders through the streets of Federal Hill, alone and disoriented, lost in the "bewildering mazes of brooding brown alleys" (CF 3.456), he is Lovecraft in the summer of 1925. By that time, the appeal of New York had faded, and Lovecraft was seeing, with open eyes, the city as it was—as opposed to the city as he had imagined it to be. As Lovecraft writes in "He," which so poignantly fictionalizes this experience:

> Garish daylight shewed only squalor and alienage and the noxious elephantiasis of climbing, spreading stone where the moon had hinted of loveliness and elder magic; and the throngs of people that seethed through the flume-like streets were squat, swarthy strangers with hardened faces and narrow eyes, shrewd

strangers without dreams and without kinship to the scenes
about them, who could never mean aught to a blue-eyed man of
the old folk, with the love of fair green lanes and white New
England village steeples in his heart. (CF 1.507)

The similarities are obvious: in both cases, the protagonists experience a painful epiphany, a realization that the city in which
they find themselves stranded does not, in daylight, resemble the
city of their dreams. "Squalor and alienage" mar the urban landscape, and the residents, who are curiously absent from the protagonists' topographical visions, are strangers, who, from the
protagonists' perspective, have displaced the original inhabitants.[4]
A stranger among strangers, Blake is doubly lost, surrounded by
signs he cannot read and people he cannot understand.

And yet, the district itself, with its cupolas and spires and
Doric porches, is not wholly alien. Indeed, it is disturbingly familiar, being nothing less than a degraded version of College
Hill. If Blake's initial vision, as he stared "dreamily" toward the
west, was of College Hill transformed from a "little garden oasis
of village-like antiquity" into a "smoke-wreathed world of
dream," then Blake's journey adheres to the logic of nightmare,
for this is College Hill corrupted and deformed. Thus, Federal
Hill, being the inversion of its twin to the east, is far more horrible than the Industrial Trust beacon—which, despite making
the "night grotesque," has no connection at all to the city's colonial past (CF 3.454)—for Federal Hill's very existence exposes
College Hill's vulnerability. What has befallen one hill may, in
other words, befall the other.

Lovecraft learned this lesson in New York, where he stum-

---

4. Paul Buhle (204) and others have touched on the xenophobia on display
here, which at first glance recalls similar passages, written a decade earlier, in
"The Horror at Red Hook" and "He." And yet, it is worth noting that HPL's
treatment of the Italians of Federal Hill is far kinder than his earlier treatment
of New York's immigrant population: Blake seems to regard them as foreigners
with whom he has little in common, but he does not despise them, nor do they
act despicably. Unlike the devil worshippers of Red Hook, they work together
to keep the Haunter at bay and, in that sense, act much more heroically than
Blake, who flees from the horror he has awakened.

bled upon the remnants of the city's colonial heritage in places like Greenwich Village. As much as Lovecraft enjoyed hunting for these relics, especially at night when his imagination could block out the "squalor and alienage" so visible in "garish daylight," their discovery must have been bittersweet, for they conveyed an awful truth: twentieth-century New York, with its skyscrapers and subways, had replaced a far older city, which, aside from a few buildings here and there, no longer existed. As Lovecraft explains in "He," "this city of stone and stridor is not a sentient perpetuation of Old New York as London is of Old London and Paris of Old Paris, but that it is in fact quite dead, its sprawling body imperfectly embalmed and infested with queer animate things which have nothing to do with it as it was in life" (CF 1.507). And if modernity could kill Old New York, it could do the same to Boston or Providence or even College Hill. It is no surprise then that, while Lovecraft was living in New York, the preservation of College Hill's historic structures began to worry him immensely. In 1925, he wrote to his aunt Lillian D. Clark again and again about various buildings marked for demolition, often lamenting that he, as an individual, could do nothing to stop the ongoing and seemingly inevitable destruction:

> The article on Westminster St. held my notice very closely, for it is with pain that I see the old houses go one by one. I had hoped that the Putney place would remain! Now to save the Clemence St. building, the Butler mansion, AND THE ARCADE! This latter business is serious, & I wish I could stir up a body of prominent people—like Chapin of the Hist. Soc.—to write about it to the *Sunday Journal*. The mutilation of that noble pile is a blow at the soul of ancient Providence, & no fate is too black for the commercial scoundrel who dares suggest it! (*Letters to Family* 361)

What Lovecraft came to realize over the course of several months in New York, Blake is learning in a few hours. The sense of alienation that Lovecraft felt, of being a "blue-eyed man of the old folk, with the love of fair green lanes and white New England village steeples in his heart" in a world without "the old folk" or "fair green lanes" or "white New England village stee-

ples," hits Blake all at once, the historic relics around him being
a cruel reminder of the home he so thoughtlessly left behind. At
this exact moment, when Blake is at his most bewildered, the
church and the horror it houses emerges.

The church, like Federal Hill itself, recalls New York, as, for
that matter, do all Lovecraft's alien landscapes. The first of
these, which are but the inverse of the Dunsanian cities Lovecraft so charmingly describes in the early and mid-1920s, appears in "He" when the first-person narrator catches a glimpse of
New York as it will someday be:

> [. . .] I saw a vista which will ever afterward torment me in
> dreams. I saw the heavens verminous with strange flying things,
> and beneath them a hellish black city of giant stone terraces
> with impious pyramids flung savagely to the moon, and devil-
> lights burning from unnumbered windows. And swarming loath-
> somely on aërial galleries I saw the yellow, squint-eyed people of
> that city, robed horribly in orange and red, and dancing insanely
> to the pounding of fevered kettle-drums, the clatter of obscene
> crotala, and the maniacal moaning of muted horns whose cease-
> less dirges rose and fell undulantly like the waves of an unhal-
> lowed ocean of bitumen. (CF 1.514–15)

This description, this vision of a "hellish black city of giant stone
terraces," heralds the emergence of what Javier Martínez Jiménez calls Lovecraft's "eldritch cities," the homes of his alien gods
(29), and thus marks a turning point in Lovecraft's work, for in
the years that would follow, his Dunsanian cityscapes would
quickly be replaced by a succession of outlandish ruins utterly
unlike anything known to humanity. References to such places,
almost invariably described as "Cyclopean," appear in almost
every story Lovecraft would write after he returned to Providence in early 1926: "The Call of Cthulhu," *The Dream-Quest of
Unknown Kadath*, "The Whisperer in Darkness," *At the Mountains of Madness*, "The Shadow over Innsmouth," "The Dreams
in the Witch House," "The Thing on the Doorstep," "The
Shadow out of Time," and, of course, "The Haunter of the
Dark." Considering how often Lovecraft slotted such descriptions into his fiction, he must have believed them to be uniquely

powerful, capable of communicating, symbolically, the themes he wished to stress. To understand what those were, we must look past R'lyeh, the most infamous of his eldritch cities, to its predecessor, the "hellish black city" of "He," which is nothing more than the symbolic expression of the alienation that New York evoked in Lovecraft, the sense, that is, of being separated from those familiar traditions that give order to the world and provide a sense of scale, of being adrift in a strange world one cannot understand. Like all Lovecraft's monsters, the Haunter comes from such a world: in the Shining Trapezohedron Blake sees "endless leagues of desert lined with carved, sky-reaching monoliths" and "towers and walls in nighted depths under the sea" and "vortices of space where wisps of black mist floated before thin shimmerings of cold purple haze" (CF 3.465). Tellingly, Lovecraft even describes the church itself as "Cyclopean" (CF 3.458), an indication that it, too, has no connection to the human-scaled world of College Hill but is—like the colossal skyscrapers of New York—built for monsters.

A fate worse than death, exposure to such places evokes a sort of vertigo. It undermines what, for Lovecraft, mattered most: "a system of anchorage which can supply standards of comparison in the fields of size, nature, distance, direction, and so on" (*Essential Solitude* 303). In Lovecraft's case, this anchorage took the form of "the continuous stream of folkways around me," which sprang from his grandfather and the Phillips family, from New England in general and Providence in particular, and from College Hill itself (303). Again and again, Lovecraft would explore this idea in different media, asserting that, because of his cosmic perspective, he needed the New England landscape to anchor him, to provide him with the comforting illusion of purpose and permanence. "I would feel lost," Lovecraft explained to Derleth, "in a limitless and impersonal cosmos if I had no way of thinking of myself but as a dissociated and independent point" (303). Lovecraft owes his fear of that sensation to New York and the two years that he spent there "as a dissociated and independent point." This fear would shape all his subsequent fiction, and in that sense, his experience in Gotham should be understood as the inverse of his discovery of Marblehead in 1922, which Lovecraft famously called "the high tide of my life" (*Letters to James F. Morton* 222). On that day, he felt himself fully immersed in "the continuous stream of folkways" that had shaped his life and his character: "In a flash all the past of New England—all the past of Old England—all the past of Anglo-Saxondom & the Western World—swept over me & identified me with the stupendous totality of all things in such a way as it never did before & never will again" (222).

If the sight of Marblehead and similar places creates a connection with the past, the sight of New York, of the Cyclopean, severs such a connection, leaving the witness paralyzed not by fear exactly, but by an awareness of the meaninglessness and impermanence of his heritage. Thus, the Cthulhu Mythos symbolizes something more than *cosmic alienation,* that sense of insignificance one feels when contemplating the cosmos, for it also symbolizes that very modern sense of *urban alienation* Lovecraft felt when, staring into his own Shining Trapezohedron, he realized just how far from home he really was. And so it is fitting that, when Blake has a similar epiphany in the church, he responds as Lovecraft did in early 1926—by fleeing "the teeming, fear-haunted alleys and avenues of Federal Hill" and racing "toward the sane central streets and the home-like brick sidewalks of the college district" (CF 3.466).

Evidence for such an interpretation can be found in Blake's fears, for he does not fear death—but a loss of identity. Note that, unlike the painter John Evans in E. F. Benson's "Negotium Perambulans," a story that also features a monster afraid of light, Blake does not bother to light any candles inside his study, a simple solution that would have kept the Haunter at bay. Blake makes no such attempt at self-preservation because the more important battle is fought in the pages of his diary, where Blake records his struggle to maintain his sense of self, which, from Lovecraft's perspective, cannot be separated from his sense of place. Thus, Blake resists the sight of "other worlds and other galaxies" that forces itself on his imagination and, in his memory, displaces his own familiar home (CF 3.476). As the

Haunter's influence grows, Blake comes close to embracing, as the protagonist of "The Shadow over Innsmouth" does, his new identity, boasting that he recalls "Yuggoth, and more distant Shaggai, and the ultimate void of the black planets" (CF 3.476). Tellingly, he resists by telling himself that "my name is Blake—Robert Harrison Blake of 620 East Knapp Street, Milwaukee, Wisconsin" (CF 3.477). He does not define himself by his occupation or his family or his achievements, but *by his address*. He is saying, as Lovecraft might, "I am East Knapp Street. I am Milwaukee. I cannot be separated from the place that shaped how I experience and understand the world." Of course, the Haunter threatens to do exactly that, to replace Blake's "system of anchorage" with one that is, to Blake, disturbingly, bafflingly alien. If Lovecraft is, through Blake, yet again asserting that "I *am* Providence" (*Letters to Family* 583), the Haunter represents his nagging fear, still troubling Lovecraft in late 1935, that his source of security and permanence was neither secure nor permanent, but disturbingly fragile.

What do we gain from such a reading? For starters, it is apparent that, despite Lovecraft's dismissal of 1924–26 as a "trivial two-year period in New York City" (*Letters to C. L. Moore* 268), he never fully recovered from the trauma of New York, the feeling that, due to his own naïveté, the world he knew and the scenes he loved had been snatched away and replaced with artificial ones that, to quote "He," "could never mean aught to a blue-eyed man of the old folk, with the love of fair green lanes and white New England village steeples in his heart." As a result, even though Blake, like Lovecraft in 1926, manages to find his way back to College Hill, he is never safe from the Haunter, which, though discovered atop Federal Hill, is not bound to it—any more than modernity and its destructive offspring, Progress, were bound to New York. They could—and would—someday come to College Hill. Just as his future wife, who visited Lovecraft in 1921, could not "fail to grasp the sensation of anticlimax involved in the abrupt transition from the ancient to the garishly modern" that one encounters when approaching downtown Providence (which Lovecraft labeled a "third-rate copy of New

York"), Lovecraft could not fail to notice that modernity, having consumed much of the city, had begun to nibble at the "soul of Providence [which] broods upon the antique hill" (*Letters to Rheinhart Kleiner and Others* 191).

Scholars have long noted that Lovecraft's realization, arrived at in 1925, that his soul, his very being, was intertwined with Providence's formed the epiphany of his life, but they have overlooked the importance of its frightening corollary: if Lovecraft's imaginative life was, like the dreams of Randolph Carter, "only the sum of what [he had] seen and loved in youth" (*CF* 2.206), then every change that affected Providence also affected Lovecraft. This fear that he might still lose what he had so desperately wanted to regain surfaces again and again in his work, for the emotional dynamo that powers stories like "The Haunter of the Dark" is not anxiety for the characters, but a sense of unease, a creeping suspicion that the setting, which Lovecraft so artfully paints, has already spoiled, its beloved spires and gables and fanlights a thin rind covering a "hellish black city" of featureless stone.

And yet, despite Lovecraft's fear that the spirit of New York, which had already established outposts downtown and on Federal Hill, would someday come for the soul of the ancient city, "The Haunter of the Dark" is not a sad story. True, Blake dies and thus pays the price for neglecting the wonders that lie behind him for the illusions that lie before, but oblivion was never something that Lovecraft feared. What is important is that College Hill survives. Indeed, after lightning dispels the Haunter, the city recovers almost instantaneously: "Half an hour later the rain stopped, and in fifteen minutes more the street-lights sprang on again, sending the weary, bedraggled watchers relievedly back to their homes" (*CF* 3.474). Life, symbolized by the return of the light and the solicitude of Blake's neighbors, rebounds, leaving the reader with a sense of hope. Despite the chaos and confusion on the other side of downtown, College Hill remains a "a little garden oasis of village-like antiquity." Here Blake's cryptic reference to Roderick Usher takes on an added meaning, for Poe's story ends with the destruction of the house of Usher, which, after the death of the family, collapses and sinks beneath the tarn. In "The Haunter of the Dark," however, Blake's home atop College Hill still stands, enchanting all those, including generations of readers and even the narrator himself, who will come after.

Works Cited

Benson, E. F. "Negotium Perambulans." In *Night Terrors: The Ghost Stories of E. F. Benson*. Ed. David Stuart Davies. Ware, UK: Wordsworth Editions, 2012. 259–71.

Bloch, Robert. "Letter to the Editor" (*Fantasy Commentator*, Summer 1945). In S. T. Joshi, ed. *A Weird Writer in our Midst: Early Criticism of H. P. Lovecraft*. New York: Hippocampus Press, 2010. 25–27.

Buhle, Paul. "Dystopia as Utopia: Howard Phillips Lovecraft and the Unknown Content of American Horror Literature." 1976. In S. T. Joshi, ed. *H. P. Lovecraft: Four Decades of Criticism*. Athens: Ohio University Press, 1980. 196–210.

Burleson, Donald R. "On Lovecraft's Fragment Azathoth.'" In *Lovecraft: An American Allegory: Selected Essays on H. P. Lovecraft*. New York: Hippocampus Press, 2015. 133–40.

Cannon, Peter. *H. P. Lovecraft*. Boston: Twayne, 1989.

Cook, W. Paul. *In Memoriam: Howard Phillips Lovecraft— Recollections, Appreciations, Estimates*. 1941. In S. T. Joshi and David E. Schultz, ed. *Ave atque Vale: Reminiscences of H. P. Lovecraft*. West Warwick, RI: Necronomicon Press, 2018. 32–88.

Haefele, John D. "Reappraising 'The Haunter of the Dark.'" *Lovecraft Annual* No. 7 (2013): 136–48.

Jiménez, Javier Martínez. "The Impact of the Eldritch City: Classical and Alien Urbanism in H. P. Lovecraft's Mythos." *Foundation* No. 131 (2018): 29–42.

Lovecraft, H. P. *The Annotated Supernatural Horror in Literature*. Ed. S. T. Joshi. New York: Hippocampus Press, 2nd ed. 2012.

———. *Letters to Family and Family Friends*. Ed. S. T. Joshi and David E. Schultz. New York: Hippocampus Press, 2020.

———. *Letters to C. L. Moore and Others*. Ed. David E. Schultz and S. T. Joshi. New York: Hippocampus Press, 2017.

———. *Letters to E. Hoffmann Price and Richard F. Searight.* Ed. David E. Schultz and S. T. Joshi. New York: Hippocampus Press, 2021.

———. *Letters to Elizabeth Toldridge and Anne Tillery Renshaw.* Ed. David E. Schultz and S. T. Joshi. New York: Hippocampus Press, 2014.

———. *Letters to James F. Morton.* Ed. David E. Schultz and S. T. Joshi. New York: Hippocampus Press, 2011.

———. *Letters to Maurice W. Moe and Others.* Ed. David E. Schultz and S. T. Joshi. New York: Hippocampus Press, 2018.

———. *Letters to Rheinhart Kleiner and Others.* Ed. S. T. Joshi and David E. Schultz. New York: Hippocampus Press, 2020.

———. *Letters to Robert Bloch and Others.* Ed. David E. Schultz and S. T. Joshi. New York: Hippocampus Press, 2015.

———. *O Fortunate Floridian: H. P. Lovecraft's Letters to R. H. Barlow.* Ed. S. T. Joshi and David E. Schultz. Tampa: University of Tampa Press, 2007.

———, and August Derleth. *Essential Solitude: The Letters of H. P. Lovecraft and August Derleth.* Ed. David E. Schultz and S. T. Joshi. New York: Hippocampus Press, 2009.

———, and Clark Ashton Smith. *Dawnward Spire, Lonely Hill: The Letters of H. P. Lovecraft and Clark Ashton Smith.* Ed. David E. Schultz and S. T. Joshi. New York: Hippocampus Press, 2017.

Poe, Edgar Allan. "The Fall of the House of Usher." In *Poetry and Tales.* New York: Library of America, 1984. 317–36.

"Uncle Eddy":
H. P. Lovecraft's Used Bookseller

David Haden

The free Internet Archive repository is increasingly useful for detailed historical research on popular culture. In 2019 I was searching its scans of old pulp magazines, runs of which usefully extend into the 1940s and 1950s. I discovered a number of letters by a Mrs. Muriel Eddy, published by several late 1940s science-fantasy magazines. In these letters Muriel fondly recalled aspects of the H. P. Lovecraft she had known. As Lovecraftians are aware, Muriel and her husband had sporadically been good friends with Lovecraft. I then discovered that her 1940s pulp magazine letters had been overlooked by Lovecraftians, since none of my discoveries were listed in S. T. Joshi's 2009 bibliography or elsewhere. Regrettably, these letters do not open a cobwebbed casket full of scintillating new details. Yet one letter in particular shines new light on an important but previously uninvestigated Providence bookseller—a man who came into frequent contact with Lovecraft, and more occasionally with the book collectors among the Lovecraft Circle, such as W. Paul Cook, R. H. Barlow, H. Warner Munn, and James F. Morton. This local bookseller was Arthur Edwin Eddy (1860–1933). He was the uncle of Lovecraft's sometime friend, collaborator, and writer Clifford Martin Eddy, Jr. (1896–1967). There are hints about this bookseller in Lovecraft's letters. For instance, Lovecraft mentions the easy and illegal Sunday access he had— gained by a clandestine knock at the door—to Arthur E. Eddy's large used bookstore. Despite the man's undoubted existence, no scholar has until now investigated him and his bookshop.[1]

It turns out that "Uncle Eddy"—as I will refer to him so as to prevent confusion with other Eddy family members—had the largest bookstore in Providence by the end of the 1920s. A press profile published toward the end of his life stated that he had around 20,000 volumes in stock, and at one point Lovecraft gleefully discovered more dusty bundles of papers in a home storage attic.

An unknown memoir of Lovecraft

The first and most important new letter by Muriel Eddy was in the pulp magazine *Thrilling Wonder Stories* for June 1948, titled "H. P. Lovecraft, Gentleman."[2]

> Lovecraft used to come over to our house and read his manuscripts night after night. Once he gave my husband a new kind of hair-cutter and advised him how to cut his own hair. It would, he averred, save many a barber's bill. He assured us he always cut his own hair and shaved himself. Lovecraft was the soul of neatness, and always looked like the old-fashioned gentleman of culture he preferred to call himself. He once visited the oldest church in Rhode Island with Mr. Eddy and signed his name in the register—"H. P. Lovecraft, Esquire, Gentleman."
>
> My hubby's uncle (now dead) owned and operated a huge second-hand bookstore on Weybosset street in Providence. His name was Arthur Eddy. Lovecraft spent hours at night, talking to our ancient uncle and poring over musty volumes in the basement. He never appeared in daylight—but always turned up around the Witching Hour of twelve. My uncle liked H.P.L. and stayed open into the wee sma' hours of morning to humour this then embryo writer. He once predicted that with the years, Lovecraft's fame would mount. How right he was! [. . .]

---

1. Chris Perridas briefly stated in a blog post that "Eddy's Bookstore is long gone" from Providence and that "In one of my next posts" its address would be revealed to readers. However, nothing further was posted about the bookstore.

2. Not to be confused with a memoir issued by the Eddys in the 1960s, titled *H. P. Lovecraft Esquire: Gentleman*, which was a six-page stencil-duplicated item for early collectors.

THRILLING WONDER STORIES

Vol. XXXII, No. 2   A THRILLING PUBLICATION   June, 1948

LETTERS FROM READERS

MAYBE we are getting young or something but the crop of letters this time seems to us to be far above average both intellectually and critically. We are opening with an excellent missive which should help to finish the laying of a feud we seem to have walked into with our eyes shut—namely the Lovecraft controversy.

H. P. LOVECRAFT, GENTLEMAN
by Mrs. Muriel E. Eddy

Editor: I've been besieged with requests for more information about Howard Phillips Lovecraft, the late

Providence writer of weird yarns—so here goes! Lovecraft used to come over to our house and read his manuscripts night after night. Once, he gave my husband a new kind of hair-cutter and advised him to learn how to cut his own hair. It would, he averred, save many a barber's bill. He assured us he always cut his own hair and shaved himself.

Lovecraft was the soul of neatness, and always looked like the old-fashioned gentleman of culture he preferred to call himself. He once visited the oldest church in Rhode Island with Mr. Eddy and, while there, signed his name in the register—"H. P. Lovecraft, Esquire, Gentleman."

My hubby's uncle (now dead) owned and operated a huge second-hand bookstore on Weybosset street in Providence. His name was Arthur Eddy. Lovecraft spent hours at night, talking to our ancient uncle and poring over musty volumes in the basement. He never appeared in daylight—but always turned up around the Witching Hour of twelve. Uncle liked H.P.L. and stayed open until the wee sma' hours of morning, to humor this then embryo writer. He once predicted that, with the years, Lovecraft's fame would mount. How right he was!

Lovecraft asked us to do much of his typing. He used an old, old machine on which he occasionally typed a story—one of the "invisible type" variety, no longer made. It is to be regretted that this typewriter was sold to a second-hand man when some disinterested outsider was cleaning his apartment after his death. I'm sure it would have been a collector's item, had it not been sold to this unknown person, to whom the name "Lovecraft" meant nothing.

I have pictures of H. P. Lovecraft as a small child, and also pictures of his mother and father. Last summer we ascertained where his grandfather had lived during his boyhood, and took interesting snapshots of the yard in which H.P.L. used to play—when he was not ill, for he was not a rugged child. I have a photo of his grandfather (who had brilliant dark eyes, a Lovecraft characteristic) and of his birthplace as well as of the grave in which he is buried (his body was placed in the ground, not in a vault).

I feel that memories of this man are precious indeed—and I even have a letter he wrote to us, congratulating our cat when she presented us with several kittens—written just as one would write to a human mother—because Lovecraft was noted for his great devotion to felines!

By the way, my favorite story in FEBRUARY TWS is: "THE SHAPE OF THINGS" by Ray Bradbury. It is written in such a manner that one wonders if—MAYBE—it couldn't be true! Fantastic but truly fascinating stuff to ponder over! I enjoyed all the stories and I loved the monstrous hairy spider (?) on the cover! I'll keep reading TWS!—135 *Pearl Street, Providence 7, Rhode Island.*

[Lovecraft's] typewriter was sold to a second-hand man when some disinterested outsider was cleaning his apartment after his death.

[. . .] Last summer we ascertained where his grandfather had lived during his boyhood and took snapshots of the yard in which H.P.L. used to play [. . .] His grandfather [. . .] had brilliant dark eyes, a Lovecraft characteristic [. . .]

Muriel Eddy's claim here—new to Lovecraftians—is that during Lovecraft's "embryo" years he spent many night hours in Uncle Eddy's basement bookstore on Weybosset Street. In using the word "embryo" Muriel is typically vague, and she might have meant anywhere from 1908 to 1924. It is well known that Muriel could confabulate memories of Lovecraft, mostly published for fans in duplicated booklets during the 1960s.[3] However, S. T. Joshi has written of her texts that "The first memoir [1945] seems on the whole quite reliable" (*IAP* 464).[4] There is then reason to trust a letter from the late 1940s. Yet her reputation means that I need to be cautious. Thus I will now test her key claims. I will begin by trying to determine the details of Uncle Eddy's early life and addresses.

Who was Arthur Edwin Eddy?

I thank Ken Faig, Jr. for kindly providing me with some of the basic genealogical details on the man and his family. Arthur Edwin Eddy[5] was born in Providence on Halloween, 31 October 1860, the son of James and Lucy Eddy. He would thus have "come of age" in the early 1880s. As a young man he established himself as a jeweler, most probably as an independent artisan rather than a bench-hand in one of Providence's immense jewelry factories. Six years later he had become established enough in life to marry, and he wed Lillian Richards Bruce in a winter

---

3. A representative list of these can be most easily found in the "Eddy, Muriel" entry in Joshi and Schultz's *H. P. Lovecraft Encyclopedia.*

4. Her memoir implies that was the Eddys who introduced HPL to *Weird Tales,* but we now know that several others had already urged him in that direction.

5. Known erroneously in several sources and archives as "Arthur A. Eddy."

wedding on 21 January 1886. The newlyweds settled into a neat and modest wooden house at 100 Gallup Street[6] in South Providence, and four years later they had a son named Harold Bruce Eddy (born 8 February 1890, died 9 August 1936), who later became a music teacher. Uncle Eddy's trade as a jeweler and then as a used bookseller, and his son's profession as a music teacher, indicate the family appreciated art and literature.

Arthur A. [sic] *Eddy*

This misnamed photo of Uncle Eddy is from the *Providence News-Tribune* (22 July 1931).[7] Lovecraft and the visiting James

---

6. The house was still to be seen until some years ago, but is now torn down or moved. Its grassy plot appears to have been divided between adjacent homes.

7. The cutting is available as a scan at the Brown University Lovecraft Collection, along with the letter. The RIAMCO listing gives: "Lovecraft, Howard P. to Wandrei, Donald. Undated, with envelope postmarked Jul. 31, 1931. Headed: 'Nether Crypts—Lammas-Eve' only. Enclosed is a clipping from The Prov-

F. Morton happened to pop in to the Eddy bookshop shortly after the item had been published. Copies were duly purchased
and the clippings sent to correspondents who knew and had pat-
ronized Eddy, and thus one was preserved. Note that what appears to be a dramatic Frankenstein-like scar on the right of his
face is probably just his heavy glasses-chain.

Faig has found that Uncle Eddy worked as a jeweler until his
fiftieth year. In 1910 he was first listed as a bookshop proprietor.
We know from his 1931 local press-cutting profile that he began
selling used books as "a sideline" to being a jeweler, which suggests that he may have practiced the jewelry craft from his
home. The *International Directory of Second-hand Booksellers and
Bibliophile's Manual* for 1894 seems to confirm this, as it gives his
home address as 100 Gallup Street in South Providence. This is
the earliest such mention of the books and indicates that he was
trading in books at that time if not before. The 1905 *A.S. of
C.C. Bulletin* (American Society of Curio Collectors) confirms
the same home address and perhaps hints that he was also trading in small curios from home. He then made his transition into
the book trade at age fifty, meaning 1910/11. Uncle Eddy appears to have very thick glasses in the 1931 photo of him that
we have, and it is then natural to suppose that failing eyesight
was a reason for his move away from jewelry work.

Eddy's Book Store on Weybosset Street

The *American Library Annual* of 1912 and 1913–14 gave his
bookstore's earliest address in the far south of the city at 852
Broad Street. This was within walking distance of his home, but
was almost certainly too far down into the suburbs of South
Providence for the young Lovecraft to have known of it, unless

---

idence News-Tribune [22 Jul 31] about Arthur A. Eddy, proprietor of Eddy's
Bookstore on Weybosset Street in downtown Providence." The July 1931 run
of this newspaper appears to have otherwise perished from history, as this cutting is all that remains. The text has information about two other key used
booksellers in the city: the Dana bookstore and Livsey and Knight. It also gives
some hints about the state of the used book trade in the city in the early years
of the Great Depression.

perhaps the shop was being advertised regularly in the local press. If it had a prominent street frontage, then some might wonder if Lovecraft noticed it on trolley-car journeys, perhaps in connection with 1906 astronomy articles for the *Pawtuxet Valley Gleaner*, which had its office at Phenix. But any long southward trolley-trips there would have been too early—the shop only opened in 1910/11.

Uncle Eddy later moved his shop up to the main retail section, on a side of the street that backed onto the cargo docks. This time the location was just over a mile from his home, easily walked. *Publishers' Weekly* (21 April 1917) usefully gives a spring 1917 date for the move, and the same edition confirms Muriel Eddy's claim of the large size by stating Uncle Eddy had "20,000 volumes in stock." She was correct on that point, and also on the basement.

Thus it is certain that Uncle Eddy had moved his large bookshop up to 260 Weybosset by April 1917.[8] A city directory of 1919 confirms the move stuck, since it also gives his new shop address as 260 Weybosset Street. This address is effectively "the top end" of Broad Street, which at its most northerly end runs into and "becomes" Weybosset. With this address to hand, I undertook further research to piece together the relevant retail history.

In the 1894 the *R. I. Medical Science Monthly* carried advertisements for one A. J. Magoon, furnace dealer, at 260 Weybosset. In 1904 the Providence Chamber of Commerce noted this business had passed to B. F. Steere. In 1914 a national automobile trade journal recorded that "The local branch of the B. F. Goodrich Co. has been removed from its former location at 260 Weybosset." Goodrich Co. was a national chain that sold vehicle tyres through dealerships. Then in July 1914 the *Jewelers' Circular* noted that the Charles S. Bush Company had moved to 260 Weybosset. Bush was there through 1916, during which

---

8. The U.S. entered the First World War on 2 April 1917, which may have some relevance. Families who were suddenly moving about, and men called up to war, would not want the cost of putting books in storage for years. There would also be war bereavements in the following years, and thus large personal libraries that needed to be sold by widows and mothers.

years the firm is described as "importers, manufacturers and dealers in drugs, dyestuffs, chemicals, paints, oils, etc., and specialize in supplies for manufacturers, bleachers, dyers, calico printers, tanners and jewelers." These points on the retail uses may seem trivial, but they help to explain certain curious present-day features still to be seen in the storefront sidewalk.

Then America entered the First World War. The heavy iron stoves, tires, and chemical barrels gave way, rather incongruously, to *music*. *Polk's Providence Directory* listed Avery Piano as trading in the ground-floor frontage at 260 Weybosset, selling pianos, sheet music, music teaching aids, and musical sundries such as strings. If the premises had once been an establishment able to sell heavy stoves, vehicle tires, and weighty barrels of chemicals, then it presumably had the sturdiness needed for heavy pianos. A bookshop in the capacious basement would be a natural fit with this piano shop. Most probably the owner invited Uncle Eddy to move farther up along the same street, in order to bring him additional passing trade. This basic retail arrangement then suggests a certain congruence with Lovecraft's fiction. For instance, one can imagine Lovecraft, while a patron of the basement bookshop, hearing the hasty scraping of a violin or random modernist jazz tinkling of a piano coming faintly through the ceilings. Lines from "The Music of Erich Zann" (1921) spring to mind:

> I heard strange music from the peaked garret overhead . . . I was haunted by the weirdness of his music. Knowing little of the art myself, I was yet certain that none of his harmonies had any relation to music I had heard before . . . (CF 1.282)

Music would be a natural fit with fine clothes, and indeed by 1920 the *Providence Magazine* noted that neighbouring 258 Weybosset had become a men's clothing shop. The row was headed "up in the world." What did the row look like? It is seen on only one 1900s postcard. The distinctive dome on the upper-right edge enables cross-checking with Google StreetView. The piano shop was in the furthermost store on the right of the card, the bookshop in the basement beneath. The piano shop can still be seen today, though its "1990s olde-style" frontage is only an emulation of the old one, just a bit shorter than before and with an inverted roof overhang.

The frontage of 260 Weybosset is half-seen on the far right
of the postcard. 261 is on the far left, half-seen,
as confirmed by another picture.

At how early a date could Lovecraft have visited this bookshop? A 1918 letter to Rheinhart Kleiner helpfully suggests that Lovecraft regularly visited Weybosset Street—possibly even late at night, or in the very early morning after long night-walks. It had a key street-car stop used by Lovecraft, and also a store where he could buy drugs and candy for his aunts as well as for himself. This was on

> the corner of Dorrance & Weybosset Streets, which is adorned & distinguished by a pharmaceutical emporium—that is, commonly speaking, a drug-store. This is the southeast corner— where you wait for the local stage-coach, or street-car, as such things are called nowadays.[9] (*Letters to Rheinhart Kleiner and Others* 113)

Thus I can establish that Lovecraft was very regularly in Weybosset Street by 1918, and may well have been aware of the newly opened bookshop there—located just 60 yards from his

---

9. This was the central stop that would convey HPL back to his then home, and which Kleiner would need to reach him.

regular homeward street-car stop and on the same side of the street. But I cannot be more certain than that, other than to observe that Uncle Eddy's shop was also about two streets over from the main Providence Public Library frequented by Lovecraft. This circumstantial topographical evidence is certainly intriguing.

Can more certainty be gleaned from key memoirs or books written by the Eddys? I acquired these, and rather curiously found no mention being made of "Uncle Eddy" or his large bookshop in Muriel Eddy's 1945 memoir. Yet she did remember him in a pulp magazine's letter pages, just a few years later. Nor is he mentioned in the detailed biographical introduction on the Eddy family to be found in the 2008 collection of Eddy's fiction and collaborations, *The Loved Dead and Other Tales*. One wonders why this should be, since we have cast-iron evidence for Uncle Eddy's existence in a number of published letters by Lovecraft.

Who Introduced Lovecraft to the Eddys?

Another mystery question seems easier to suggest an answer to: was it this uncle who introduced Lovecraft to the Eddys in the summer of 1923? On this point S. T. Joshi asks: "But how did Lovecraft come into contact with the Eddys at all? There is some doubt on the matter" (*IAP* 464). Joshi then finds the fanciful 1960s claims of Muriel Eddy to be questionable. Muriel claimed then, and only then, that the Eddys had known Lovecraft and his mother from c. 1918 and had been amateur journalists published in the *Tryout*. Decades of scholarship have now shown this to be highly unlikely. But Joshi stated in the biography that he still remained puzzled as to how the fateful connection actually happened (*IAP* 464–65).[10]

I now suggest that the Weybosset bookseller offers a simple and plausible mechanism for the meeting. My theory runs as follows:

---

10. Joshi also notes a vague and then-recent claim by descendant Jim Dyer of an extant correspondence between HPL and the Eddys dating "as early as 1918." But in early 2022 these supposed letters have still not been revealed to the world.

1) Aware of *Weird Tales* and with story acceptances in hand, around June 1923 Lovecraft is seen in Eddy's bookshop. He is browsing and then asking for "sensational" literature published in recent magazines, trying to get a feel for markets. He modestly explains to the curious bookseller that he has just had five stories provisionally accepted by *Weird Tales*. He naturally then bemoans "the torture of typing" that he must now endure, in order to see these stories published.

2) The intrigued bookseller mentions that his nephew writes stories like that, and indeed just last year had landed a paid ghost story in *Action Stories*.[11] Then the bookseller cannily figures that nephew Eddy and his wife could use any paid typing work that Lovecraft might care to send their way. After all, five stories in a national newsstand magazine might bring a tidy sum for this young Phillips gentleman. Uncle Eddy swiftly writes out the address and phone number and hands over the paper. The address turns out to be relatively near to Lovecraft's home.

3) Lovecraft then feels obliged to contact the Eddys, but is perhaps cautious of social entanglements quite so close to home, especially with those living in what he recalls—from his old bicycle rides as a youth—as being a somewhat down-at-heels neighborhood on the "wrong" side of the Seekonk River. Also, he does not wish to damage his relationship with a key bookseller by "getting off on the wrong foot" with his nephew. Thus he is cautious, seeking only to sign up the Eddys for his cherished amateur journalism movement. But after a few such letters and a few phone calls, in the pleasant late summer weather he decides to stroll over the bridge one evening and to meet them in person. By 7 October he tells Frank Belknap Long that Eddy is the "new Providence amateur" (*SL* 1.254).

That would be my theory.

Yet the first relatively firm evidence for Lovecraft knowing this bookshop only comes in late November 1923. Nephew Eddy was by then known to and good friends with Lovecraft, and evidently knew the ancient back-alleys behind his uncle's

---

11. The ghost story "Moonshine" was published in the July 1922 issue of *Action Stories* (Fiction House).

bookshop. These hoary alleys went threading down toward the docks from the back of Weybosset. Lovecraft was introduced to this atmospheric quarter in a heavy river-fog on 22 November 1923, as he recalled a few weeks later in a letter:

> There are [in the city of Providence] whole sections in which I had never set foot; & some of these we [HPL and nephew Eddy] have begun to investigate. One southwesterly section I discovered from the 1777 powder-horn map ... Not a stone's throw from that 1809 Round-Top church[12] that I shew'd you, lies the beginning of a squalid colonial labyrinth in which I moved as an utter stranger, each moment wondering whether I were indeed in my native town or in some leprous, distorted witch-Salem ... there was a fog, & out of it & into it again mov'd dark monstrous diseas'd shapes ... narrow exotick streets and alleys ... grotesque lines of gambrel roofs with drunken eaves and idiotick tottering chimneys ... streets, lines, rows; bent and broken, twisted and mysterious, wan and wither'd ... claws of gargoyles obscurely beckoning to witch-sabbaths of cannibal horror in shadow'd alleys that are black at noon ... and toward the southeast, a stark silhouette of hoary, unhallowed black chimneys and bleak ridgepoles against a mist that is white and blank and saline—the venerable, the immemorial sea. (*Letters to James F. Morton* 60)

It would be natural for nephew Eddy to have used Uncle Eddy's bookshop as a warm base from which to depart and return on winter explorations into this "squalid colonial labyrinth." Again, this is not definitive evidence, but the chances of Lovecraft knowing the bookshop at this point seem very high. Equally high are the chances that his new close friendship with Uncle Eddy's nephew meant that he received a warmer welcome than before.

Given all this, Muriel Eddy's talk of night visits to 260 Weybosset in Lovecraft's "embryo" years is unlikely to refer to the mystery years of 1908–13. It is implausible that Lovecraft ever regularly visited Uncle Eddy's first bookshop far down in

---

12. This church was at 300 Weybosset St., some 40 doors down from Uncle Eddy's bookstore and on the same side of the street.

South Providence at 852 Broad Street, in existence there from 1910/11 to 1916. The various dates of his bookshop must then limit Muriel's claim of regular night visits to sometime after the springtime of 1917. But how early? An avid local newspaper reader like Lovecraft must surely have heard news of the opening of a large bookshop at 260 Weybosset. A store which advertised an enticing 20,000 used volumes, located only two streets over from the Public Library. Given this, one can quite easily envision a twenty-seven-year-old Lovecraft rattling the catch and jangling the doorbell on the evening of the grand opening day. But sadly there is no evidence for an early date, unless perhaps we accept Muriel's implied claim that Uncle Eddy knew of Lovecraft before she and her husband met him (i.e., when he was still an "embryo" writer).

To summarize then: Lovecraft probably knew of the bookshop's existence by 1917/18, may have been a patron by summer 1923, and he must surely have set foot in the place and also have become somewhat more friendly with the proprietor by November 1923.

Secret Knocks and Late-Night Opening

Muriel Eddy's claim of night opening is directly relevant to the evidence for visits to the shop by Lovecraft's friends, a matter I will come to in a moment. But first I must note some evidence for a general late-night trade on Weybosset. For instance, directories place the Musician's Union office and several newspaper offices just around the corner from the bookshop. Local newspapermen and dance-hall musicians were then semi-nocturnal, which may have made it more viable for a used bookstore to open quite late at night on certain evenings of the week. If the piano store was open late on "dance nights"—supplying emergency strings, sheet-music, and minor repairs to the city's dance-hall and theatre musicians—then the bookshop below might also profit from being open late.

I have also discovered that by the 1930s the Avery piano store sold advance tickets for big Boston concert performances, another reason to be open in the early evenings at times when showgoing crowds were strolling to the nearby theatres. Consider also that the nearby Public Library opened in the evenings, and that postcards liked to imply that Weybosset was then abundantly lit up at night.[13]

Postcard of a night scene on Weybosset Street, c. the 1910s.

On Lovecraft's return home from the "pest zone" of New York City, this Providence bookshop became a fixture on the city tour given to key book collectors in his circle. The evidence for this is found in Lovecraft's letters. By the end of late 1920s, once he was regularly bringing amateur journalist and bookish friends to visit Providence, we even start to see him introducing some quite "high roller" buyers to Uncle Eddy: Lovecraft expects "as guest the amiable James Ferdinand Morton, who in the next four days will probably do to our local mineral quarries what Cook did to Eddy's bookshop" (*Letters to Wilfred B. Talman* 112).

---

13. There are a few other mentions of Weybosset in the materials to which I have access. HPL mentioned to Galpin that the stationery store "Neilan in Weybosset Street always charges me fiendish rates for my [typewriter] paper" (*Letters to Alfred Galpin and Others* 31). That was the Neilan Typewriter Exchange, 43 Weybosset (Prop. Francis H. Neilan), which adds a little more data to the story of HPL's typewriter. HPL's future wife Sonia also stayed at a hotel on Weybosset when she first came to Providence.

Lovecraft here means that W. Paul Cook had made such a large and careful pick of the best older weird and supernatural items that he left very few gems for others to glean. Cook was a major book collector and connoisseur at that time, termed by some in the Lovecraft Circle as "The Colossus of the North." Further details on Cook and Uncle Eddy are found in a letter to Frank Belknap Long:

> Cook has been down twice this autumn—once on the 15th and 16th of October, and again last Sunday. On each occasion we have made trips to Eddy's (Arthur E. Eddy, uncle of the celebrated theatrical man and weird author whom you had the inestimable honour of meeting [when he was in New York City]) Book Store—Cook nearly buying the old fellow out, and I purchasing a good deal more heavily than my purse and recent custom would ordinarily justify. I am now trying to complete my family file of the *Old Farmer's Almanack* . . . Eddy evades the Sabbath closing [Sunday closing] law by keeping his shop door locked and admitting customers individually as they knock . . . (*SL* 2.185–86)

Evidently there were special arrangements for favored customers, and at odd times too. I imagine that such clandestine openings were probably facilitated by the basement location, and Lovecraft's letter also usefully indicates that access was not dependent on the piano shop above being open. The bookshop must have had its own access door. The Sunday opening also indicates that Uncle Eddy was not a religious man. This fact is further confirmed by the 1931 local newspaper profile of him. It notes his willingness to sell large numbers of unspecified "paperback" items, which I would suggest were perhaps the Little Blue Books paperback line that were churned out after 1919 by Haldeman-Julius. They were anyway the sort of item that brought at least one fulminating religious minister down into the store to berate him. He would, it was reported in the newspaper, stand up to the fulmination and make a cogent case for the material.

Of course, none of this can quite confirm Muriel Eddy's claim of late-night opening, or that "He [Lovecraft] never appeared [at Eddy's shop] in daylight—but always turned up around the Witching Hour of twelve." Yet that question was then somewhat solved for me by finding an advert in the October 1930 edition of the *Providence College Alembic:* "OPEN EVENINGS." P.C. = Providence College. This 1930 ad proclaims "Largest Collection of Old Books in Rhode Island," but a 1931 press article was more cau-

Eddy's Book Store

260 Weybosset Street

Largest Collection of Old Books in Rhode Island

P. C. Men
Always Welcome to Look
Them Over
OPEN EVENINGS

tious—the shop was "probably the largest of its kind in the city."

Here we see "open evenings" very clearly stated, albeit in 1930, and no other times stated. Possibly there was a "noon to midnight" opening? Of course, a skeptic might argue that evening opening was merely a product of the start of the Great Depression and the need for cash. But on balance all the available evidence suggests Eddy was habitually open into the evenings, and was also found there on Sundays. Again, Muriel Eddy's memory is found to be broadly correct. Indeed, if Lovecraft appeared there very late, as she presumably recalled being told once by Uncle Eddy, then it may even be further evidence for his undertaking night-walks in his city.

The Nature of Uncle Eddy's Stock

This bookstore was not the only local "store" to which Lovecraft was specially admitted. Uncle Eddy had yet more items stored at home in his attic. We know that Uncle Eddy and his family continued to live at 100 Gallup Street, and that the home attic was being used as book overflow storage by early 1928, and probably since 1917.[14] This use is known because Lovecraft engaged in a sort of friendly competition with his collecting friend Paul Cook. A 1928 letter reveals that Cook had purchased "a vast supply of *Farmer's Almanacs* in order to bring his file into competition

---

14. Not near the 1923 address of the Eddys, who then lived on Second Street on the other side of the river that divides the lower half of Providence. However, by 1929 the Eddys had moved and were living just a half-mile from Uncle Eddy.

with mine" (*Letters to Maurice W. Moe* 465). Cost appears to have meant that Lovecraft had not previously been able to bolster his own cherished collection of the *Old Farmer's Almanack*. Vrest Orton and Samuel Loveman once had friends who might have sold collections to Lovecraft, but nothing more is heard of these after the letters that initially mention them—and thus we must assume the deals fell through because of high prices or other bidders. But in 1928 Cook's purchases were the spur that Lovecraft needed to begin collecting old issues in earnest, and he now firmly resolved to "begin striving ultimately for a full set back to the very first number." For this task he found that

> [Uncle] Eddy proved just the right man for the purpose. In his [home] attic there are uncounted and unclassified oceans of ancient numbers, and he gave me the free run of the place at a nickel a copy. In this manner I made my personal file complete back to 1839, and scattering back to 1805—not bad as a starter. [. . .] All this has aroused the genial Eddy to a sense of value of his once despised wares, so he has just "boosted" the price of old almanacks up to a dime each! The good old law of supply and demand! (*Letters to Maurice W. Moe* 465)[15]

This shows that Lovecraft found Uncle Eddy "genial," even if by Christmas 1927/28 he may have distanced himself from the man's nephew. On the latter point consider that their joint patron Houdini was dead by October 1926, and that nephew Eddy appears to have been sending questionable "begging letters" to Lovecraft while in New York City (see *Letters to Family and Family Friends* 520). Nephew Eddy did attend—invited or not—a "gang" meeting in Providence on 20 July 1927 (*IAP* 686),[16] but that does not mean that friendly relations were immediately or fully restored. Also, for Uncle Eddy to offer Lovecraft the run of his home attic and presumably some refreshments from his wife,

---

15. By "numbers" HPL may mean to indicate collections of old serials of various kinds.

16. Nephew Eddy next makes an appearance in *IAP* as a Providence witness for HPL's divorce proceedings in January 1929, willing to testify to Sonia's supposed "abandonment" of HPL.

all for the sake of a few nickels, suggests a certain level of trust.

Interestingly, this 1928 home visit sends Lovecraft south and into the residential suburbs of Lower South Providence. Muriel Eddy and her family were then living not far away. I discovered this new address data because the *Ghost Stories* magazine for April 1929 printed a letter from Muriel Eddy and gave her address as "317 Plain Street," Providence. The content is of no interest, but the address is. Muriel talked of living on "Second Street, East Providence" in late summer 1923,[17] in her 1945 memoir of the first meeting with Lovecraft.[18] Then her 1961 memoir recalls that "shortly after" this initial meeting she and her family moved to an unspecified address on "Fox Point" and thus into the eastern core of the city. Yet "317 Plain Street" is actually in Lower South Providence and about a half-mile from Uncle Eddy and his family at 100 Gallup Street. That said, if one walked a mile east from 317 and across the river-bridge, one would indeed step over into the railyards and passenger docks of the Fox Point district—and thus be rather nearer to College Hill and Lovecraft. According to Google StreetView, the old house still exists in its well-preserved original shape as "315–317." It would be interesting if other Lovecraftians could establish the precise dates for the Eddy family at this location, which could then be tallied with any exact dates at which Lovecraft is known to have visited the Eddys at their new home, if visit he did after April 1926.

Back at Uncle Eddy's bookshop, what was the stock like? We have already seen that it held much that was of interest to the weird fiction collectors Cook, Munn, and Morton.[19] Later Bar-

---

17. Joshi and Schultz (*H. P. Lovecraft Encyclopedia* 84) put the meeting later than the "August" 1923 stated in her 1945 memoir. The "Eddy, Muriel" entry there has the meeting as happening in "fall 1923," and a later date does seem more plausible to me than August.

18. By 1945 the address she gave when writing personally to the early Lovecraftian researcher Winfield Townley Scott was "125 Pearl Street."

19. Lovecraftians may not think of Morton as much of a collector. Yet consider that HPL found Morton's personal library very impressive when fully assembled and shelved at Paterson, and thought it better even than that of Cook. "I've never seen so fine a private Library" he wrote (*Letters to Family and Family Friends* 657–58).

low and Wandrei also visited. I have already established that the shop carried unspecified "paperback" items that at least one local churchman frowned on and fulminated about, but Lovecraft's letters also reveal that it carried runs of respectable magazines from the 1890s. The magazines are mentioned in connection with visits by Munn: "I trust Munn has by this time looked you up. He was here yesterday, & we had a very pleasant session—went down to Eddy's Bookstore & nosed around until he found an old story by Camille Flammarion in some 1893 *Cosmopolitans*" (*Letters with Donald and Howard Wandrei* 217); and "when Munn and I were in Eddy's bookshop Monday, (this Eddy is uncle of the C. M. Eddy, Jr who writes for W.T.) we met the venerable Joseph Lewis French, editor of the anthology 'Ghosts, Grim and Gentle'. He is a quaint, peppery-voiced old codger of 70" (*Essential Solitude* 151).

The 1931 local press profile of Uncle Eddy reveals strong demand for primers in learning English, and for poetry books. Eddy observes that "modern"[20] poetry was "much in demand" by the general public, an idea that may faintly amuse contemporary poets. But recall that poetry was then still accessible and popular, and paid poems adorned many print publications. Indeed, Lovecraft's New York friend and fellow British Empire loyalist Ernest La Touche Hancock (1857–1926) was even able to make his living as a professional light versifier. A 1933 store card with some verse by Uncle Eddy also indicates that he kept poetry, declaring that among his ample stock: "The poetry is very good." This self-proclaimed specialism probably implies that Uncle Eddy was himself partial to poetry.

The letters also note book purchases by Lovecraft himself, implying that the stock had various points of interest despite his own large home library. Thus he was not merely an impoverished onlooker while his Providence visitors went on strip-mining spending sprees. He purchased as freely as his purse allowed, something always likely to increase the garrulousness of an otherwise taciturn bookseller.

---

20. The word "modern" in the press profile may not necessarily mean modernist "jazz"-type poetry, since we are talking about the tastes of Providence in 1931.

The Passing of Uncle Eddy

Uncle Eddy died on 13 April 1933 and his massive used bookshop appears to have died with him, vanishing from the available historical record. Evidently his nephew Eddy was not left the business in the will, and Uncle Eddy's musician son did not take it on either. Possibly the deepening Great Depression complicated any continuation of the business, even if it might have been run from a home address. Lovecraft does not mention a public "per-book" closing sale in his letters, at least in the various volumes of letters that I have had access to. I assume that dealers and perhaps even libraries in Rhode Island vied to have first pick. At a guess, the remains might have gone, as the remains of the Lovecraft library were soon destined to go, into the local Dana bookshop's vast overflow storerooms. These took up the entire top two floors of the Wilcox building on Weybosset Street and were totally burned out in a large fire circa 1970.[21]

Uncle Eddy's musician son—the same age as Lovecraft—died in August 1936, without marriage or children. Uncle Eddy's younger brother, Clifford Martin Eddy[22]—the namesake father of Lovecraft's friend Clifford Martin Eddy, Jr.—died four years on, in 1937. Uncle Eddy's wife Lillian lived on as a widow until 1953. The nephew and Lovecraft's writer friend Clifford Martin Eddy, Jr. lived until 1967, and his wife Muriel Eddy until 1978.

Did Lovecraft acknowledge the death of Uncle Eddy in the spring of 1933? Not in any poem in the current *The Ancient Track*—I recently created and published a full index to the most

---

21. The Dana's Old Corner Book Shop was at 44½ Weybosset St., a.k.a. the Wilcox Building, Providence. By the 1960s each upper storeroom offered the favored initiate "an enormous warehouse-like room filled with thousands of books, all neatly categorized and shelved, just as in an open bookstore. My jaw dropped at the sight—for me it was like stumbling into King Tut's tomb, or Ali Baba's cave." Martin J. Murphy, "Recollections of a Providential Bibliohaven," *Fine Books* (May 2011). In the 1940s–60s this housed the remaining bulk of HPL's library.

22. Other brothers and sisters were Howard Moody Eddy (1877–?) and the late arrival Mary Bennett Eddy (1882–1938). I again thank Ken Faig, Jr. for his genealogical information.

recent edition of *The Ancient Track* and I found no trace of such.[23] This seems a little surprising, as we might have expected at least a short memorial, meant for local publication and private circulation among those in Lovecraft's circle who had known Uncle Eddy. Before his death Lovecraft had called him "a great favourite" of the circle. In a 1931 letter to Talman he wrote:

> Here's a good newspaper picture of our local bookseller Eddy, whom you probably know through many transactions. It was in the *News-Tribune,* and I would have missed it if Morton and I hadn't happened to visit the shop—by sheer coincidence—the day after it appeared. I got a dozen copies, since the old boy is a great favourite with all Kalemites who visit Providence. (*Letters to Wilfred B. Talman* 181)

But perhaps the family of the deceased demurred at the prospect of a final public poem from Lovecraft. It is, however, possible that Lovecraft said more about the death of Uncle Eddy in letters that I have not seen. The only mention I can find to indicate the passing is the word "late" being used in one letter of 1934, when Lovecraft remarks on reading "A. Merrit's old yarn 'The Metal Monster', which I had never read before because Eddy told me it was dull. The damn'd fool! (nephew—not our late bibliophilick friend)" (*Letters to James F. Morton* 347–48).

Do any of Lovecraft's "Christmas greetings," to unknown recipients, fit well with Uncle Eddy and his bookshop situation? No, again a blank is drawn, unless Uncle Eddy was the

> Illustrious Monarch, in whose lofty mind
> the scholar and executive are joined,
> see round the throne thy docile subjects kneel (*AT* 314)[24]

Nor is there any short and purring poem to a hypothetical bookshop cat that might once have done "mouse-patrol duty" at 260 Weybosset.

---

23. The free Index can be found on my Tentaclii blog, in PDF.

24. Kneeling is something done in a large floor-to-ceiling book shop, though admittedly there is no evidence of Uncle Eddy being a published scholar.

The Afterlife of the Store

When last heard of, Uncle Eddy's cellar bookshop was known as the "Gallery Flux," being usefully noted as such on resumes in the 2010s by a few former Rhode Island School of Design (RISD) art students. It has since vanished as a student graduation-show gallery, though if RISD still hold the keys they may be interested to learn of its small place in the history of the weird.

The Avery Pianos store is still there today at ground level, in a rebuilt "1990s olde-style" frontage that closely emulates demolished frontages. Yet by using Google StreetView one can still see some original remains of the old place, and these hint at the dark basement that still lurks below. Two block shapes are embedded in the original sidewalk, each containing four large old "street hatches." Lovecraftian tourists will see that the blocks are today sealed up with concrete, but once they must have allowed sets of four Goodrich tyres to be jacked up to the street level. Hence their unusual shape and configuration. It would then make sense for the openings to have later been fitted with iron grids with inset glass cubes, so as to let a little natural light down *into Uncle Eddy's bookshop. One can't help thinking here of the cellar in Lovecraft's story "The Shunned House": "the dank, humid cellar . . . with only a thin door and window-pierced brick wall to separate it from the busy sidewalk" (CF 1.454).

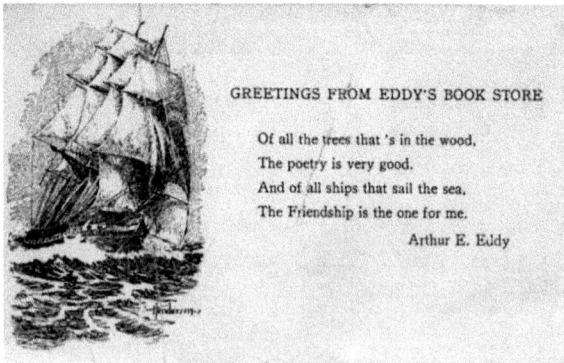

GREETINGS FROM EDDY'S BOOK STORE

Of all the trees that 's in the wood,
The poetry is very good.
And of all ships that sail the sea,
The Friendship is the one for me.

Arthur E. Eddy

Greetings from Eddy's Book Store. Probably 1933.

Some Surviving Words

Above we see a "Greetings from Eddy's Book Store" card, with lines by Arthur E. Eddy himself. It appears to be the only writing he has left us.[25] Note that the first line has a slight Scots feel to it, and also recall Muriel Eddy's memory that his store "stayed open into the *wee sma' hours* of morning" (my emphasis)—these two small hints suggest that Uncle Eddy may have spoken with a Scots accent and a touch of the old Scottish dialect.

How much personal rather than professional "Friendship" he ever extended to Lovecraft, especially in the "embryo" years of 1917–21, we cannot now know. But we do know that Lovecraft was welcome to visit Uncle Eddy's home in 1928 and that he was named in passing as "friend" in at least one late letter. According to Muriel Eddy, writing in the late 1940s, Uncle Eddy also read and admired Lovecraft's early fiction. Her other claims on the bookseller stand up under close scrutiny, and thus we might be inclined to believe her on this.

Other Magazine Letters by Muriel Eddy

I earlier mentioned that I had found other letters written to pulp magazines by Muriel Eddy. Here are my brief notes on these. One such letter can be found in the magazine *Fantastic Adventures* (October 1948), titled "Shaver and Lovecraft." Here we learn that Lovecraft liked to watch husband Eddy writing his music ("my husband has composed music for years," she notes), and that he and Lovecraft talked about setting "weird poems" to music. Again this is possibly interesting because of the early date of the memory. Curiously, I don't see this point mentioned in either the 1945 or 1961 Muriel Eddy memoirs, though Lovecraftians do know from other sources that Eddy liked to write songs and had a talent as an actor and impersonator. In his early 1920s ventures undertaken for Houdini, for instance, he did brave undercover work in disguise—and thus helped to expose

---

25. This card is dated in the Brown archives as 1938, but is far more likely to be from the year of Eddy's death in 1933. There has probably been a misreading by an archivist of "33" as "38" from a handwritten date.

the ghoulish fraud of spiritualism.

Muriel briefly appears again in the letters column of *Fantastic Adventures* (December 1948), this time writing on "Lovecraft's Wife." This letter is only of very slight interest, merely noting for the benefit of readers that her local newspaper had published a long article and memoir by Lovecraft's wife Sonia. This presumably is the well-known memoir first printed in the *Providence Journal*.

Kittens in the Bathtub?

The pulp magazine *Startling Stories* printed Muriel's "More Love-craftiania" letter in March 1949. This notes the theatrical ges-tures Lovecraft used when he read his stories aloud in the Eddy household, and there is one other genuine-sounding memory that helps to confirm a very curious detail of Lovecraft's everyday life.

After Lovecraft went away to be married, "his two aunts gave our children over 100 empty chocolate boxes to play with! (In fact, a bath-tub full!)" These boxes, from his Angell St. address, are known from Muriel Eddy's much later and very unreliable 1961 memoir. My new 1949 discovery show that the boxes were not one of Muriel's 1960s confabulations.[26] Her memory also has some supporting evidence from others.[27] What then are we to make of Muriel's curious and apparently accurate memory? It hardly seems evidence of some slovenliness on Lovecraft's part, though some visitors may have taken "candy boxes discarded in the bath-tub" as evidence for that during his final years. Yet a little research showed me that, as the confectionary and ice-cream trades emerged in their modern forms, by 1920s chocolate boxes were becoming almost works of art in themselves. Their front illustrations depicted fine "ye olde" eighteenth-century

---

26. Muriel Eddy's 1945 memoir talks only of two items of furniture being taken over to the Eddys, apparently arranged by HPL himself on a visit to the Eddys made just before his departure for New York and (then-secret) marriage.

27. L. Sprague de Camp's *Lovecraft: A Biography* (1975) has it as follows: "A caller once found Lovecraft's bathtub full of empty candy boxes." But I regret I cannot find the actual source for this—despite my recalling that it occurs elsewhere. Harry K. Brobst is not the source, as given in Cannon, *Lovecraft Remembered* (Arkham House, 1998).

British coaching-road scenes, flowery sunset gardens, or adorable kittens in colour lithography—all just the sort of pictures that Lovecraft liked and the new modernists hated ("chocolate box-y" became a term of dismissive opprobrium used by leftist critics and modernist artists at this time). These pictures alone might then be good reason for his preserving the boxes. Yet I suggest that the more likely possibility is that these empty boxes formed a ready supply of somewhat shower-proof and damp-proof containers, being glossy outside and lined with grease-proof inserts. They could have been used for holding letters and papers when working outdoors in parks and on the Seekonk riverbank during the summer, as Lovecraft did on an almost daily basis. It may also be thought by some that the boxes would have been equally useful for mailing books and manuscripts, and indeed they would have been. In that case, however, it is then curious that we appear to have no letter in which Lovecraft's correspondents mention such boxes. So far as I know, despite the many cat-lovers among his correspondents, none of the circle ever expressed their delight at encountering a kitten picture on a chocolate-box mailing box sent to them by Lovecraft. The purpose of these bathtub boxes must thus remain something of a mystery, unless more evidence for them can be found.

Finally, I suggest there may still be other memoir letters from Muriel Eddy to be found in rare and as yet un-scanned science-fantasy pulps from c. 1946–51. Also home addresses in *Ghost Stories* (1926–32) and perhaps other pulps of that period. I urge those with large pulp magazine collections to peruse the likely letter pages.

Works Cited

Cannon, Peter, ed. *Lovecraft Remembered.* Sauk City, WI: Arkham House, 1998.

de Camp, L. Sprague. *Lovecraft: A Biography.* Garden City, NY: Doubleday, 1975.

Eddy, Arthur E. "Greetings from Eddy's Book Store, 1933." (Store card, with lines of his poetry.) Online as part of the "Harris Broadsides" at the Brown Digital Repository. repository.library.brown.edu/studio/item/bdr:272274/

Eddy, C. M., Jr. *The Loved Dead and Other Tales.* Ed. Jim Dyer. Narragansett, RI: Fenham Publishing, 2008.

Eddy, Muriel. "H. P. Lovecraft, Gentleman" (letter). *Thrilling Wonder Stories* 32, No. 2 (June 1948): 125–26.

———. "Howard Phillips Lovecraft." 1945. in S. T. Joshi, ed. *A Weird Writer in Our Midst: Early Criticism of H. P. Lovecraft.* New York: Hippocampus Press, 2010.

———. Letter to the Editor. *Ghost Stories* 6, No. 4 (April 1929): 84.

———. "Lovecraft's Wife" (letter). *Fantastic Adventures* 10, No. 12 (December 1948): 147.

———. "More Lovecraftiania" (letter). *Startling Stories* 19, No. 1 (March 1949): 152.

———. "Shaver and Lovecraft" (letter). *Fantastic Adventures* 10, No. 10 (October 1948): 147.

Joshi, S. T. *H. P. Lovecraft: A Comprehensive Bibliography.* Tampa, FL: University of Tampa Press, 2009.

———, and David E. Schultz. *An H. P. Lovecraft Encyclopaedia.* 2001. New York: Hippocampus Press, 2004.

Lovecraft, H. P. *Letters to Alfred Galpin and Others.* Ed. S. T. Joshi and David E. Schultz. New York: Hippocampus Press, 2020.

———. *Letters to Rheinhart Kleiner and Others.* Ed. S. T. Joshi and David E. Schultz. New York: Hippocampus Press, 2020.

———. *Letters to Family and Family Friends.* Ed. S. T. Joshi and David E. Schultz. New York: Hippocampus Press, 2020.

———. *Letters to James F. Morton.* Ed. David E. Schultz and S. T. Joshi. New York: Hippocampus Press, 2011.

———. *Letters to Maurice W. Moe and Others.* Ed. David E. Schultz and S. T. Joshi. New York: Hippocampus Press, 2018.

———. *Letters to Wilfred B. Talman and Helen V. and Genevieve Sully.* Ed. David E. Schultz and S. T. Joshi. New York: Hippocampus Press, 2019.

———. *Letters with Donald and Howard Wandrei and to Emil Petaja.* Ed. S. T. Joshi and David E. Schultz. New York: Hippocampus Press, 2019.

Perridas, Chris. "A Visit by Munn" (12 August 2009). *H. P. Lovecraft and His Legacy,* chrisperridas.blogspot.com/2009/08/visit-by-munn.html.

The Ripple Effect:
Star Trek and the Lovecraft Mythos

Cecelia Hopkins-Drewer

This paper identifies some Lovecraftian motifs used in *Star Trek: The Original Series* and investigates whether the creator of *Star Trek*, Gene Roddenberry, had access to Lovecraftian material. It will also highlight connections between Lovecraft correspondent August Derleth and fantasy collector Samuel Peeples, together with Robert Bloch and writer Dorothy C. Fontana. The ripple effect of creative influence emanating from the Lovecraft Circle will be observed, and comparisons made to one of Lovecraft's science fiction offerings, "The Whisperer in Darkness," in order to confirm the resemblance.

A number of fans have noticed the remarkable similarity between the opening teaser of *Star Trek: The Original Series* and Lovecraft's phraseology. (See Lovecrafttherpg.com) Each episode of *Star Trek: The Original Series*—excluding the pilots—begins with the voiced motif: "Space: the final frontier. These are the voyages of the Star Ship *Enterprise*. Its five-year mission: to explore strange new worlds, to seek out new life and new civilizations, *to boldly go where no man has gone before*" (CBS Studios, *Star Trek: The Original Series: Season 2,* cover blurb, emphasis added). Lovecraft's actual phrasing in *The Dream-Quest of Unknown Kadath* is: "At length, sick with longing . . . Carter resolved *to go with bold entreaty whither no man had gone before*" (CF 2.100).

The inclusion of the Lovecraftian phrase in *Star Trek* is attributed to a collaboration between Samuel A. Peeples, Gene Roddenberry, John D. F. Black, and Bob Justman (Hiskey; Solow and Justman 144–49). Possible sources for the motif are thought to include a 1958 White House pamphlet on the space

49

program, Captain Cook's journal, and Lovecraft's stories (Hiskey). Some modification was required for non-sexist political correctness, so "no man" became "no one," and this phrase continued to be used by *Star Trek: The Next Generation* (Jacob).

Star Trek: The Original Series also appears to contain a number of Lovecraftian motifs and concepts. Themes shared between television episodes and Lovecraft stories include: the harvesting of brains, which is featured in "Spock's Brain" (Season 3, Episode 1) and Lovecraft's "The Whisperer in Darkness." An attack by globes of color occurs in "The Lights of Zetar" (Season 3, Episode 18) and Lovecraft's "The Colour out of Space." Materialized dreams of ancient cities are featured in "Plato's stepchildren" (Season 3, Episode 10) and Lovecraft's "Polaris."

Other shared themes appear to comprise: alien encounters among ruined cities in "Wink of an Eye" (Season 3, Episode 11) and Lovecraft's *At the Mountains of Madness;* unnatural longevity in "Requiem for Methuselah" (Season 3, Episode 19) and several of Lovecraft's stories ("The Alchemist," "The Picture in the House," *The Case of Charles Dexter Ward*); and finally body switching in "Turnabout Intruder" (Season 3, Episode 24) and *The Case of Charles Dexter Ward* and "The Thing on the Doorstep."

Of course, there are differences between Lovecraft's weird tales and *Star Trek: The Original Series* episodes. *Star Trek* has a team of crew members and is therefore more social in its setting than a Lovecraft story, which typically has a narrator and one or two main characters. The *Enterprise* flies through space, landing on new planets, and has unlimited access to new situations, whereas Lovecraft has to set up a plausible premise for each encounter. *Star Trek* is not horror; although the team encounters ships full of dead crews and occasionally loses an officer from the *Enterprise*, the audience generally feels safe watching the action-oriented captain.

According to his biographer, *Star Trek* creator Gene Roddenberry read "pulp magazines" during his youth, and was especially fond of the stories of Edgar Rice Burroughs, including "John Carter of Mars" (Alexander 34–37). He also enjoyed the "Skylark series" by E. E. "Doc" Smith. Alexander reports that his friend Ray often found Gene "deeply absorbed in *Amazing*

Stories or its arch-competitor, *Astounding Stories*" (31). Lovecraft usually published in *Weird Tales,* but "The Colour out of Space" notably was featured in *Amazing Stories* in 1927, while *At the Mountains of Madness* and "The Shadow out of Time" appeared in *Astounding Stories* in 1936.

Some of the information regarding Roddenberry is anecdotal and speculative. However, a stronger and more verifiable connection appears to exist in the involvement of Samuel Peeples. Roddenberry and Peeples had been friends since 1958, when they were both nominated for the same award (Alexander 203). According to Fandom, Peeples was "a fount of ideas" and served as an adviser during the creation of the 1964 first pilot, "The Cage" ("Samuel A. Peeples"). Moreover, it was Peeples's script that launched the successful second pilot in 1965 (Solow and Justman 66–67). Peeples was offered the position of producer in 1966, but appeared happy with *Tarzan* and his own Western series, while supporting Roddenberry unconditionally in the *Star Trek* venture (see Alexander 229, 270; Fandom, "Samuel A. Peeples").

Samuel Peeples has been officially credited with writing "Where No Man has Gone Before" (Season 1, Episode 3). He was furthermore asked to write "Beyond the Farthest Star," Season 1, Episode 1 of *Star Trek: The Animated Series* (1973). He also wrote a story outline, "Worlds That Never Were," and unutilised script for *Star Trek II: The Wrath of Khan* (1982) (James 208; Fandom, "Samuel A. Peeples").

In addition to being a writer, Samuel Anthony Peeples was a great collector of pulp science fiction and fantasy, publishing an article entitled "The Technique of Fantasy Collecting" in *Fantasy Advertiser.* (See Lone Star Comics). Robert Weinberg reports that Peeples was an acquaintance of August Derleth and in 1961 requested that a copy of Lovecraft's novella *The Shunned House* be bound in hardcover ("The Truth about the Shunned House Hardcover").

Peeples apparently followed the establishment of Arkham House closely, writing that he felt "a peculiar form of gratitude for the tremendous job you've already done with Arkham House in rescuing such fine writers from the limbo of the lost pulps." He promptly ordered copies of all new Lovecraft material, as well as the works of Robert E. Howard (Peeples, "Correspondence": letter dated 29 August 1961).

In another letter to August Derleth dated 25 June 1963, Sam Peeples complains his order of *The Dunwich Horror* is running late: "After spending a small fortune to complete my Lovecraft set, it is somewhat annoying to have visitors look at it and remark, 'Oh you don't have the latest one . . .' especially after ordering it in advance" ("Correspondence"). Peeples was a longterm fan of the weird and remarked that he "grew up with the field" but "never felt" such tales ought to be limited to a particular group of readers. He suggested a "WEIRD BOOK CLUB" to promote the tales to a wider audience ("Correspondence": 12 September 1961).

Peeples's extensive science fiction collection included a full set of *Weird Tales*, which he sold prior to his death (see Greenberger 147; Weinberg, "Collecting Fantasy Art #7"). The remainder of his library is housed at the American Heritage Center, University of Wyoming, and the catalogue includes a number of paperback books by Frank Belknap Long, another of Lovecraft's peers (see Peeples, "Samuel Anthony Peeples Papers," collection list).

Berkmann (ch. 1) reports that Roddenberry looked through Sam Peeples's science fiction magazine collection for ideas when planning his *Star Trek* series. Peeples (cited in Alexander 230) also allowed Roddenberry to browse the magazines and borrow a rare book around October 1963. In August 1964, Roddenberry requested access to the magazine collection for himself and his designer. Apparently, "Peeples happily invited Gene and his designer over" (Alexander 203–4).

Samuel Peeples may likewise have been instrumental in the hiring of Lovecraft associate Robert Bloch to write for *Star Trek*. On 2 July 1963, Peeples wrote to August Derleth regarding the closed doors of Hollywood: "Outside talent is rarely admitted. This is a wall I am determined to crumble. That's why I brought Bob Bloch out. And others" ("Correspondence").

According to IMDB, *Star Trek* episodes written by Robert Bloch include: "What Are Little Girls Made Of?" (1966), "Catspaw" (1967), and "Wolf in the Fold" (1967). (See also Gerrold and Sawyer 205–6.) The alien villains in "What Are Little Girls Made Of?" and "Catspaw" both mention "the Old Ones," who are a higher authority presumably from the planet Exo III. This is thought to be a tribute by Robert Bloch to "the Old Ones" of Lovecraft's stories (Fandom, "Old Ones (Exo III)").

Pioneer female scriptwriter Dorothy Fontana wrote a selection of *Star Trek* episodes and functioned as story editor for others, eventually becoming associate producer of ensuing series and "spin-offs" (Gerrold and Sawyer 38, 40; Huver; Robb 41). According to the Bowie interview (Shout! Factory), she initially worked in the "typing pool" at Revue Studios, transcribing a copy of Robert Bloch's *Psycho* for Alfred Hitchcock. Then, in 1959, she worked as "production secretary" on *Overland Trail,* produced by Samuel A. Peeples. (IMDbPro; Shout! Factory). In an interview with Moviefone (Huver), she recounts selling her first script to television in the spring of 1960, for production in another series created by Samuel Peeples. Fontana confirmed to Stephen Bowie that she came to consider Peeples her mentor as well as a friend (Shout! Factory; see also Solow and Justman 15).

When Gene Roddenberry asked Fontana to work with him on *Star Trek: The Original Series,* he likewise required her to read a selection of emerging science fiction writers. According to the Bowie interview, these included "25 or 30 books," but according to the Moviefone interview, she "must have gone through about 50 books, reading the short stories" and making notes (Huver; Shout! Factory). Prior to that research, Fontana had little interest in science fiction, although *Forbidden Planet* and *The Thing* were among her favourite movies (Shout! Factory).

Whether the volumes Fontana read for research were from Sam Peeples's collection or included stories by members of the Lovecraft circle remains a matter for conjecture unless specific titles are identified. However, it is notable that "By Any Other Name" (Season 2, Episode 22), written by Jerome Bixby, Gene Roddenberry, and Dorothy Fontana (Gerrold and Sawyer 207; IMDB), appears to reference the shared Lovecraftian mythos.

The episode begins with the *Enterprise* answering a distress call and subsequently being hijacked by aliens from Andromeda. Although the aliens are in human form, when Spock attempts to mind-probe one he gets an impression of what they looked like back on Kelva: "A series of bizarre and exotic images bursting on my mind and consciousness. Colors, shapes, mathematical equations fused and blurred. I've been attempting to isolate them, but so far I've been able to recall clearly only one. Immense beings, a hundred limbs which resemble tentacles" (CBS Studios, "By Any Other Name").

Compare the vision glimpsed by Spock with Lovecraftian beings correspondingly described as a combination of color, suggestive geometry, and tentacles. In "The Call of Cthulhu," the alien statue is made of "greenish" stone and covered in strange glyphs. Lovecraft depicts an "octopus-like" creature "whose face was a mass of feelers" (CF 2.31–32). Likewise, in Wilcox's dreams the "geometry" was "abnormal, non-Euclidean, and loathsomely redolent of spheres and dimensions apart from ours" (CF 2.51). Moreover, in another Lovecraft story, "From Beyond," the narrator sees "a pale outré colour or blend of colours" (CF 1.195) and "a seething column of unrecognisable shapes," including "jellyish monstrosities" (CF 1.198–99).

The plot from "Return to Tomorrow" (Season 2, Episode 20), written by Gene Roddenberry and John T. Dugan (a.k.a. John Kingsbridge; see Gerrold and Sawyer 207; IMDB), sounds Lovecraftian as it utilizes the "prehistoric aliens" theme developed in Lovecraft's stories. In "Return to Tomorrow," the *Enterprise* receives communication from a being on a dead planet. The being, identified as "Sargon," calls Kirk, Spock, McCoy, and Mulhall his "children," and claims to be an alien ancestor:

> Because it is possible you are our descendants, Captain Kirk. Six thousand centuries ago, our vessels were colonising this galaxy, just as your own star-ships have now begun to explore that vastness. As you now leave your own seed on distant planets, so we left our seed behind us. Perhaps your own legends of an Adam and an Eve were two of our travelers. (CBS Studios, "Return to Tomorrow")

Sargon's people are no more, having perished in "a struggle for such goals and the unleashing of such power that you could not comprehend."

Sargon explains that "there comes to all races an ultimate crisis," mouthing a statement that sounds much like the theory of declining cultures Lovecraft derived from Spengler (see *SL* 2.121). The theory is embodied fictionally in the short novel *At the Mountains of Madness*, where the Miskatonic University geology expedition investigates the ruins of an alien civilization which predated modern man's existence on Earth.

Sargon describes the nature of the crisis in terms of blasphemy, as "one day" the Arretian "minds became so powerful" that they "dared think of" themselves "as gods." This reminds us that in Lovecraft's stories, characters often expand their research until they encounter esoteric knowledge so immense that it destroys them. For example, in "The Other Gods" Barzai challenges the gods: "The wisdom of Barzai hath made him greater than earth's gods . . . they fear the coming of Barzai the wise, who is greater than they" (CF 1.277). However, this provokes "the gods of the outer hells that guard the feeble gods of earth" (CF 1.278), and Barzai is lost into "the abyss."

The final and most significant Lovecraftian element is that Sargon no longer has any physical existence and survives as "a glowing sphere elegantly poised on an angled support." It is "the essence" of his mind, in the form of "pure energy" and "matter without form." In another room, there are several more such glowing spheres containing "Henoch and Thalassa," the last of the surviving beings from Arret. The Arretians wish to take over the bodies of key members of the *Enterprise* crew, and the situation is resolved using a ruse that forces the aliens to leave the bodies. Sargon and Thalassa share one last kiss before they accept their journey into oblivion.

The encapsulated brains are similar to the contraptions employed in Lovecraft's "The Whisperer in Darkness," first published in the August 1931 issue of *Weird Tales*, where the narrator is offered the opportunity to travel between worlds in a capsule-like form:

> *It seemed that complete human bodies did not indeed make the trip* . . ..There was a harmless way to extract a brain . . . the bare compact cerebral matter was then immersed in an occasionally replenished fluid within an ether-tight cylinder of metal mined

in Yuggoth, certain electrodes reaching through and connecting at will with elaborate instruments. For the winged fungus-beings to carry the brain cylinders intact through space was an easy matter. (CF 2.522)

At the commencement of Lovecraft's tale, all evidence of "horrible cylinders and machines" has been cleared away (CF 2.467). The narrator of the tale is a man by the name of Wilmarth, who is employed as "an instructor of literature at Miskatonic University in Arkham, Massachusetts" (CF 2.468). After the "Vermont floods of 3 November 1927," reports are made regarding "pinkish things about five feet long" found floating in the swollen rivers (CF 2.468–69).

The organisms are referred to as "old ones" and are "not native to this earth" (CF 2.471). They "come from the Great Bear in the sky" and have established outposts on earth to mine stone, and fly cargo back to their home planet (CF 2.471–72). Wilmarth receives a letter from Henry Akeley, and the correspondence continues with Akeley reporting hearing buzzing voices in the woods (CF 2.478–90).

Akeley becomes increasingly paranoid, recounting that he feels spied upon, the dogs bark, and strange footprints are found nearby (CF 2.492–93); when he is attacked during the night, green stuff is left on the ground (CF 2.495–96), and there is a suggestion that this is "blood or juice" (CF 2.498), thus bringing into doubt whether the creatures are animal or vegetable in nature. We are later told more explicitly that the Mi-Go are more vegetable than animal, having a "fungoid structure" (CF 2.502). The choice of the classification of fungi is inspired. Fungi are often associated with plants, but they are so unique they are often given a taxonomic "kingdom" of their own.

Akeley says the creatures will not let him leave and want to take him away: "not only to Yuggoth, but beyond that—away outside the galaxy and *possibly beyond the last curved rim of space*. I told them I couldn't go where they wish *or in the terrible way they propose to take me*" (CF 2.496; emphasis in original).

Then suddenly Akeley writes in a "curiously different and calming" manner, asking Wilmarth to visit and bring all the photographs and recordings (CF 2.500–503). The letter is typed and betrays a suspicious amount of knowledge regarding the alien creatures. This sounds like a trap designed to gather and destroy all the evidence.

There are several hints that "Yuggoth," which the Mi-Go use as a staging point in our galaxy, is an undiscovered ninth planet from the sun (CF 2.503). This is another inspired choice, scientifically speaking, as the story was written in 1930, after Pluto was discovered; but the action is set in 1927, before the discovery of Pluto! Furthermore, now that Pluto has been reclassified as a dwarf planet, Lovecraft's mysterious ninth planet is still being speculated about based on the behavior of neighboring space bodies (Phys.org).

Our suspicions remain high as Wilmarth is met by the mysterious Noyes (CF 2.509), and no dogs survive around Akeley's residence (CF 2.513). Claw prints are evident, however, and Wilmarth begins to feel uneasy (CF 2.513–14). He visits Akeley in a darkened room, where only his host's face and hands are visible. Akeley describes Yuggoth and announces that he expects "to visit other planets, and even stars and galaxies" (CF 2.516–18). Wilmarth is shown a neat row of metal cylinders and is told they contain three humans, six fungoids, two Neptunians, and several creatures from "a dark star beyond the galaxy" (CF 2.523). The brain in cylinder "B-67" is activated and proves especially well traveled, saying: "I have been on thirty-seven different celestial bodies—planets, dark stars, and less definable objects—including eight outside our galaxy and two outside of the cosmos of space and time" (CF 2.525). Wilmarth is invited along on a series of similar voyages, and the extent of the space travel described in "The Whisperer in Darkness" does appear to anticipate the wide-ranging voyages of the starship *Enterprise* in *Star Trek: The Original Series*.

Wilmarth overhears a conversation in the night, and an ominous reference is made to a "fresh cylinder" (CF 2.533). The reader is not sure whether this fresh cylinder is intended for the capture of Wilmarth, but the suggestion is enough to create a sense of danger. Wilmarth tiptoes downstairs and discovers wax replicas of Akeley's face and hands—thus implying the Akeley he met in the living room was a mere puppet (CF 2.536–38).

Wilmarth locates Akeley's old Ford car and escapes. When he sends the sheriff back to investigate, his team only finds a dressing gown, gloves, and bandages (CF 2.529).

The analysis reveals that in Lovecraft's tale, space travel is indelibly associated with horror, whereas in *Star Trek: The Original Series* space travel represents a combination of duty, excitement, and risk for the crew. The closest thing to Lovecraft's fear of space travel is represented by "space sickness" as diagnosed by McCoy in "Lights of Zetar" (Season 3, Episode 18). Tales such as Lovecraft's "The Whisperer in Darkness" cautiously explore the concepts of space travel and future technology, but later writers, like Gene Roddenberry, Sam Peeples, D. C. Fontana, and Robert Bloch were able to thoroughly embrace their space themes.

In conclusion, if you are watching *Star Trek: The Original Series* and think you have seen something that reminds you of Lovecraft, you may be correct, as the creator of *Star Trek*, Gene Roddenberry, was an avid reader of pulp magazines. Fellow writer Samuel Peeples owned a full set of *Weird Tales* and original editions of Lovecraft. Lovecraft's correspondent Robert Bloch contributed several episodes to the original series, while other writers, including D. C. Fontana, followed the themes established by Gene Roddenberry.

Works Cited

Alexander, David. *Star Trek Creator: The Authorized Biography of Gene Roddenberry*. New York: Penguin/Roc, 1995.

American Association of Variable Star Observers, (2010) "The Myths of Ursa Major, The Great Bear" (2010). AVVSO, Cambridge, MA, www.aavso.org/myths-uma. Accessed 5 July 2021,

Berkmann, Marcus. *Set Phasers to Stun: 50 Years of Star Trek*. London: Hachette UK, 2016.

CBS Studios. "By Any Other Name." Original airdate: 23 February 1968. *Chrissie's Transcript Site* www.chakoteya.net/StarTrek/50.htm. Accessed 13 January 2021.

———. "Return to Tomorrow." Original airdate: 9 February 1968. *Chrissie's Transcript Site* www.chakoteya.net/StarTrek/51.htm. Accessed online on 3 July 2021.

———. *Star Trek: The Original Series: Season 2.* CBS Broadcasting & Paramount Pictures, 2009. Distributed by Paramount Home Entertainment (Australia).

———. *Star Trek: The Original Series: Season 3.* CBS Broadcasting & Paramount Pictures, 2009. Distributed by Paramount Home Entertainment (Australia).

Fandom. "Old Ones (Exo III)." *Memory Alpha,* wikia.memory-alpha.wikia.com/wiki/Old_Ones_(Exo_III). Accessed 5 July 2021.

———. "Samuel A Peeples." *Memory Alpha,* wikia.memory-alpha. wikia.com/wiki/Samuel_A._Peeples. Accessed 5 July 2021.

Gerrold, David, and Robert J. Sawyer, ed. *Boarding the Enterprise.* Dallas, TX: Smart Pop, 2006.

Greenberger, Robert. *Star Trek: The Complete Unauthorized History.* Minneapolis, MN: Voyager Press, 2012.

Hiskey, Daven. "'To boldly go where no one has gone before' is thought to have been inspired by a line from a White House pamphlet on space" (2012). *Today I Found Out.* www.todayi foundout.com/index.php/2012/02/to-boldly-go-where-no-one-has-gone-before-is-thought-to-have-been-inspired-by-a-line-from-a-white-house-pamphlet-on-space/. Accessed 5 July 2021.

Huver, Scott. "Writer D. C. Fontana Looks Back on 50 Years of 'Star Trek'" (2016). *Moviefone.* www.moviefone.com/2016/09/07/d-c-fontana-star-trek-interview/. Accessed 5 July 2021.

IMDB.com. "Robert Bloch: 1917–1994." www.imdb.com/name/nm0088645. Accessed 5 July 2021.

———. "Samuel A. Peeples: 1917–1997." www.imdb.com/name/nm0670268/. Accessed 6 July 2021.

———. "Star Trek (1966–1969): By Any Other Name." www.imdb.com/title/tt0708422. Accessed 3 July 2021.

———. "Star Trek (1966–1969): Return to Tomorrow." www.imdb.com/title/tt0708445/. Accessed 3 July 2021.

IMDbPro. "Overland Trail: (1960–1960)." pro.imdb.com/title/tt0053528/?rf=cons_tt_btf_cc&ref_=cons_tt_btf_cc. Accessed 6 July 2021.

Jacob, S. "TNG: Opening Credits Monologue." www.sjtrek. com/trek/quotes/STheNextGeneration/Monologue/. Accessed 5 July 2021.

James, Carl. *Science Fiction and the Hidden Global Agenda*. 2014. pdfcoffee.com/science-fiction-and-the-hidden-global-agendapdf -pdf-free.html. Accessed 4 July 2021.

Joshi, S. T., and David E. Schultz. *An H. P. Lovecraft Encyclopedia*. Westport, CT: Greenwood Press, 2001.

Lone Star Comics. "Fantasy Advertiser Vol. 3 #1 (1948) Comic Books." *My Comic Shop.com*. www.mycomicshop.com/search? minyr=1948&maxyr=1948&tid=50555490&mingr=0. Accessed 6 July 2021

Lovecraft the Role Playing Game. "Did Lovecraft Provide Star Trek with 'Where No Man Has Gone Before'?" (2015). *Word-Press*. www.lovecraftrpg.com/2015/12/21/did-lovecraft-provide-star-trek-with-where-no-man-has-gone-before/. Accessed 5 July 2021.

Morgans Lists. (2014) "6 Organisms That Can Survive the Fall-out from a Nuclear Explosion" (2014). Accessed online on 6 July 2021 from morgana249.blogspot.com.au/2014/08/6-organisms-that-can-survive-fallout.html.

Paramount Pictures. (1996) *Special Collectors Edition: Star Trek 30 Years*. Ed. Lee Ann Nicholson. New York: Viacom Consumer Products, 1996.

Peeples, Samuel A. "Correspondence between August Derleth and Sam Peeples." August William Derleth Papers, Wisconsin Historical Society, Library-Archives Division. Box 38, folder 3.

———. "Samuel Anthony Peeples Papers." American Heritage Center, University of Wyoming, Collection Number 07498. rmoa.unm.edu/docviewer.php?docId=wyu-ah07498.xml. Accessed 6 July 2021. Container List (old format): www.uwyo. edu/ahc/_files/pdffa/07498.pdf.

Phys.org. "Hunt for Ninth Planet Reveals New Extremely Distant Solar System Objects" (2016). phys.org/news/2016-08-ninth-planet-reveals-extremely-distant.html. Accessed 4 July 2021.

Robb, Brian J. (2012) *Star Trek: The Essential History of the Classic TV Series and the Movies*. Philadelphia: Running Press Book Publishers, 2012.

Shout! Factory. "An interview with D. C. Fontana (1939–2019)" (2019). www.shoutfactory.com/blog/an-interview-with-d-c-fontana/. Accessed online on 5 July 2019.

Solow, Herbert F., and Robert H. Justman. *Inside Star Trek: The Real Story*. New York: Pocket Books, 1996.

Weinberg, Robert. "Collecting Fantasy Art #8: Sam and the Scientologists" (2011). *Tangent*. tangentonline.com/columns/articles/collecting-fantasy-art-8-sam-and-the-scientologists/. Accessed 4 July 2021.

———. "The Truth about the Shunned House Hardcover." *The Battered Silicon Dispatch Box*. www.batteredbox.com/ArkhamHouse/ShunnedHouse.htm. Accessed 5 July 2021.

Briefly Noted

The publication of Lovecraft's complete extant correspondence by Hippocampus Press is, incredibly, coming to a close. With the issuance this year of *Miscellaneous Letters* and *Letters to Woodburn Harris and Others*, all that remains is the publication of *Letters to Hyman Bradofsky and Others* (which will contain several batches of correspondence to amateur figures of the 1930s, exhibiting Lovecraft's extensive involvement in the field even late in life) and, climactically, the joint correspondence of Lovecraft and Frank Belknap Long, based on original manuscripts recently acquired from the book dealer L. W. Currey. A volume of the letters to R. H. Barlow was published in 2007 by University of Tampa Press and remains in print from that firm; Hippocampus will attempt to secure a licensing arrangement so that that volume can appear in its series as well. The end result will be a 24-volume set that contains every known scrap of Lovecraft's correspondence, thoroughly annotated by David E. Schultz and S. T. Joshi.

Solitary Conversation: A Bakhtinian Exploration of H. P. Lovecraft's "Dagon"

Isaac Aday

Contemporary scholarship on the life and works of H. P. Lovecraft is highly variegated in both scope and reception. Scholars have attacked outright the lackluster plots and forms of Lovecraft's stories (Robinson), while others have mounted exceptional defenses of his purported prosaic flaws (Berruti). Critics have delved deeply into the uniquely social and cultural components of his world-building and lore (Simmons), while others have pulled back and investigated the underlying philosophical positions within them (Palinhos; Harman). Lovecraft's racism and personal beliefs (both in his work and outside of it) are frequent topics of contention (Guarde-Paz; Joshi), as is his place in academic canon, as Steffen Hantke points out. Feminist scholars have observed the role of women in Lovecraft's fiction (Williams; Wisker), while still others have studied the relationships and connections between his work and folklore in the 1920s and '30s (Evans).

However, even with this wide range of fruitful discussion, very few critics appear dedicated to engaging with the more formal, language-oriented aspects of Lovecraft's writing—that is, more specifically, their underlying structures, language patterns, and modes of discourse.[1] Critics seem hesitant, in other words,

---

1. This is not to say that they are nonexistent. Massimo Berruti's article on "Dagon" does look intensively at language and form—noting, among other things, that HPL's "persistent recourse to qualifying adjectives" is not a flaw or ineptitude of his writing, but rather a success: the "proliferation of adjectives has the same aesthetic goals as aphasia . . . Language gets nowhere, as an en-

to treat Lovecraft's form as worthy of deeper investigation—preferring, as many of the above scholars illustrate, to focus on the effects and ideas of his works' content. This is, as I see it, a glaring oversight. Indeed, while an analysis of Lovecraft's content (theme, character, philosophical nuance, or biography) is certainly useful, ignoring the more formal concerns of his writing represents a serious gap in the present scholarship.

The present paper seeks to begin filling this gap. Engaging with Mikhail Bakhtin's concept of "polyphony,"[2] the present paper articulates a new reading of Lovecraft's "Dagon" that reveals the deeper literary structures, questions, and psychological nuances of this story that have been overlooked. Beginning with a detailed analysis of the narrative elements of "Dagon" in conversation with some of Lovecraft's critics, the present analysis will progress into an interrogation of these narrative elements through Bakhtin's notion of the "polyphonous"—prompting new questions about "Dagon" and ultimately establishing a fresh understanding of the text itself. In so doing, I aim to establish Lovecraft's form and language as something more worthy of literary investigation than it is currently treated.

I would like to begin here with a discussion of psychology in "Dagon." It is, after all, precisely the psychological depths of the story's narration that allow for its nuance (and perhaps also its polyphonous nature) to be seen most clearly. From the very first passages of the short story, Lovecraft portrays the narrator as an individual with a tremendously complicated psychological profile. The story opens with an immediate glimpse into his tortured thought process:

I am writing this under appreciable mental strain, since by tonight I shall be no more. [At] the end of my supply of the drug

gine that goes out of phase" (7). Articles like these are, however, a minority in the larger picture of scholarship on HPL.

2. Though the related terms "heteroglossia" and "dialogism" are most certainly related to the present analysis, and some of its concepts might also apply here, the primary emphasis of this study will be upon the polyphony as Bakhtin understood it within the prose of Fyodor Dostoevsky. I provide a definition of this term in the pages to follow, to help clarify the concept.

> which alone makes life endurable, I can bear the torture no long-
> er; and shall cast myself from this garret window . . . Do not think
> from my slavery to morphine that I am a weakling or degenerate.
> When you have read these hastily scrawled pages, you may guess
> . . . why it is I must have forgetfulness or death. (CF 1.52)

Even in these first few lines, a few facts are made available to
readers that cannot be ignored. First and perhaps most obviously, the narrator is writing this manuscript under "considerable
mental strain": this document is, to a certain degree, not only a
recollection of a traumatic (but hitherto undisclosed) event, but
also a suicide note from a man on the brink of mental collapse.
Second and perhaps more subtly, the narrator admits to the regular use of morphine—a drug associated with dissociations from
reality, hallucinations, and general impairment of the mind and
cognitive faculties. These details, taken together, appear to
problematize the validity of the narrator's impressions in this
story. Indeed, even in this first passage the protagonist is plainly
established as an unreliable narrator: any information that the
reader might receive through him may or may not be blurred or
falsified by his emotional instability or his drug addiction. Everything in the manuscript to come must be, therefore, questioned
for its authenticity.

Some critics who have spoken on this "unreliability" have
suggested that the narrator's failure to establish credibility is
simply the mark of poor storytelling. Lovecraft scholar James Arthur Anderson, for instance, attributes the lack of narratorial credibility to the earliness and inexperience of Lovecraft's career, and
ultimately recognizes it as a "major flaw" of the story's structure:

> While many of Lovecraft's later protagonists tell incredible tales
> [as does the protagonist in "Dagon"], Lovecraft is careful to
> make them credible narrators. As [can be seen in] "The Call of
> Cthulhu," which closely resembles "Dagon" in plot structure,
> the narrator's accounts are verified by newspapers, professors,
> and other reliable sources. One of Dagon's major flaws lies in
> Lovecraft's failure to make this narrator reliable. In the very first
> paragraph, the narrator attempts to legitimize himself . . . but
> this self-testimonial is not, in itself, enough. (Anderson 66)

Of course, Anderson is right to recognize that the narrator's "self-testimony" is not enough: the narrator is obviously unreliable. Still, Anderson's vision of the narrator of "Dagon" as a self-insisting and "self-testimonial" character prompts a third observation about the introductory passage that Anderson and other critics appear to have neglected: the narrator appears to address someone in this first paragraph. Indeed, although Anderson's observation correctly recognizes that the protagonist's language is "self-testimonial" (e.g., "do not think from my slavery to morphine that I am a weakling or a degenerate" [CF 1.52]), his analysis ultimately overlooks the fact that this self-testimony necessarily requires an external "other" (real or imagined) as the object of this testimony. When the narrator writes, for instance, that "you may guess" why he must have "forgetfulness or death" (CF 1.52), it is impossible to imagine that he is writing to himself—*he* already knows why it is he must have forgetfulness or death. The narrator appears, in such phrases, to defend himself actively against what he presumes to be a judgmental externality: a person, multiple people, or society in general which will read his manuscript and form perceptions about both him and the manuscript itself.[3] This document is written, in other words, with an "audience" of some sort in mind: there is an implied and tangible (though vague) "readership" of the manuscript within the story itself.

Here, a major break is made from previous criticism of "Dagon."[4] Indeed, for what might be the first time in the criticism of this story, the present analysis understands the tale's narration

---

3. This "other" is hinted at elsewhere in "Dagon" as well. Though never named outright, this "other" is implied at the end of "Dagon" to be the narrator's "fellow-men"—a very vague address that might be read as representatives of several different groups or people (CF 1.58). In a similar vagueness, the narrator likewise recognizes that such "fellow-men" may both take his claims seriously or laugh at them: whether his writing will be read as "information or contemptuous amusement" (CF 1.58) remains unclear to both the narrator and the readership of the story.

4. One exception, perhaps, can be made for Salonia, whose analysis of "Dagon" implies Dagon's falsity. Still, one might argue that Salonia's treatment is itself too certain in promising the falsity of the narrative. As this paper argues, Dagon's existence or nonexistence is never solidified.

as having certain qualities inherent to a multi-person conversation as opposed to a simple, internalized, and monolithic articulation of solitary thought. Seen in this way, one is no longer reading the errant and wholly internal thought processes of a suffering man, but rather a message written to someone or something external, some "other," which is understood to be capable of forming judgments and opinions.

It is here, with this "conversational" reading of "Dagon" in mind, that we might introduce the concept of "polyphony" to examine this relationship further. In Bakhtin's analysis of Dostoevsky in *The Problems of Dostoevsky's Poetics*, a few major qualities of polyphony might serve as the grounding for definitive purposes:

1. "[One] is dealing not with a single author-artist ... but with a number of philosophical statements by several author-thinkers" (5).
2. Such characters are "fully valid" and "ideologically authoritative" even though their ideas are "disparate, contradictory philosophical stances, each defended by one or another character" (5).
3. Each voice takes part in the "plurality of independent and unmerged voices and consciousnesses" and each has "equal rights" and "his own world" (6). They do not serve, for instance, as the "vehicle for the author's own ideological position" (7).

Polyphony might be described, therefore, as an ideological "multi-voicedness" present in fictional texts where characters are not "mouthpieces" of their authors, but free-thinking and individual entities with their own unique sets of beliefs and "worlds." Each "voice" in this multi-voicedness is not used to define or establish another voice's truth; each are, rather, an unmerged and independent voice in "conversation" other voices.

There are, of course, some immediate issues that arise in applying this term to the passages that have hitherto been described. Perhaps most strikingly problematic is the fact that the protagonist of "Dagon" is indeed the only explicitly speaking character in the story—which, one might imagine, would exclude him from the possibility of partaking in a "polyphonic" dialogue that requires "a plurality of independent and unmerged voices" (Bakhtin 6). Still, with the mention of this external "other" to which "Dagon" is being written, we might challenge this notion: is this "other" a character in itself, who might exert an influence upon the narrator's writing? Is the "other," though not itself a speaker, still capable of a certain kind of implicit speech? Does this "other" ultimately possess its own ideology from which the author feels the need to break away? Here one might turn once again to Bakhtin, who acknowledges that, even in certain single-author (single-speaker) passages,

> . . . [the] hero's self-awareness [is] penetrated by someone else's consciousness of him, the hero's own self-utterance [is] injected with someone else's words about him; the other's consciousness and the other's words then give rise to specific phenomena that determine the development of [the hero's] self-awareness, loopholes, protests . . . interruptions . . . repetitions, [and] reservations . . . Let us imagine two rejoinders . . . which, instead of following one after the other and being uttered by two different mouths, are superimposed one on the other and merge into a single utterance issuing from a single mouth. (209)

Bakhtin seems to suggest here that it is possible, indeed, to think of certain single-author passages as being made in response or relation to some (hidden?) external entity even when this entity is not present—for the hero's "self-utterance" to be "injected with someone else's words about him" (209). Bakhtinian scholar Augusto Ponzio elaborates upon this idea: "one's own word alludes always and in spite of itself, whether it knows it or not, to the word of others . . . Consciousness of self is reached and perceived against the background of the consciousness that another has of it . . . Therefore, dialogism also presents itself in a single voice, in a single utterance" (8). As in Dostoevsky's *Notes from the Underground*—where the underground man "fears that the other may think that he fears the other's opinion . . . but such fear reveals his dependence upon the other's consciousness" (Ponzio 9)—these authors seem to argue that the definition of the self, and the very foundation of consciousness, is reached through one's awareness of themselves as they are perceived through others in their situated social world. One can speak, whether one knows it or not, in response to someone (or something) other than the self even in solitary speech. In such instances as Ponzio describes, the single speaker may therefore create an active response to the words of someone else (we might add: be they real or imagined through internalized interlocutors) even when one is speaking alone. A "merging" of sorts might be said to occur between the author's own person (and all their thoughts, beliefs, and so forth) and the author's surrounding others—resulting in the creation of a multi-voiced speech, even from a solitary individual.

Is a process such as this taking place in "Dagon"? Indeed, the narrator of "Dagon" is certainly addressing a general but quite tangible "other" in his speech, after all—and this "other" does have a concrete effect upon the manuscript itself, as we can see through his self-testimony. The "other" is vague and faceless, but nonetheless present to such a degree that the narrator feels the need to defend himself and his manuscript explicitly: he does not wish to be perceived by this "other" as a weakling or degenerate, and therefore takes up a concrete defense against this perception in his writing. Indeed, like Bakhtin's treatment of Dostoevsky's *Poor Folk*, one might be able to construct a rudimentary image of this "other" in conversation with the narrator with a little imagination:[5]

> Narrator: I have something to tell you, and it must be taken seriously.
> Other: But you are addicted to morphine—you are surely a weakling and degenerate.
> Narrator: I am addicted, yes—but nonetheless hear me out, and do not think me a weakling or degenerate. I am under considerable strain.

---

5. On p. 210 of *Problems of Dostoevsky's Poetics*, Bakhtin creates an imaginary dialogue between one of the characters from *Poor Folk* and the mysterious "other" that the character appears to respond to in his letters. The dialogue presented in this paper mimics this dialogue.

Other: Why? Why should I listen to you, and read your "hastily scrawled pages" (CF 1.52) even after you admit to being a morphine addict?

Narrator: After you have read these pages, you will realize why "I must have forgetfulness or death" (CF 1.52).

Truly, one might argue that the opening lines of this text represent an implicit conversation between the narrator and this "other" in a sense similar to (though perhaps not perfectly) what Bakhtin describes. Each line that the narrator writes in the opening paragraph of "Dagon" appears to relate somehow to the narrator's expectations of how his manuscript shall be received or understood. His language reflects, in other words, the *anticipation* of his manuscript being read by someone other than (and external to) himself. His writing then concretely caters to the perceived demands of this external being through self-defense and ultimately appears adjusted to the degree that the document becomes a form of discourse. Seen in this way, this tangible "other," who is not only addressed but is addressed explicitly ("you may guess . . ."), is indeed a "character" in this short story that, though unspeaking itself, is capable of speaking through the narrator's own mouth. Whether or not this qualifies as polyphonic in the sense that Bakhtin describes—it may not be "polyphony proper" as is seen in Dostoevsky's oeuvre—one might nevertheless argue that there is something certainly "multi-voiced" in this passage, even though it comes, again, from only one narrator.

The notion that "multi-voicedness" might occur even within one solitary speaker prompts one further observation of "Dagon." Indeed, in the latter moments of the story, another singularly spoken "conversation" appears to occur when, suddenly, the narrator simultaneously begins to doubt his own impressions of Dagon while assuring himself (contradictorily) of their complete and undeniable validity: "Often I ask myself if it could not have all been a pure phantasm—a mere freak of fever as I lay sun-stricken and raving in the open boat after my escape from [a prisoner's vessel]. This I ask myself, but ever does there come before me a hideously vivid vision in reply" (CF 1.58). Here too, one might notice the presence of two separate perspectives emerging from one mouth—and, in this case, one mind. The first voice appears to doubt whether Dagon has ever existed: perhaps, indeed, it was all a trick of a fevered mind, or a hallucination brought about by the sun or the stress of his seafaring journey, and the entirety of the present manuscript is completely imagined. The second, by contrast, appears completely convinced of its validity, and brings to mind the image of the beast that, for all the fear it inspires, cannot be doubted. Here, though shorter for the sake of avoiding redundancy, one might offer a similar imaginary dialogue:

> Narrator 1: There are other factors to consider, here. Are we sure we were not simply hallucinating? The sun was hot that day, and we had a fever.
> Narrator 2: Have you forgotten that image—that terrible image? Can you truly doubt such an impression?

It is important to note that, as in many of Dostoevsky's works that Bakhtin analyzes, there is never any emerging "finality" in this conversation. Indeed, though the narrator "sees" Dagon once again at the end of the story, his impressions are problematized by the unreliability of his narration that has hitherto been recognized: it is possible, at any moment in the text, that the narrator is hallucinating (from stress or morphine or both), but it is simultaneously possible that everything he is describing is indeed real. The reality of one or the other is, however, never made clear through Lovecraft's writing. Neither one of these "voices" is solidified or confirmed as the one and only "true" reality. Rather, in alignment with Bakhtin's conception of polyphony, each voice has "equal rights" and is treated as "fully valid" (5–6).

With this information in mind, one is prompted to wonder as to the extent to which one might understand an internal "dialogue" such as the one in "Dagon" as possessing the necessary attributes of being called "polyphonic" in the Bakhtinian sense. While again there is only one person in this dialogue, there might be said to be many voices that compete, argue, and debate against one another with no ultimate confirmation of "truth."

While this might or might not be understood as "polyphonic" in the sense that one typically understands Bakhtin (i.e., it lacks several "separate" author-thinkers as one sees in Dostoevsky, and it is not strictly ideological or philosophical in nature), it nonetheless opens up a variety of new questions. Is one's "inner dialogue" truly a dialogue in the Bakhtinian sense? Is more than one separate, philosophical worldview contained in each embattled "position" of the solitary (but contradictory and uncertain) mind? Can internal dialogue be seen as polyphonic, under certain, definable conditions?

Here, perhaps, questions are just as fruitful as answers: thinking about what constitutes a "voice" in a polyphony (especially in reference to newer stories such as this, where Bakhtinian models might or might not be applicable) is itself a promising direction for both scholarship on Lovecraft and literary criticism in general. Even if we ignore any connection to Bakhtin's conception of polyphony in "Dagon," such a conversation nevertheless prompts one to consider what might be made of these "voices" within the protagonist's solitary (though contradictory) mind. Indeed, while these perspectives do not appear to be inherently full, philosophical, or "complete" worldviews as such, they remain, at a bare minimum, two ways of seeing the world and understanding reality in conversation with each other: either Dagon is real or he is not.

This new reading of Lovecraft's "Dagon" radically breaks the mold of previous criticism. Far from being seen as a story "about" a man and a (very "real") fish-person, this reading prompts one to view this story as a complicated psychological narrative between a man, a multiplicity of contradictory thoughts, and a societal "other" that are all in conversation with one another. It becomes, in other words, a story whose emphasis upon discourse and unreliability is central to uncovering its deeper structures and meaning. Seen in this way, the story becomes, like Edgar Allan Poe's "Ligeia," less of a mere arousal of the senses and more of an investigation of character, structure, and form, and thereby warrants investigation rather than (or perhaps in addition to) sensation.

The above analysis, though far from a universal establishment of the polyphonous nature of "Dagon," allows for a reading of the text that is, arguably, far more interesting, nuanced, and literary than it is often understood to be. This new understanding of "Dagon" requires, however, the ability to treat it as a text whose language and formal characteristics—and not simply its plot or philosophical worth—actually warrant further investigation. It is quite certain that many of Lovecraft's other stories—which frequently contain a variety of modes of discourse, from letters to dialogues to ancient runes—may be analyzed similarly.6 It is my hope, in fact, that such analyses as this ought to become more common. But to reveal the deeper nuances of these and other texts, one must recognize the falsity of the implicit notion that Lovecraft's writing—and perhaps even weird fiction in general—is devoid in some capacity of linguistic merit. Lovecraft's prose and form are not simply weak vessels through which contemplative ideas or spinal shudders are procured; they are important aspects of their storytelling that, when analyzed, allow for deeper understanding of his works themselves. The hallmarks of "the weird" and all its fish-people and mysterious islands, madness and death, must not distract future criticism from the willingness to engage with these texts' language and form on a deeper, analytical level.

Works Cited

Anderson, James Arthur. *Out of the Shadows: A Structuralist Approach to Understanding the Fiction of H. P. Lovecraft.* Holicong, PA: Wildside Press, 2011.

Bakhtin, Mikhail. *Problems of Dostoevsky's Poetics.* Ed. and tr. Caryl Emerson. Minneapolis: University of Minnesota Press, 1984.

Berruti, Massimo. ""Dagon": Shipwreck to Nowhere." *Lovecraft Studies* No. 45 (2005): 1–9.

---

6. "The Statement of Randolph Carter" in particular might be said to share some of the characteristics of "Dagon" explored in this paper.

Evans, Tim. "A Last Defense against the Dark: Folklore, Horror, and the Uses of Tradition in the Works of H. P. Lovecraft." *Journal of Folklore Research* 42, No. 1 (2005): 99–135.

Guarde Paz, Cesar. "Race and War in the Lovecraft Mythos: A Philosophical Reflection." *Lovecraft Annual* No. 6 (2012): 3–35.

Hantke, Steffen. "From the Library of America to the Mountains of Madness: Recent Discourse on H. P. Lovecraft." In David Simmons, ed. *New Critical Essays on H. P. Lovecraft.* New York: Palgrave Macmillan, 2013. 135–56.

Harman, Graham. *Weird Realism: Lovecraft and Philosophy.* Winchester, UK: Zero Books, 2012.

Joshi, S. T. "Why Michel Houellebecq is Wrong about Lovecraft's Racism." *Lovecraft Annual* No. 12 (2018): 43–50.

Palinhos, Jorge. "Architectures of Madness: Lovecraft's R'lyeh as Modernist Dystopia." In Maria Monteiro, Mario Kong, and Maria Neto, ed. *Utopia(s)—Worlds and Frontiers of the Imaginary.* Boca Raton, FL: CRC Press, 2017. 325–28.

Ponzio, Augusto. "Otherness, Intercorporeity, and Dialogism in Bakhtin's Vision of the Text." *Language and Semiotic Studies* 2, No. 3 (2016): 1–17.

Robinson, Christopher. "The Abysmal Style of H. P. Lovecraft." In Maylis Rospide and Sandrine Sorlin, ed. *The Ethics and Poetics of Alterity: New Perspectives on Genre Literature.* Newcastle upon Tyne, UK: Cambridge Scholars Publishing, 2015. 126–41.

Salonia, John. "Cosmic Maenads and the Music of Madness: Lovecraft's Borrowings from the Greeks." *Lovecraft Annual* No. 5 (2011): 91–101.

Simmons, David. "A Certain Resemblance: Abject Hybridity in H. P. Lovecraft's Short Fiction." In David Simmons, ed. *New Critical Essays on H. P. Lovecraft.* New York: Palgrave Macmillan, 2013. 13–30.

Williams, Sara. ""The Infinitude of the Shrieking Abysses": Rooms, Wombs, Tombs, and the Hysterical Female Gothic in "The Dreams in the Witch House."" In David Simmons, ed. *New Critical Essays on H. P. Lovecraft.* New York: Palgrave Macmillan, 2013. 55–72.

Wisker, Gina. ""Spawn of the Pit": Lavinia, Marceline, Medusa, and All Things Foul: H. P. Lovecraft's Liminal Women." In David Simmons, ed. *New Critical Essays on H. P. Lovecraft.* New York: Palgrave Macmillan, 2013. 31–54.

Briefly Noted

The extent to which Lovecraft's work permeated American and world culture, even at a time when he was relatively little-known, is a continual source of amazement. It is known that the French artist and writer Jean Cocteau discussed Lovecraft briefly in "Books of 1954: A Symposium" (*Observer* [London], 26 December 1954), where he cited the first French volume of Lovecraft's stories, *La Couleur tombée du ciel* (1954). Now we learn that in 1951 he executed a pencil drawing that he titled "Homage à Lovecraft": it apparently depicts a Deep One from "The Shadow over Innsmouth." Even more remarkably, the late Stephen Sondheim (1930–2021) exhibited an interest in Lovecraft early in his career, writing an adaptation of "The Rats in the Walls" for radio at the age of nineteen. The typescript of this item has recently surfaced. Whether the script was actually broadcast in 1949 or at any other time is unknown.

"The Essence of Cosmic Mystery": The Appeal of John Martin's *Paradise Lost* Pictures to H. P. Lovecraft

Christopher Cuccia

H. P. Lovecraft harbored a profound admiration for the seventeenth-century poet John Milton, drawing much inspiration from Milton's epic masterwork, *Paradise Lost* (1667/1674) (see Cuccia). Lovecraft also greatly admired one of Milton's most famous illustrators, Gustave Doré, who produced the masterful engravings for an 1866 edition of *Paradise Lost,* which Lovecraft's family owned, and which in turn inspired a Lovecraftian creature: "I began having nightmares of the most hideous description, peopled with things which I called 'night-gaunts,'" Lovecraft revealed in a letter of 1916, explaining, "I used to draw them after waking (perhaps the idea of these figures came from an edition de luxe of 'Paradise Lost' with illustrations by Doré, which I discovered one day in the east parlour)" (*Letters to Rheinhart Kleiner and Others* 66). Doré's gloomy engravings remain the most popular Milton illustrations to this day, but prior to Doré it was the English painter and printmaker John Martin (1789–1854) who could boast the most celebrated illustrations of *Paradise Lost,* and Lovecraft professed in a letter of 1928, which we will return to throughout, that he preferred these:

> Under Lovemanic guidance I looked up engravings of his work in the N.Y. Public Library, & was enthralled by the darkly thunderous, apocalyptically majestic, & cataclysmically unearthly power of one who, to me, seemed to hold the essence of cosmic mystery . . . He was, in a sense, a Milton among painters . . . It is . . . fitting to compare him with Gustave Doré, since his

scenes were always conceived in the external spirit of classic naturalism, the element of terror, mystery, or sublimity being infused by a process much subtler than mere distortion. . . . Martin illustrated Milton—much better than did Doré later on, in my opinion . . . (Letter to Vincent Starrett, 10 January 1928; *Letters to Maurice W. Moe and Others* 527–28)

Lovecraft's preference for Martin over Doré appears to have rested on the bleak Martinian vision of the Miltonic cosmos—an already bleak vision, profoundly inhospitable to man, at least in Lovecraft's view—coming closest to the spirit of Lovecraftian cosmicism.

A proper understanding of why Martin appealed to Lovecraft's sensibilities requires a thorough exploration of the nature of the artist's profoundly unique approach to the pictorial arts. John Martin emerged from rather humble origins: born in Northumberland, he was the youngest of four eccentric sons of a working-class family no one would have expected to produce an artist of worldwide renown. At the age of fourteen, Martin was apprenticed to a coachbuilder, followed by the minor Italian artist Boniface Musso, in Newcastle upon Tyne. In 1806, with little artistic training, the seventeen-year-old Martin relocated to London, supporting himself for five years through china and glass painting, supplementing his meager income through the sale of watercolor and sepia drawings. In the early 1810s, Martin boldly moved on to painting pictures with apocalyptic themes, sending these to the Royal Academy of Arts. He first garnered critical attention with *Sadak in Search of the Waters of Oblivion* (1812), a positively infernal picture, with a minuscule subject in the foreground completely dwarfed by his sublime surroundings. (Incidentally, this is the picture that graced the cover of the 1999 Penguin Classics edition of Lovecraft's *The Call of Cthulhu and Other Weird Stories*.) Expansive landscapes depicting fantastical scenes of natural disaster and divine destruction—populated by puny people often facing impending doom—were to become Martin's trademark. Naturally, this was what endeared Martin to Lovecraft:

Night; great desolate pillared halls; unholy abysses & blasphemous torrents; terraced titan cities in far, half-celestial back-
grounds whereon shines the light of no familiar sky of men's
knowing; shrieking mortal hordes borne doomward over vast
wastes & down cyclopean gulfs where Phlegethon & Archeron
flow [see *PL* 2.578, 580–81]; these are the dominant impressions
one (i.e., myself, at least!) carries away from the study of a set of
Martin engravings. (*Letters Maurice W. Moe and Others* 528)

Martin, securing critical acclaim with *Joshua Commanding the
Sun to Stand Still upon Gibeon* (1816), would throughout the
1820s produce a series of these cataclysmic canvases, often of
biblical scenes, such as his famous *Belshazzar's Feast* (1820),
which was so wildly popular that it "had to be roped off to pro-
tect it from the crowds" (Wees and Campbell 2). So central was
the motif of the apocalyptic to Martin's oeuvre that when York
Minster was set on fire in 1829, the conflagration conjured up
the works of Martin for a woman watching the terrifying spectacle. (Ironically enough, unbeknownst to her the perpetrator was
Martin's mentally unstable brother Jonathan, who would thereafter be known as "Mad Martin.")

With his penchant for the apocalyptic, Martin was inevitably
drawn to that Bible of the Romantics, *Paradise Lost*, ambitiously
launching his printmaking career in the mid-1820s with his mezzotints of Milton's masterwork. The ambitious publisher Septimus Prowett commissioned Martin to singlehandedly illustrate
Paradise Lost in full, paying the handsome sum of 3,500 guineas
for a large and smaller set of twenty-four mezzotint engravings
for an edition of Milton's epic poem to be issued in eight different formats, the prints published monthly between 1825 and
1827 and to be assembled by the subscriber.[1]

This Martin-illustrated edition of *Paradise Lost* was profoundly unique in various ways. For one, whereas most Milton illustrators traditionally produced only one picture for each of the

---

1. For the complicated matter of the publication of Martin's Miltonic mezzotints
and their assemblage, see Balston 95–97; Altick 360; Wees and Campbell 18,
19n1; Hanley et al. 25n1; Woof et al. 20–21, 188. On the differences between
Martin's separate sets of *Paradise Lost* mezzotints, see Collins Baker 112–13.

twelve books of *Paradise Lost*—or fewer, as publishers often employed multiple artists for a single edition—Martin enjoyed the
privilege of illustrating twice this number. More significant still,
while illustrated editions typically featured an engraver's prints
after a painter's pictures, Martin's Milton pictures were engravings, executed solely by the artist himself. Prowett promoted this
as a selling point in his prospectus, claiming that it "cannot fail
to be highly appreciated by the Connoisseur, that Mr. Martin, by
a rare effort of art, has wholly composed and designed his sub-
jects on the Plates themselves; the Engravings therefore possess,
as originals, the charm of being the first conceptions of the Artist, and have all the spirit and finish of the Painter's touch" (*Literary Gazette* No. 426). And most significant of all, Martin's
engravings were executed in the unique method of mezzotint,
the engraving style allowing for extremes of dark and light,
working from the former rather than the latter.

    Given the great darkness of his mezzotints, Martin's sublime
hellscapes naturally made for his most impressive Milton illustrations. It was duly noted in contemporary criticism that *Paradise Lost's* paradoxical notion of "darkness visible" (1.63) was
masterfully realized by Martin. For instance, in 1829 the poet
Edwin Atherstone, commenting on his friend Martin at the
close of the decade that brought his greatest artistic success,
wrote, "none has like him painted the "darkness visible" of the
infernal deeps" (quoted in Wees and Campbell 2). Indeed, with
his print of *Pandemonium* (1824), which depicted "the high Cap-
itol / Of Satan and his Peers" (1.756–57), Martin managed
something no other Milton illustrator had ever ventured to envision. Martin's "gigantic and lurid Pandemonium," as Richard
D. Altick describes the resplendent infernal palace in *Paintings
from Books,* serves as "the sister palace of the one he made famous in *Belshazzar's Feast*" (361).

    So magnificent was Martin's rendering of hell's "*Pandæmoni-
um*, City and proud seat / Of *Lucifer*" (10.424–25) that a reviewer in the *Athenaeum*, commenting on Martin's larger, standalone
mezzotint of *Pandaemonium* (1831), remarked, "Satan seems far
more magnificently lodged than any potentate of upper air. We

wish the Government would desire Martin to design a palace for our kings" (460). Interestingly enough, when Martin revisited this subject a decade later in his painting of *Pandemonium* (1841)—for which he would also design a rather fetching frame, decorated with serpents and dragons—the infernal pile would now more than a little resemble the new Palace of Westminster, the construction of which began the year prior, prompted by the destruction by fire of the Old Palace in 1834.

The "gloomy Deep" (*PL* 1.152) within which Martin's Pandæmonium towers is also profoundly unique. Martin harbored serious engineering ambitions, so much so that, as J. Dustin Wees and Michael J. Campbell note, from 1827, the year he completed the mezzotints for Prowett's edition of *Paradise Lost,* to 1849 Martin "devoted a considerable amount of time and money to engineering schemes" for the purpose of "beautifying London" (3). It should then perhaps come as no surprise that, as has often been observed, Martin infused these engineering elements into his images of the Miltonic hell, Martin's cavernous underworld calling to mind early nineteenth-century architectural innovations, such as mineshafts and sewer tunnels (Svendsen 65, 67, 71–72).

Martin's profoundly original *Paradise Lost* illustrations were fabulously popular,[2] both with the public and with the critics. "We know no artist, whose genius so perfectly fitted him to be the illustrator of the mighty Milton," read an early review of the Miltonic mezzotints in the *Literary Gazette,* and the review goes on to read,

> in what we have seen of his conceptions he has more than realized the highest of our hopes. There is a wildness, a grandeur, and a mystery about his designs which are indescribably fine:—

---

2. See Balston 98: "The publication was a complete success, and Martin's plates won a lasting renown. In the next forty years Charles Whittingham (1846) and Sampson Low (1866) published editions of *Paradise Lost* with the larger series, Charles Tilt (1837 and 1838) and Henry Washbourne (1849, 1850, 1853 and 1858) with the smaller. But even steel plates would not stand up to so many impressions; in Washbourne's later editions they appear much worn. There was a curious revival in 1876, when Bickers & Sons published *The Poetical Works of John Milton* with small photographic prints of the larger series."

the painter is also a poet. It may be that the figures cannot possess the force and dignity with which the imagination clothes them: but the sweeping elements; the chaos come again; the wonders of that Heaven and Hell which existed before earth was made, are magnificently embodied. In short, we look upon these engravings to belong to the foremost order of true genius: beyond this there is no praise. (No. 428)

The English poet Robert Montgomery, in his 1830 poem *Satan,* went as far as to deem Martin, for his mastery of "the dark sublime," as in fact a "second Milton" (344)—a sentiment echoed by Lovecraft nearly a century later, when he referred to Martin as "a Milton among painters."

Not all were impressed with Martin's efforts, however. As magnificent as the landscapes were, in Martin's *Paradise Lost* pictures Milton's larger-than-life characters—even the hellish epic hero Satan, who sought to scale the heavens and unseat the Almighty Himself—are completely dwarfed by the landscapes they inhabit. Even the extraordinarily laudatory review in the *Literary Gazette* cited above conceded, "the figures cannot possess the force and dignity with which the imagination clothes them." Thomas Babington Macaulay lambasted Martin for this undeniable fact, asserting that he was completely unfit to picture Milton, and simply scorning his *Paradise Lost* pictures when skewering Montgomery's *Satan* in a review of April 1830. Macaulay would elaborate in another review written eight months later, wherein he derided Martin's *Paradise Lost* pictures for precisely the reason they were so popular:

He should never have attempted to illustrate the Paradise Lost. There can be no two manners more directly opposed to each other than the manner of his painting and the manner of Milton's poetry. Those things which are mere accessories in the descriptions become the principal objects in the pictures; and those figures which are most prominent in the descriptions can be detected in the pictures only by a very close scrutiny. Mr. Martin has succeeded perfectly in representing the pillars and candelabras of Pandemonium. But he has forgotten that Milton's Pandemonium is merely the background to Satan. In the

picture, the Archangel is scarcely visible amidst the endless colonnades of his infernal palace. (1.523)

In *Paradise Lost,* the lower-ranking devils diminish themselves so
as to fit within Pandæmonium (I.775–92), with the chief devils
retaining "thir own dimensions" in council "far within" (1.792–
98). Macaulay's complaint is essentially that Martin has taken
Milton's Satan—"thir mighty Paramount," indeed "Hell's dread
Emperor with pomp Supreme, / And God-like imitated State"
(2.508, 510–11)—and diminished him just the same.

One of the reasons for the fact that "in Mr. Martin's picture
the landscape is everything," as Macaulay complains, is that
Martin's figure drawing skills were deficient. But Martin transformed this disadvantage into an advantage, vast vistas with diminutive figures that seem so insignificant in comparison serving
as the heart and soul of Martin's illustrations. Lovecraft picked
up on this characteristic feature, which, he expressed, endeared
Martin to him: "His greatest weakness was the rendering of the
human figure, but this was no major defect because with him
figures were only slight & subsidiary parts of great landscape &
architectural conceptions" (*Letters to Maurice W. Moe and Others* 528). Lovecraft goes on to enumerate the Martinian features
of "unholy abysses & blasphemous torrents," the "terraced titan
cities," and the "shrieking mortal hordes borne doomward over
vast wastes & down cyclopean gulfs" quoted above. For Lovecraft, the cosmos is not "merely the background" to man, as religious worldviews hold; no, man's insignificance is betrayed by
the vastness of the cosmos, and hence the rather colorless human characters of Lovecraft's stories merely help to illustrate the
infinitely greater power of the cosmic entities indifferent to
man's impending destruction. This is the lifeblood of Lovecraftian cosmicism, and precisely the reason Lovecraft found Martin's
illustrations of Milton so appealing.

The idea of Milton's magnificently sublime Satan being depicted in a manner that renders him "slight & subsidiary" is
what is difficult to digest for those who fail to appreciate Martin's *Paradise Lost* pictures. This can, however, be read in a
counter-Romantic way, i.e., as Martin bringing Milton's Satan

down to size. In their article on Septimus Prowett and the Martin-illustrated *Paradise Lost,* Howard J. M. Hanley, Margaret Cooper, and Susan Morris make just this point, referring specifically to Martin's plate of *Satan Arousing the Fallen Angels* (1824). This scene of Satan summoning his defeated legions in the depths of hell was a favorite among artists ever since Milton illustration commenced in 1688, and Romantic artists around the turn of the nineteenth century simply reveled in this moment, picturing Satan at his most heroic. This is not necessarily the case with Martin:

> Martin's illustrations are the first to attempt to portray the immensity of Milton's universe. In a radical departure from his predecessors, Martin's figures are dominated by the landscape, both natural and architectural. Even Satan is no exception . . . : gone are the aggressive overwhelming images of Fuseli, Westall and their contemporaries drawn 20 years before . . . True, as we can see, Martin makes Satan the focal point, as he must be: his pose is of aggressive command, essential for an artist seeking an effect of the sublime. But he is none the less subordinate to the vastness of the surroundings and here overlooks a cavernous swirling tunnel of rocks and water which totally swamp his diminutive followers. (21)

In order to understand how this vision clashes with the impressions made by Milton's verse, consider the simile Milton employs when giving the reader a sense of the "monstrous size" (1.197) of Satan:

> His Spear, to equal which the tallest Pine
> Hewn on *Norwegian* hills, to be the Mast
> Of some great Ammiral, were but a wand,
> He walkt with . . . (1.292–95)

Contrast this with Martin's image, wherein Satan instead appears like a tiny toy soldier wielding a toothpick. This is not a problem for Lovecraft, of course, as Lovecraft did not read Milton's *Paradise Lost* as the so-called "Romantic Satanists" did—with Milton, unconsciously or otherwise, on the side of Satan, so to speak—simply because, as leading Lovecraft scholar Robert

H. Waugh put it, "Lovecraft was not of the party of Satan but of the party of Chaos" (16). Lovecraft could therefore feel much more at home—in Miltonic Chaos—in Martin's *Paradise Lost* pictures, for while Romantic artists produced plentiful outsized Miltonic Satans, Martin laid claim to what none of these illustrators produced: a vast vision of the Miltonic cosmos, in all its terror and wonder.

Certain critics have, however, insisted that Milton's Devil was indeed given his due in Martin's mezzotints. Martin's Satan is, after all, another installment in Romantic art's many Miltonic Satans insofar as he is a winged heroic nude male equipped with shield, spear, ornate helmet, and/or crown. And as minuscule as the Martinian Satan may appear in the infernal episodes, he is represented as one among many, with this increased focus on Satan's fellow fallen angels improving upon Romantic renditions of the Miltonic Satan in a quite significant respect. While supremely sublime, the Romantic Satan often indeed "seem[s] / Alone th' Antagonist of Heav'n" (*PL* 2.508–9), which is to say, with very few exceptions the figure of the fallen archangel was dominant to the point of isolation, and the deep bond of brotherhood shared between the "great Commander" (1.358) and his "Companions dear" (6.419) in Milton's text was undeniably lacking. Martin does not achieve the levels of Gustave Doré in terms of capturing that splendid sense of brothers-in-arms among the rebel hosts, which, as in *Paradise Lost* itself, serves to enhance Satan's noble air, but Martin does indeed anticipate Doré in increasing the scope beyond Satan himself. This is the rationale behind the aforementioned reviewer in the *Athenaeum,* when responding to Martin's larger, standalone mezzotint of *Satan in Council* (1831), ranking Martin's Satan above those of prior Romantic Milton illustrators.[3]

---

3. See the *Athenaeum* No. 246: "The great enemy of mankind, seated on his infernal throne, and surrounded by myriads of his fallen companions, and meditating the renewal of war against Heaven, is a subject worthy of the highest powers; and it cannot be said that John Martin is deficient in matters which belong to imagination. It is not, however, in magnificent light and shade, and supernatural splendour alone, that Milton excels; he is a great painter of char-

Undeniably diminished within Martin's *Paradise Lost* pictures, however, are Adam and Eve—the representatives of the human race—and this gets to the essence of their likeness to Lovecraftian cosmicism. The most diminishing picture Martin provided was a profoundly bleak treatment of the expulsion from Eden scene, *Adam and Eve Driven out of Paradise* (1827). The conclusion of Milton's epic, while somber, is meant to be at least somewhat reassuring to the reader, who of course occupies the fallen world Adam and Eve now enter:

> Some natural tears they dropp'd, but wip'd them soon;
> The World was all before them, where to choose
> Thir place of rest, and Providence thir guide:
> They hand in hand with wand'ring steps and slow,
> Through *Eden* took thir solitary way. (12.645–49)

The crucial concluding lines of *Paradise Lost* stress that while Adam and Eve are "solitary" (12.649)—and "wand'ring" (12.648), like the philosophizing fallen angels (2.561) or Satan himself journeying across the cosmos (2.830, 973)—the expelled parents of the human race still have "Providence [as] thir guide" (12.647) along their treacherous journey through the fallen world. Martin's vision of this scene is far bleaker: Adam and Eve are pitifully diminutive figures against the backdrop of what appears a not merely fallen but genuinely apocalyptic world. Kester Svendsen, while conceding the gloominess of Martin's picture, insists upon other positive elements (71–72), but really the negativity is overwhelming. Wendy Furman-Adams and Virginia James Tufte have made much of the bleakness of Fuseli's treat-

---

acter—particularly those of a melancholy and gloomy kind—and we think his Satan a masterpiece. Now we have seen sundry Satans in our day—Fuseli, Lawrence, Stothard, and Blake, tried their talents on the great apostate, and all, in our opinion, more or less failed; nor can we say that the fiend of Martin, as a solitary figure, is successful: it is not, however, as a solitary figure that the painter has exhibited him; he is seated on his throne in the centre of his new palace; lights, to which Greek fire was as a will-o'-wisp, burn overhead; while ranked in order round, his comrades in evil are seated, gloomily listening to the words of the great anarch; the scene fills and satisfies the imagination" (459–60).

ment of *Paradise Lost's* expulsion scene (269), wherein the arch-angel Michael, as representative of Providence, comes off as remarkably petulant, reassuring the crestfallen human couple—and, more importantly, the viewer—he coldly turns his back on that Paradise is truly lost, with no hint of any "paradise within," as Michael promised, certainly not "happier far" (12.587). And yet in Fuseli's picture Adam and Eve are still the focus, their dramatic embrace expressing the picture's own positive elements: Fuseli's Eve is an emotional wreck, but Adam supports her as they balletically make "thir solitary way" (12.649) out of Eden; what's more, Adam's left hand over Eve's womb would seem to gesture toward the prophetic reassurance that "her Seed" will produce man's salvation.[4] Martin's interpretation is infinitely bleaker, calling to mind his famous cataclysmic biblical canvases.

It is certainly true that Milton's illustrators from the very beginning proved to be some of the great skeptics with regards to *Paradise Lost's* supposedly uplifting ending, artists routinely depicting the expulsion scene rather sadly, albeit in varying degrees. While Martin's may arguably be the bleakest, the fact is that he was hardly alone in interpreting the scene in such a fashion; therefore, what is perhaps more notable about Martin's depictions of Eden is that this supposed Paradise is a rather gloomy place even before the expulsion—even before the Fall. This is naturally what captivated Lovecraft, given his thoughts on "the miserable denizens of a wretched little flyspeck on the back door of a microscopic universe," his misanthropic scorn for the "accursed flyspeck-inhabiting lice which we call human beings . . ." (*Against Religion* 16).

Macaulay had complained that, in Martin's Hell, "the Archangel is scarcely visible amidst the endless colonnades of his infernal palace," but his criticism of Martin's *Paradise Lost* pictures is far more appropriate in sight of Eden: "Milton's Paradise, again, is merely the background to his Adam and Eve. But in Mr. Martin's picture the landscape is everything. Adam, Eve, and Raphael attract much less notice than the lake and the

---

4. See *Paradise Lost*, 10.179–91, 1028–40; 11.112–17, 153–58; 12.232–35, 324–30, 375–400, 537–51, 594–605, 620–23. See also Svendsen 69–70.

mountains, the gigantic flowers, and the giraffes which feed upon them" (1.523). This same criticism was made of Martin even
before his Miltonic mezzotints of the 1820s. While these are the
Milton illustrations he is best known for, Martin had actually
turned to *Paradise Lost* a decade earlier with a series of oil paintings of the great English epic, depicting mostly paradisiacal
scenes, interestingly enough.[5] It was noted, however, that Martinian bleakness permeated even these pictures, *The Times* writing
of Martin's 1823 painting of *Adam and Eve Entertaining the Angel
Raphael,* "Mr Martin! Where does your colourman live? Where do
these trees grow? Where such *lapis lazuli* mountains and skies?
Where such figures to be met with? We forgot that the whole picture is antediluvian" (quoted in Myrone 116). William Hazlitt
would voice similar, more bluntly expressed grievances about
Martin's *Adam and Eve Asleep in Paradise,* a lost Miltonic picture:

> It has this capital defect, that there is no *repose* in it. You see
> two insignificant naked figures, and a preposterous architectural
> landscape, like a range of buildings over-looking them. . . . They
> ought to have been painted imparadised in one another's arms,

---

5. In 1813, Martin exhibited *Adam's First Sight of Eve* (1812) at the Royal
Academy; a decade later, he exhibited *Adam and Eve Entertaining the Angel
Raphael* (1823), as well as a larger version of *The Expulsion of Adam and Eve
from Paradise* (1823–27), a lost work, at the British Institution; two years later,
Martin's *Creation of Light* (1825) canvas, another lost work, was exhibited at
the Society of British Artists. See Altick 359–60; Wees and Campbell 18, 24;
Woof et al. 199. Martin not only painted *Paradise Lost* pictures prior to his
mezzotint engravings for Septimus Prowett's critically and commercially successful edition of *Paradise Lost,* but afterward as well. Two of the Miltonic
prints were recreated in oil, *The Conflict Between Satan and Death* (1832) and
Pandaemonium (1841), but Martin also pictured a variety of original Paradise
Lost scenes on canvas: at the British Institution he exhibited *The Deluge* in
1826 (and won a gold medal at the Paris Salon in 1835 for a larger version of
this picture painted the year before); at the Royal Academy of Arts, he exhibited *The Eve of the Deluge* (which ended up in the Royal Collection) in 1840,
followed by *The Celestial City and the River of Bliss* in 1841, and *The Fall of
Man, Morning in Paradise* (or *Adam and Eve in Paradise: Morning Hymn*), and
Evening in Paradise in 1844, and lastly *The Judgement of Adam and Eve* in 1845.
See Altick 360.

shut up in measureless content, with Eden's choicest bowers closing round them, and Nature stooping to clothe them with vernal flowers. . . . [O]n the contrary, you have a gaudy panoramic view, a glittering barren waste, a triple row of clouds, of rocks, and mountains, piled one upon the other, as if the imagination already bent its idle gaze over that wide world which was so soon to be our place of exile, and the aching, restless spirit of the artist was occupied in building a stately prison for our first parents, instead of decking their bridal bed, and wrapping them in a short-lived dream of bliss. (2.233n.)

Yet Adam and Eve are not only Eden's genuinely "puny habitants" (*PL* 2.367); the imposing landscape that looms ominously over the helpless human couple is, if not nearly as dark as hell, undeniably pervaded by a profound gloomth. *The Times'* review of Martin's *Adam and Eve Entertaining the Angel Raphael* quoted above quipped that it was unclear whether this Edenic scene took place before the Flood; this criticism is even more appropriate when applied to his Miltonic mezzotints, which appear to invite suspicions that perhaps Milton's Eden was not the Paradise—that "short-lived dream of bliss" Hazlitt describes—the reader is meant to imagine.

Milton aspired with *Paradise Lost* to "justify the ways of God to men" (1.26), but Lovecraft found in the epic poem a profoundly bleak vision of the cosmos, hence the Miltonic looming large over Lovecraft's oeuvre. Lovecraft favored John Martin's dark mezzotint illustrations of Milton because he sensed that Martin captured his own misanthropic interpretation of *Paradise Lost;* indeed, he felt Martin went even further, producing with his "insignificant figures" and "preposterous architectural landscape" a kind of proto-cosmicism, a profoundly bleak vision quite akin to his own, with primordial man and woman genuinely "accursed flyspeck-inhabiting lice." Lovecraft felt Martin "was, in a sense, a Milton among painters," and by the same token Lovecraft himself aspired to be, in a sense, not only a Milton but a Martin among writers of weird fiction and cosmic horror.

Works Cited

Altick, Richard D. *Paintings from Books: Art and Literature in Britain, 1760–1900*. Columbus: Ohio State University Press, 1985.

Athenaeum. No. 246 (14 July 1832): 459–60.

Balston, Thomas. *John Martin 1789–1854: His Life and Works*. London: Duckworth, 1947.

Collins Baker, C. H. "Some Illustrations of Milton's *Paradise Lost* (1688–1850) (*Continued*)." *The Library*, Fifth Series, 3, No. 2 (September 1948): 101–19.

Cuccia, Christopher. "A Bridge through Chaos: The Miltonic in 'Dagon' and Lovecraft's Greater Cthulhu Mythos." *Lovecraft Annual* No. 15 (2021): 102–27.

Furman-Adams, Wendy, and Virginia James Tufte. "Anticipating Empson: Henry Fuseli's Re-Vision of Milton's God." *Milton Quarterly* 35, No. 4 (December 2001): 258–74.

Hanley, Howard J. M.; Cooper; Margaret; and Susan Morris. "The Mysterious Septimus Prowett: Publisher of the John Martin *Paradise Lost*." *British Art Journal* 2, No. 1 (Autumn 2000): 20–25.

Hazlitt, William. *The Plain Speaker: Opinions on Books, Men, and Things*. London: Henry Colburn, 1826. 2 vols.

Literary Gazette, and Journal of Belles Lettres, Arts, Sciences, &c. No. 426 (19 March 1825): 191; No. 428 (2 April 1825): 220.

Lovecraft, H. P. *Against Religion: The Atheist Writings of H. P. Lovecraft*. Ed. S. T. Joshi. New York: Sporting Gentlemen, 2010.

———. *Letters to Maurice W. Moe and Others*. Ed. David E. Schultz and S. T. Joshi. New York: Hippocampus Press, 2018.

———. *Letters to Rheinhart Kleiner and Others*. Ed. S. T. Joshi and David E. Schultz. New York: Hippocampus Press, 2020.

Macaulay, Thomas Babington. *Miscellaneous Works of Lord Macaulay*. Ed. Lady Trevelyan. New York: Harper & Brothers, 1880. 5 vols.

Milton, John. *Complete Poems and Major Prose*. Ed. Merritt Y. Hughes. 1957. Indianapolis: Hackett, 2003.

Montgomery, Robert. *Satan: A Poem*. London: Samuel Maunder, 1830.

Myrone, Martin. *John Martin: Apocalypse*. London: Tate Publishing, 2011.

Svendsen, Kester. "John Martin and the Expulsion Scene of *Paradise Lost*." *Studies in English Literature, 1500–1900* 1, No. 1 (Winter, 1961): 63–73.

Waugh, Robert H. "The Blasted Heath in 'The Colour out of Space.'" In Waugh's *A Monster of Voices: Speaking for H. P. Lovecraft*. New York: Hippocampus Press, 2011. 15–37.

Wees, J. Dustin, with Michael J. Campbell. *Darkness Visible: The Prints of John Martin*. Williamstown, MA: Sterling & Francine Clark Art Institute, 1986.

Woof, Robert; Hanley, Howard J. M.; and Hebron, Stephen. *Paradise Lost: The Poem and Its Illustrators*. Grasmere, UK: Wordsworth Trust, 2004.

———

Briefly Noted

We are saddened to note the death on 1 February of Richard L. Tierney (b. 1936). Poet, critic, and novelist, Tierney deserves eternal commemoration in the Lovecraft community for his one-page article, "The Derleth Mythos" (in Meade and Penny Frierson's anthology *HPL* [1972]), which began the dismantling of August Derleth's seriously erroneous view of Lovecraft's pseudo-mythology—work that was carried on by Dirk W. Mosig ("H. P. Lovecraft: Myth-Maker") and others. Tierney also wrote other important essays on Lovecraft, such as "Lovecraft and the Cosmic Quality in Fiction" (in S. T. Joshi's *H. P. Lovecraft: Four Decades of Criticism* [1980]). Many of his novels, tales, and poems reflect Lovecraftian themes.

Lovecraft and the Folklore of Glocester's Dark Swamp

Stephen Olbrys Gencarella

A century ago, in the waning months of 1923, H. P. Lovecraft and C. M. Eddy, Jr. set out to visit an area of Glocester, Rhode Island known as the Dark Swamp. Although the results of their sojourn were mixed—the pair eventually found the location of the swamp but did not venture into it—the excursion inspired Eddy's story "Black Noon" (unfinished at his death in 1967) and the opening of Lovecraft's "The Colour out of Space" (Joshi and Schultz 84).[1] Recently, their journey has induced Lovecraft enthusiasts to share rumors of a creature roaming the swamp, introduced by the name "IT" in one of Lovecraft's letters. Legend tripping and dark tourism to the area have commenced in earnest as well and only promises to increase in the decades ahead, with growing attention to Lovecraft's work and regional conferences such as NecronomiCon Providence. These recent practices have borne narrative germinations that are, in the technical parlance of Folklore Studies, proto-legends: raw materials that may eventually coalesce into a coherent legend and narrative tradition passed along by raconteurs. While it remains unclear if tales of IT will become a viable contemporary legend, a greater question remains concerning Lovecraft's assertion that such a folk narrative was circulating in the early 1900s. The historicity of that claim is the subject of this article.

Throughout this essay, I explore the question of whether Lovecraft tapped into the remnants of a narrative tradition or simply invented IT. I examine the accounts composed by Love-

---

1. Muriel Eddy employed similar imagery for her story "The Dark Road" (2017).

craft and the Eddys concerning the search for the Dark Swamp and the potential folk narratives that provoked their interest. I focus especially on a tale set near the swamp concerning a "burning beast," which recent enthusiasts have cited as testimony for Lovecraft's depiction of IT. I trace the historical context of that story and its relationship to other regional folklore, especially a cycle of treasure tales that thrived in the nineteenth century. I also examine the tradition of swamps in the folklore of Indigenous peoples of southern New England in order to compare Lovecraft's statement regarding precolonial beliefs about IT. Although I draw upon the methods of Folklore Studies to analyze numerous texts—several of which have been unexamined for more than a century and will be novel to Lovecraft scholars—I must admit that this essay is speculative by necessity. There are simply not enough data in the form of records from an oral tradition to render an incontestable judgment concerning the folkloric origins of IT, but I do offer a conclusion in accord with the best available evidence. My analysis contributes to Lovecraft scholarship by assessing his powers and practices of invention and adaptation and to Folklore Studies by catching a folkloric production process in the act, as it transmutes fiction into folklore.

The Dark Swamp

To get our bearings among the several narrative processes involved, it makes sense to begin geographically. The Dark Swamp lies in the southwest quadrant of the rectangular-shaped town of Glocester. Its contours have never been explicit and have shifted over time. Today it roughly consists of a cedar wetland bordered by the Ponaganset Reservoir to the south, Pine Hill to the southwest, and Durfee Hill (the second highest elevation in Rhode Island) to the northeast. The Ponaganset Reservoir took shape starting in 1856; its engineers instigated a flooding that united two bodies of water, Ponaganset Pond and its nearby southern and smaller neighbor Walton Pond. The Dark Swamp does not appear on the 1831 or 1851 maps of Glocester, the former of which shows both ponds still divided and the latter the home of one D. Page (David Page), just north of Ponaganset

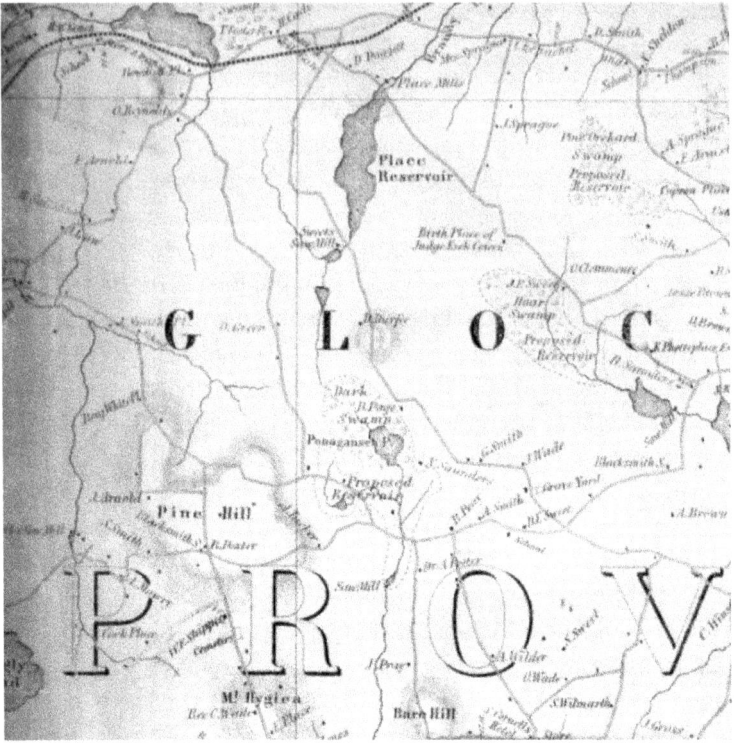

Pond and south of Durfee Hill. The swamp does appear on an
1855 map, however; it encompasses an area to the west of the
Page homestead and surrounds the entire "Proposed Reservoir,"
which includes the ponds. It is not present on a 1870 nor a 1895
map, both of which illustrate the reservoir; the former further
pinpoints the Page homestead and the latter the home of A. F.
Potter and the Ponaganset Mining and Smelting Company at the
same place near the reservoir. This location—formerly the Page
homestead and later that of Albert Potter and his company—was
the site of a gold mine, shafts of which were not formally closed
until the 1980s. Chepachet, the main village of the town, lies a
few miles to the east. All these features will come into consideration of the folklore associated with Lovecraft's report.[2]

2. See Faig (2017; originally composed c. 1973) for an earlier identification of
the Dark Swamp.

Discrepancies in the Accounts of Dark Swamp

The first mention of Dark Swamp—and of IT—occurs in a letter Lovecraft sent to Edwin Baird, the editor of *Weird Tales*. Baird published it in the March 1924 issue of the magazine.[3] The relevant passage appeared thus:

> Next Sunday we are going on a trip which may bring you echoes in the form of horror-tales from both participants. In the northwestern part of Rhode Island there is a remote village called Chepachet, reached by a single car line with only a few cars a day. Last week Eddy was there for the first time, and at the post office overheard a conversation between two ancient rustic farmers which inspired our coming expedition. They were discussing hunting prospects, and spoke of the migration of all the rabbits and squirrels across the line into Connecticut; when one told the other that there were plenty left in the *Dark Swamp*. Then ensued a description to which Eddy listened with the utmost avidity, and which brought out the fact that in this, the smallest and most densely populated state of the Union, there exists a tract of 160 acres which has never been fully penetrated by any living man. It lies two miles from Chepachet—in a direction we do not now know, but which we will ascertain Sunday—and is reputed to be the home of very strange animals—strange at least to this part of the world, and including the dreaded "bobcat", whose half-human cries in the night are often

3. Necronomicon Press republished HPL's letter in *Uncollected Letters* (1986). Its listing as c. August 1923 therein appears to be a minor error. The letter otherwise follows a chronological sequence in the collection and lies between another to Baird c. October 1923 and one to Farnsworth Wright c. January 1926. It also references HPL's pleasure in learning that the readers of *Weird Tales* "are taking kindly to my tenebrous effusions, as represented by 'Dagon'" (7–8). "Dagon" appeared in the October 1923 issue of the magazine. Finally, HPL mentions his impending visit to Dark Swamp with Eddy "next Sunday" (9); in his subsequent letter to Long dated 8 November, HPL identifies the date of the trip as Sunday, 4 November. Given this information, one may assume that HPL composed the letter around Sunday, 28 October. More pressing, this establishes that HPL and Eddy visited Glocester in November 1923, not August, as is sometimes reported, based on Eddy's recollection.

heard by neighboring farmers. The reason it has never been fully penetrated is that there are many treacherous potholes, and that the archaic trees grow so thickly together that passage is well-nigh impossible. The undergrowth is very thick, and even at midday the darkness is very deep because of the intertwined branches overhead. The description so impressed Eddy that he began writing a story about it—provisionally entitled "Black Noon"—on the trolley ride home. And now we are both to see it . . . we are both to go into that swamp . . . and *perhaps* to come out of it. Probably the thing'll turn out to be a clump of ill-nourished bushes, a few rain-puddles, and a couple of sparrows—but until our disillusion we are at liberty to think of the place as the immemorial lair of nightmare and unknown evil ruled by that subterraneous horror that sometimes cranes its neck out of the deepest potholes . . . It. (91–92)

There are numerous items to observe in this brief contribution. First is that Eddy—not Lovecraft—was present in the Chepachet post office a week prior to their trip, where he overheard two men discussing hunting plans, one of whom invoked the Dark Swamp, where game remained ample. Eddy further learned that the swamp was named because of its thick canopy—"dark" implying lack of light, not a sinister nature. That is, essentially, the gist of the contribution of those "ancient rustics" in this account. The men do not identify a legendary inhabitant nor any reason for fear. Although recent commentators (following Lovecraft's fancy) have assumed that the squirrels and rabbits fled for Connecticut to escape a lurking creature, there is no support for that interpretation here; indeed, the quip just as easily might have been in jest between the two men.

In this letter it is Lovecraft, not the two farmers, who introduces the concept of "It" with its craning neck, and he does so explicitly stating his and Eddy's interest in visiting the location to find inspiration for horror tales. It is Lovecraft, furthermore, who pronounces the animals of the Dark Swamp to be "very strange" for that part of the world, seemingly unaware that his specific example, the bobcat, is native to Rhode Island. And it is Lovecraft who suggests—albeit playfully with his interjection *"perhaps"*—a reason to consider the Dark Swamp a foreboding place. In this description, the author's imagination rather than the conversation between the "ancient rustics" raises suspicions about the locale.

Lovecraft's second foray into the matter occurs in a letter to Frank Belknap Long dated 8 November 1923. This contribution is a classic Lovecraftian epistle, nearly 1500 words in length, the bulk of which describes his and Eddy's journey from house to house in search of directions to the Dark Swamp. The framing paragraph borrows from Lovecraft's earlier letter but introduces significant changes:

> It was a quest of the grotesque and the terrible—a search for Dark Swamp, in northwestern Rhode-Island, of which Eddy had heard sinister whispers among the rusticks. They whisper that it is very remote and very strange, and that no one has ever been completely thro' it because of the treacherous and unfathomable potholes, and the antient trees whose thick boles grow so closely together that passage is difficult and darkness omnipresent even at noon, and *other* things, of which bobcats—whose half-human howls are heard in the night by peasants near the edge—are the very least. It is a very peculiar place, and no house was ever built within two miles of it. The rural swains refer to it with much evasiveness, and not one of them can be induc'd to guide a traveller through it; although a few intrepid hunters and woodcutters have plied their vocations on its fringes. It lyes in a natural bowl surrounded by low ranges of beautiful hills; far from any frequented road, and known to scarce a dozen persons outside the immediate country. Even in Chepachet, the nearest village, there are but two men who ever heard of it. Eddy discover'd its rumour at the Chepachet post office one bleak autumn evening when huntsmen gather'd about the fire and told tales and exprest wonder why all the squirrels and rabbits had left the hills and fled across the plain into Connecticut. One very antient man with a flintlock said that IT had mov'd in Dark Swamp, and had cran'd ITS neck out of the abysmal pothole beneath which IT had ITS immemorial lair. And he said his grandfather had told him in 1849, when he was a very little boy, that IT had been there when the

first settlers came, and that the Indians believed IT had always been there. This antient man with the flintlock was the only one present who had ever heard of Dark Swamp. (SL 1.265)

In detailing the trip, Lovecraft recollects numerous local citizens, each of whom sends him and Eddy to the next in pursuit of information. They comprised the following:

- The proprietor of a tavern and others in the taproom at Chepachet, who had "never heard of Dark Swamp."
- Henry Sayles, the town clerk (unnamed in Lovecraft's letter), who remarked that "the Dark Swamp had a very queer reputation, and that men had gone in who never came out; but confest he knew little of it, and had never been near it."
- A Mr. Sprague, initially thought to have been a guide into the swamp for an expedition from Brown University for botanical specimens in 1911.
- Fred Barnes, the actual guide of that party, who "had not much to say." Lovecraft and Eddy waited for him to arrive "all of thirty-five minutes in his squalid kitchen."
- The innkeeper and patrons of Cady's Tavern, where Lovecraft and Eddy lunched.
- James Reynolds, who directed them to the owner of the Dark Swamp.
- Ernest Law, the owner, who informed them of the location of the Dark Swamp two miles from his home and who added that "the peasants have a little exaggerated its fearful singularities, tho' it is yet a very odd place, and ill to visit by night."

With knowledge of the location attained for a subsequent visit, Lovecraft and Eddy returned to Chepachet and then to Providence. Akin to his letter to Baird, Lovecraft identified a motive for their undertaking. "We now know how to reach the swamp most expeditiously," he wrote, "and will not again lose time in devious inquiries. It will be a pleasing day's trip, and even tho' we discover no unsuspected horror, we shall surely behold enough of the darkly picturesque to furnish out a dozen tales apiece" (SL 1.267).

In comparison with the note to Baird, Lovecraft rewrote the narrative with more dramatic flair in this later letter. It was now the "rusticks" who provide sinister whispers, identify the location as very strange, and imply that the squirrels and rabbits fled to Connecticut in fear. In this rendition, an "antient man with the flintlock" rather than Lovecraft introduces IT (now capitalized) with its craning neck. Additionally, and quite unlike the initial letter, Lovecraft characterizes that man as passing along a narrative tradition from his grandfather, a tale in which precolonial Indigenous people believed that the creature had always inhabited the swamp.

None of the actual interlocutors during their visit narrated a legend or otherwise invoked IT. To the contrary, most were unaware of the Dark Swamp. Only Henry Sayles fed the impression of it being a strange place, although his point was that like all large swamps, it could be dangerous; at no point did he raise the potential of supernatural lore. Ernest Law, the best equipped to pass along any folk stories, tamped down that promise although he did suggest (if Lovecraft is to be believed) that some exaggerated its "fearful singularities." The source for any tale about IT, then, is a single, unidentified man whom Lovecraft never personally encountered, and whose description varies widely in two accounts—and that man did not describe the creature with any sense of detail.

The discrepancies alone are enough to disqualify either as a legitimate source of historical information, but there are several other challenging issues that arise immediately. Although Lovecraft correctly asserts the Dark Swamp lies in a natural bowl between hills and is technically accurate that the people with whom he spoke did not know of it, he is woefully mistaken in his assertion that "no house was ever built within two miles of it." The aforementioned maps incontrovertibly reveal numerous homesteads throughout the area. The 1895 map further demarcates two schoolhouses (numbers 8 and 9) within a mile. And despite Lovecraft's implications of concerned evasion, the fact that no homes stood in the swamp is simply common sense: the ground is too wet to build there.

Similarly, his assertion that the swamp is "far from any fre-

quented road" requires explication. Snake Hill Road, the artery
through southern Glocester, had once run through the swamp.
The creation of the Ponaganset Reservoir cleaved a section, but
a network of roads remained. The road itself was ancient, likely
first a path forged by precolonial Indigenous people. Admittedly,
it was a typical country road in comparison to those in Providence, but it did not suffer lack of use. And although most of
the inhabitants in the area were engaged as farmers or colliers—
an activity that resulted in the cutting of vast swaths of forest to
furnish coal and pasture—newspapers recommended tourism to
Durfee Hill and the reservoir as early as the late 1800s, especially following the opening of the gold mine.[4] By 1923, the mine
and the coal pits had ceased operation and nature had begun to
reclaim unfarmed land, but Lovecraft's depiction of the swamp's
isolation is the product of his limited—and arguably motivated—perception.

Eddy's commentary complicates the matter even more as it
shifts numerous elements, including the responsibility for learning about the location onto Lovecraft:

> One other jaunt with Lovecraft is retained rather vividly in
> memory, for all that it was in a way a frustrating one. It was a
> trip made into the country in August 1923, in search of a
> blighted area called "The Dark Swamp"—a place of such stygi-
> an darkness that the sun reputedly never shone there, never
> penetrated its fastnesses, even at high noon. Lovecraft had no
> very clear idea of its setting, but had been told that it was locat-
> ed off the Putnam Pike, about halfway between Chepachet,
> Rhode Island and Putnam, Connecticut.
>
> The day we set out was blistering hot; though we took the first

---

4. The Special Features and Fashions section of the Sunday edition of the
Providence Journal for 9 July 1922, for example, published a two-page essay entitled "Daring Explorer Scales State's Highest Peak." Illustrated with amusing
cartoons and written in a playful style that hearkens to explorer's tales of un-
charted mountainous forests, the essay follows the expedition of Minerva
Braithwaite to scale Durfee Hill. It includes mention of seeing the remains of
"Potter, or Gold Mine, Farm" and "the faraway waters of Ponneganset [*sic*],
nestling like a turquoise gem in an emerald field" (47).

trolley in the morning to the end of the line in Chepachet, it was already very warm at that hour. In Chepachet, we started out on foot on the road to Putnam. The heat increased as the day wore on. We had brought sandwiches with us, and from time to time we stopped at farmhouses along the way for water and to inquire about the Dark Swamp. But no one seemed to have heard of it, and after four miles, Lovecraft, considerably wilted by the heat, decided reluctantly that we would have to give up the quest. So we found some reasonably comfortable stones at the side of the road and sat there until one of the Putnam—Providence cars stopped for us and put an end to our search. We never afterward took it up again, though, despite the discomfort of the summer day, it was as rewarding as any walk with Lovecraft, in that he found many of the old farm buildings fascinating and conveyed that fascination to me. (*Gentleman from Angell Street* 49–50)

Eddy's recollection was initially published in 1966 in *The Dark Brotherhood and Other Pieces*, a collection edited by August Derleth. While it is reasonable to give precedence to Lovecraft's detailed letter, composed soon following the hike, over Eddy's brief memory pulled four decades after the event, there are three other portrayals to consider, all by Eddy's wife Muriel. She wrote the first in 1945. It follows her discussion of the initial face-to-face meeting between Lovecraft and the Eddys on a sweltering Sunday afternoon in August 1923:

It was during the hot summer months that Lovecraft expressed the desire to have Mr. Eddy accompany him on a quest to find a so-called "Black Swamp" somewhere, it was said, in the wilds of Chepachet, R.I.—a swamp so overhung with trees that no sunlight ever penetrated it. Always on the lookout for oddities of nature, the idea of seeing such a swamp intrigued Lovecraft to such an extent that he took the whole day off, leaving his writings, as eager as any schoolboy to witness nature's phenomenon. The whereabouts of that swamp—if such a swamp truly exists—is still a mystery—at least, it was never located, and Mr. Eddy almost had to carry Lovecraft back from the rural excursion, at least a mile, to the trolley line, for, unaccustomed to such vigorous jaunts at that time, the writer of tales macabre

soon became so exhausted he could hardly move one foot after
the other. It was a great disappointment to Lovecraft that the
trip was a failure, as far as finding the swamp was concerned;
but the rural characteristics of the village delighted him, and
found place, I am sure, in many of his later stories. ("Howard
Phillips Lovecraft" 18)

The second account appeared in 1961. The essay, entitled
"The Gentleman from Angell Street," also details their first
meeting in August.[5] She continues:

It was during the summer of 1923 that Lovecraft expressed
the desire to have Mr. Eddy accompany him on a quest to find a
so-called "Black Swamp" somewhere near the small village of
Chepachet, Rhode Island. It was said to be a swamp so overhung by trees that sunshine never penetrated it.

The thought of visiting such a swamp intrigued H.P.L. and
he discarded his habit of staying in during the bright hours of
the day to join my husband in the long hike. They took a trolley
to Chepachet, and from then on they were on their own. It was a
long walk to any kind of swamp land from the civic center of the
community, and hours later, after viewing several small swamps
but not finding any to answer the description of Black Swamp,
they were about to turn back when Lovecraft suggested they stop
in and rest at one of the farmhouses dotting the section. Besides,
he averred, some of the farmers in that region might possibly
know where (and if) there was such a swamp in the vicinity.

The wife of one farmer invited them into the kitchen and offered them refreshment in the form of a glass of milk and gin-
gerbread. H.P.L. eagerly accepted it, and he listened attentively
as their hosts assured them that Black Swamp was virtually unknown to them, and it must have been a pipe dream somebody
had, writing up a non-existent place. There were plenty of
swamps, but none, they were sure, through which sunlight never filtered. Sometimes their cows got lost in the swamplands,
but they always found them sooner or later.

---

5. This pamphlet was the basis for another, trimmed version entitled *H. P.
Lovecraft, Esquire, Gentleman*, which referenced the "Black Swamp" but removed the account (4).

Lovecraft, later, jotted down in a little notebook he carried, tidbits of their quaint Yankee talk, saying the trip was not entirely a failure, as he had gleaned quite a bit from hearing the antiquarians converse. It would come in handy when he wrote his next story, he assured my tired-out husband. (*Gentleman from Angell Street* 11–12)

Muriel Eddy's third account appeared in the pamphlet "Howard Phillips Lovecraft: The Man and the Image," from 1969.[6] The essay confirms:

My husband often accompanied Howard on trips to get new ideas. One day they took a trolley car from Providence to the village of Chepachet, Rhode Island, to find a black swamp. It was said to be so overhung by trees that sunshine could not penetrate it.

They hiked for hours, and saw several swamps, but found nothing to answer the description.

But H.P.L. made many notes for future reference. He told Cliff that no trip was ever wasted.

Although Howard never wrote a story about the nonexistent swamp, my husband used this as a basis for the last story he wrote during his retirement. Entitled "Black Noon," it will be published in 1970 by August Derleth of Arkham House, Sauk City, Wis. (4)

Eddy's memory was not perfect—she erroneously credited a walk with her husband in "in the western part of Rhode Island" (*Howard Phillips Lovecraft: The Man and the Image* 5) as inspiration for "The Picture in the House," when Lovecraft wrote that story in 1920. Nevertheless, her reminiscences help reconstruct the apparent error in her husband's: C. M. Eddy simply misremembered the day of their first encounter in person on a hot summer in August 1923 with the later date of their hike in November. With that matter resolved, all six are relatively similar, and the defining feature that consistently runs through them is

6. This pamphlet was reprinted with minor revision as "H. P. Lovecraft among the Demons" in the *Rhode Islander*, the magazine of the Providence *Sunday Journal*, on 8 March 1970.

not IT but the notion that the swamp was dark due to the canopy. Hence, the notion of a folklore concerning a supernatural creature circulating in the community appears only in Lovecraft's stylized letter to Long. Such contradiction would warrant consideration of Lovecraft as an unreliable narrator, but a curious folkloric tradition from the 1800s gives reason to pause on that judgment.

The Burning Beast, a Jolly Old Ghost

In mid-January through early February 1896, the following article appeared in several newspapers throughout the Northeast of the United States, including the *Boston Globe:*

COW, MONSTER OR GHOST?
Reappearance of the Fearsome Thing that
Pirate Hicks Discovered Fifty years Ago.
Neil Hopkins Says It Was as Big as an Elephant
and Seemed to Be All Afire.

Putnam, Conn., Jan. 11—Neil Hopkins, of Glocester, R.I. was returning from his work on Dandelion Hill a few nights ago, when, at the darkest spot in the road, a strange beast gave him chase.[7] He cannot exactly tell what it was, as he caught only a glance of it as he ran. Hopkins is certain that the creature was some supernatural beast that lives in Glocester forest.

"It seemed to be all a-fire; it had a hot breath," Hopkins told his neighbors. "There was a metallic sound, like the clanking of steel against steel. The beast didn't seem to be strong in the wind, for it chased me only a short distance and then plunged off into the woods. I could hear the dead branches and twigs crackling under the heavy tramp."

Hopkins says it was as big as an elephant, and that he is certain it had no tail.

Opinion is divided as to what it was that scared Hopkins. Some think that it was only the escaped circus bear that held up several

---

7. Both "Neil" and "Nell" appear as Hopkins's name in various newspapers. Similarly, there is no Dandelion Hill in Glocester, but given the context, the reference culls from Durfee Hill.

farmers and scared their horses in the Glocester wood last fall.

The bear was seen in Buck Woods, near Webster, Mass., and as far south as Glocester. Others believe that it was the famous Glocester monster, the "burning beast," that Hopkins saw.

The "burning beast" has been seen only once before. That was fifty-seven years ago last summer, when it appeared to four Glocesterites, John Jepp, Ben Cobb, Ben Saunders and Albert W. Hicks, the pirate, who was afterward hanged on Liberty Island, in New York Bay.[8] Hicks was a native of Glocester. He and his companions were digging up the Page farm one night, trying to find Capt. Kidd's supposed buried gold, when the monster frightened them away. They dropped picks and shovels and run for life. Some Spanish doubloons had been previously found on the Page farm, but the gold diggers never cared to search further after their awful experience.

Hicks used to describe the beast thus:

---

8. Albert Hicks (1820?–1860), often known by the moniker the Last of the Pirates, was raised near southwestern Glocester. In 1860 Hicks was arrested in Providence for three murders in New York, for which he was hanged. Hicks left a confession, published after his execution, in which he detailed a life of crime that included piracy, mutiny, robbery, and the murder of potentially a hundred people throughout his travels from the Sandwich Islands to South and Central America to California and the southern United States. His trial became a national sensation and he was the subject of numerous ballads and folk poetry. Hicks's reputation has greatly diminished in recent decades, but for more than a century after his death he was a celebrated sinister figure in American folklore and popular culture. In 1963, for example, he was one of the five serial killers reanimated in a wax museum in an episode of *The Twilight Zone*. Locally he remained a folk figure as well. The *Providence Journal* published a detailed narrative concerning his infamy on 16 February ("Rhode Island Criminals") and 23 February 1890 ("History of the Hicks Family," which mentions a "knoll west of Walton's Inn" and conflates John Walton's story with that of Joseph Hicks, Albert's ancestor). On Halloween 1954, the Journal published a survey by Robert Wheeler of ghosts and their haunts in Rhode Island. The first image was of a stone chimney, the remnant and relic of a fallen house swallowed by the woods. Underneath the caption reads: "Pirate Hicks will be here tonight, counting ill-gotten gains" (17). Elsewhere, Wheeler explained that on Snake Hill Road in Glocester, near the Connecticut border, "Old Pirate Hicks, who was hanged on Bedloe's Island in New York Harbor in 1860, will be perched on the chimney counting his money" (18–19).

"It was a large animal, with staring eyes as big as pewter bowls. The eyes looked like balls of fire. When it breathed as it went by flames came out of its mouth and nostrils, scorching the brush in its path. It was as a big as a cow, with dark wings on each side like a bat's. It had spiral horns like a ram's, as big around as a stovepipe. Its feet were formed like a duck's and measured a foot and a half across. The body was covered with scales as big as clam shells, which made a rattling noise as the beast moved along. The scales flopped up and down. The thing had lights on its sides like those shining through a tin lantern. Before I saw it I felt its presence and I smelled something that was like burnt wool as it went by. I had a feeling of suffocation when it came near me. The monster seemed to come from nowhere and to go away in the same manner."

There are many people in Glocester who believe that the burning beast still haunts the forest not far from the Providence turnpike, and that it was it that scared Hopkins.

A reprint of this story appeared in 2017 on *Strange New England*, a blog and podcast by New England outdoor enthusiast Michael Girard, under the title "Glocester Ghoul." Although Girard made no connection to Lovecraft's IT, certain similarities are promising, as the Page farm abutted the Dark Swamp. Indeed, the temptation to link the two proved powerful. Rhode Island based author and self-described "paranormal investigator" Thomas D'Agostino leapt at the opportunity in the *Smithfield Times* of July 2020. In an essay entitled "Dark Swamp's IT," D'Agostino details Lovecraft and Eddy's search for the monster—he suggests both that IT actually existed and that "a few folks" were willing to share their stories about it with the traveling duo—before inquiring how they came to learn of the creature in the first place. "Perhaps it was the account by local pirate Albert Hicks," D'Agostino proposes, "or a later account by Neil Hopkins that sparked their curiosity." D'Agostino then proceeds to recount the narrative of the burning beast, directly correlating it with Lovecraft's creature. "Is the beast called IT still lurking in the woods of West Glocester?" D'Agostino ponders, before concluding that "[t]here are some who still believe that something eternally resides in the area of Dark Swamp, waiting for an unwary traveler to enter the domain of IT."

D'Agostino repeated this claim in an interview for *The Rhode Show*, a lifestyle and entertainment program for WPRI, the CBS affiliate for Rhode Island. The segment, entitled "The Haunted Tale of the Dark Swamp," aired on 30 October 2020 and continues broadcast online as of this writing in December 2021. Therein, D'Agostino claimed "actual documentation of a few people who encountered IT," including Albert Hicks and Neil Hopkins, and again narrated the tale of the burning beast as if it had occurred in reality. D'Agostino conflated the two creatures without pause. He then recalled Lovecraft and Eddy's investigation, once more suggesting that several "old timers" shared stories with them about IT, and thereby implied a longstanding tradition of narratives in the Glocester area concerning a monster in the Dark Swamp—as well as the existence of the creature itself.

Time will tell if D'Agostino's reinterpretation influences future raconteurs to continue this hasty merger, but it bears observation that the entry for the Dark Swamp on The H. P. Lovecraft Wiki now links to D'Agostino's *The Rhode Show* interview. The description of the creature at that popular website also borrows from the burning beast narrative:

> The Dark Swamp is the location of many local legends going back to before white settlement. The location is believed to be the home of a foul-smelling creature with flaming eyes and clam shell scales. Some say it breathes fire. It is referred to simply as "IT". There have been, as of 2021, recent reports of a skunk ape type creature wading in the swamp. It should be noted that due to the depth of the liquid mud and the thick screening foliage, passage into the swamp itself is all but impossible even in winter. A final real-world phenomenon remarked upon by visitors is that The Dark Swamp is a zone of silence - no bird or animal sounds are heard within its boundaries although they are common beyond it. ("The Dark Swamp")

Put simply, we are witnessing the birth of a contemporary legend, one whose elements suture Lovecraft's IT of the Dark Swamp with the burning beast tale from 1896.

A serious issue, however, plagues the veracity of that linkage. The 1896 tale of the burning beast did not originate in Glocester. It was concocted by a writer as a special to the newspaper the *New York World* (published by Joseph Pulitzer), where it first appeared under the title "Cow, Monster or Ghost?" on 12 January. The *New York World* was, like many of its rivals in New York City, an unabashed proponent of yellow journalism—tabloid and sensationalist narratives designed to grab attention and make a quick dollar, often with little or no basis in factuality. This is a perfect example of such journalism, a thrilling story for readers who in all probability would have no idea where Glocester was. As is typical with such tales, this one traveled the United States in newspapers as far away from northwestern Rhode Island as Kansas, Kentucky, Montana, Nebraska, Ohio, and Wisconsin in an abbreviated form entitled "Jolly Old Ghost." No names appear in the second version, but the basic elements remain. A ghost as large as an elephant with scorching breath accosted a man walking home from work on Dandelion Hill. His report provoked "the old inhabitants of Gloucester"—the editor used the old spelling of the town in Rhode Island or preferred the one in Massachusetts—to recall the "burning beast" of fifty-seven years prior, which assaulted four men during their attempt to dig up Captain Kidd's treasure on the Page farm. The pirate Hicks does not turn up in this version, but his description of the creature appears without change, which the anonymous journalist opines as one "to be recommended to novelists, poets, and playwrights who wish to produce a sensation."

Although narratively appealing in its simplicity, D'Agostino's rush to judgment to connect the burning beast tale of 1896 with Lovecraft's IT is precisely that: a rush to judgment.[9] His desire to

---

9. To state it diplomatically, D'Agostino routinely commits amateurish mistakes in his recounting of New England folklore and history. In what amounts to a single page in his Haunted Rhode Island, for example, his explanation of HPL's visit to Dark Swamp is strewn with errors, even as it borrows language

correlate the two and to suggest that a creature genuinely lurks in Dark Swamp is deeply problematic. D'Agostino further seems unaware of both the tale's origins in *New York World* and the historical and social context of its publication. Such ignorance and imprecision are regrettable, as that context could provide evidence—again, speculative—of a tradition of legends of which informants to Eddy and Lovecraft may have had access. A careful analysis of that publication history is required to present the best case that Lovecraft tapped into a local folk narrative tradition rather than simply inventing IT and shifting rumors he made up into the mouth of the "antient man with the flintlock."

Context for the Publication of the Burning Beast Tale

The publication of the burning beast tale in 1896 in *New York World* was the culmination of a decade of stories—authentic news, historical reminiscences, folk narratives, and fictional musings—by which Glocester became celebrated throughout the Northeast. It began innocently in the pages of Elizabeth Perry's history of Glocester, published in 1886. Therein she observed in passing that "[o]n the Page farm, not far from Poneganset pond, a mine was opened a few years since, where some quartz and a little gold were found, but thus far little has been done to find out its resources" (76). It is the sole mention of the farm and the mine in her book. There are no chronicles of the "Glocester monster" that purportedly attacked treasure hunters in 1839, nor are the specific names of John Jepp, Ben Cobb, Ben Saunders, or Albert Hicks present among the hundreds that she includes, although the family names were among the community. Testimonies of Captain Kidd's treasure are similarly absent, but Perry included legends and quasi-historical tales of counterfeiters in nearby caves; the Dark Day of 1780; the "Darned Man" (a nineteenth-century itinerant around whom copious lore gravi-

---

from HPL's letter to Long. Among them is a claim that HPL "made several trips to the area in search of the horrible swamp and its creature," that "[o]ld-timers shared various tales of IT with HPL," and a description of the monster's activities that are creations of D'Agostino's imagination rather than citations of HPL (68).

tated); and a haunted brook near Chepachet, where the ghost of a murdered Indigenous woman lurked. She took pains to detail other folk traditions such as corn huskings and funeral practices. If there were a thriving tradition about the burning beast circulating at the time, in all probability Perry would have recorded them.

That is not to suggest that Perry meticulously gathered every item of folklore in Glocester. On 3 March 1889, the *Providence Journal* published an article entitled "Up-Country Superstitions" that featured the people of the southwest corner of the town closer to the swamp than to Chepachet. It commences with mention of Hicks the pirate, born and raised on "Sodom Street," the historical name for a road running through Sodom Plain near Pine Hill.[10] The predominant legend, however, did not concern Hicks but John Walton, whose name adorned the pond. According to the article, Walton kept a hostelry in the 1700s, remnants of which were still visible. The tale continues:

> He lived with an Indian squaw for his wife. She was called Matonia, and Durfee Hill used to bear her name. She was Walton's abject slave. She belonged to the Narragansetts, and to this day is referred to by the up-country people as "Walton's old squaw." When Matonia died her lord and master wanted to throw her body into the pond to save the expense of burial, and, as he expressed it, "for the sharks to eat." But the neighbors dug her grave on the north brink of the water just south of the house. Nobody knows now where the spot was . . . [T]he building of the Ponagansett reservoir in 1857 caused the grave to be overflown, sweeping the resting place of her bones, but not the memory of Walton's old squaw, out of existence.

One of the people who knew the precise location of Matonia's grave was Harris Bowen, who had since died.

The remainder of the essay chronicles various folk beliefs

---

10. The name has since changed, but it was employed as late as the 1940s. An article in the Providence Journal dated 19 December 1948, for example, records both Sodom Street and Dark Swamp Road, the latter of which ran "from near James Reynolds homestead, south to Snake Hill Road" ("Glocester Now Has Legal Names . . .").

among the locals, including an idea that informed the image of sharks consuming Matonia's body in Walton Pond, namely that saltwater fish (specifically herring) came up the rivers to the source of the Pawtucket River. This, incidentally, is factually true, as herring, salmon, shad, and other anadromous fish return to New England rivers to spawn. The litany of their other beliefs "in wizardry," however, are genuine folklore, mostly typical superstitions regarding actions taken under the full moon or certain constellations; black snakes; and prophetic children whose presence could prevent a ship from sinking.

This minor legend and list of superstitions might have passed into oblivion were it not for its reprinting in the *New York Times* on 7 April, which itself lent to republication throughout the nation for subsequent weeks. The *Times*, however, altogether dropped the tale of John Walton and Matonia and renamed the remaining essay "Ghosts and Witchcraft." Precisely why the *Times* took an interest in the lore of this small community in Rhode Island is unclear, although as an educated guess I would propose a rising interest in the gold mine, on which Albert Potter began excavations and mining operations as early as 1877. In the early 1890s he established the aforementioned Ponaganset Mining and Smelting Company and the operation became, in the words of the 21 August 1893 *Providence Journal*, "the chief topic of conversation" throughout the region ("Searching for Gold"). The *Journal* routinely covered events concerning the mine, which prompted New York newspapers to follow suit.[11]

The mining operations inspired and arguably rekindled certain legends in the area. On 5 May 1889, the *Journal* published a lengthy article entitled "Glocester Gold Digging," examining Potter's efforts. It contained the earliest version in print of the story that would grace *New York World* in 1896, along with related tales. The first concerned a "robber gang"—two men and an old woman—who in the 1700s lived on what would become the Page farm. They were surviving members of Captain Kidd's crew, es-

---

11. In addition to articles mentioned in the main body, see *The Sun of New York* ("Hunting for Gold in Glocester, R.I.") and *Providence Journal* ("The Glocester Gold Mine").

sentially in hiding following their life of crime. One day they entertained a disgraced Englishman—presumably a fellow crew member—who decided to purchase a plot of land nearby, known by an (undisclosed) Algonquian word that translated to "winter's camping pond." That man was none other than (John) Walton. Picking up from the 3 March article, this essay explained that Walton operated a hostelry and owned several enslaved people, including an Indigenous maiden whom he purchased from the Narragansett. Walton was, however, even more severe in this version. He forced the woman into marriage, abused her mercilessly, and whipped her to death, whereupon he ordered the others to dispose of her body in the pond. (They buried her on the shore instead, taking advantage of Walton's own illness at the time.) All four of these former pirates, the *Journal* continued, purportedly buried treasure throughout the area.

When David Page came to own the land, he spent thousands of dollars searching for the pirate gold. He never found that buried treasure, but he—or, more precisely, his son Rhodes—hit across another one in 1847, namely the gold mine "that by a coincidence had been discovered and worked by old Walton and his followers in the last half of the 18th century."[12] The Walton mine, the *Journal* further explains, "is near the scene of some ghostly and hair-raising adventures that have befallen those who delved at night and worked thus that they might live without work." One of these "weird stories" is that of Rhodes Page's suicide—he cut his own throat in desperation over a mortgage debt—but the most harrowing was the adventure of a gang consisting of John Jepp, Ben Saunders, Gussie Smith, Ben Cobb, Harris Bowen, and Albert Hicks before he became a pirate.

One night they set out to excavate the pirate treasure buried somewhere on the Page farm. The *Journal* proffers a specific date: 13 November 1833, when Hicks was a mere lad of fourteen. That was the night the Leonid meteor shower illuminated the sky

---

12. According to this account, Walton "shipped several barrels of the ore to England to have it assayed" and cited for support *The Industrial History of Rhode Island* published in Philadelphia by Hogg & Co., but no such book exists. The article also claims that Potter discovered the tools once used by Walton.

throughout the United States, during which fifty to hundred and fifty thousand meteors appeared every hour.[13] As they dug "an immense white light suddenly shot out of the sky and hovered over them like a sheet, continuing to illuminate the pond, the ravine and all the oaks as it seemed to the frightened sense of the men for several seconds." Harris Bowen, "who was well versed in witchcraft and wizardry," took it as a positive omen and urged them to continue. They did as directed and while

> the men were intent upon their labors, a meteor of enormous size dropped into Walton pond, causing the water to bubble, seethe and boil, and spurt upward like a geyser, six feet high or more in the air. Remarkable as it may appear the superstitious band were not scared this time, but seemed to think it was only a natural phenomenon connected with the success of their undertaking.

Soon thereafter, the men discovered an iron scuttle buried deep within the earth. They carried it in triumph to John Jepp's cabin not far from Cady's tavern, but upon opening it, discovered trash—a hoax revealed more than two decades later when Niles Page and Rhodes Saunders admitted to "having some fun with the gold diggers." Undeterred by this prank, the gang returned to their pursuit on the next full moon. The tale continues:

> But a very strange thing happened the next season, which so terrified the two "Bens," John and "Gus," and Harris and Hicks, that they never durst go by that place again, excepting in the day time. One full-moonlit night the gang were at their midnight exertion with pick and cider jug, on the border of Niles Page's pasture, when a strange beast appeared, like those described in the Apocalypse. Harris Bowen, in speaking of the adventure afterwards, would say: "By——, it was a kind of something; it went by me. I didn't see it, but I felt it. I was kneeled down on one knee, when all of a sudden it felt dark. I saw nothin', but I smelled somethin' that was like burnt wool as it went by. It dis-

13. The Leonids are an annual occurrence; the 1833 shower was an extraordinary spectacle. HPL published an essay on the Leonids for the *Pawtuxet Valley Gleaner* on 9 November 1906, and mentions the "very brilliant display" (*CE* 3.38) that occurs every thirty-three years, but did not reference the 1833 event.

appeared, and then it felt as if a big weight had been lifted up, and I felt free from a feeling of half-suffocation. It seemed to us all to come from nowhere and to go away the same."

Bowen thereafter avoided the area at night and only once travelled the route that crept past the "winter's camping pond," doing so weighted with great trepidation. As for his companions:

"Ben" Saunders and John Jepp did not feel its presence, but saw the creature as a horrible object. They said it was a large animal with big staring eyes, that looked like balls of fire, as large as pewter bowls. They said that when it breathed as it went by, there were flames that came out of its mouth and nostrils, scorching the brush in its path. John [sic, but from context should be Ben] claimed it was as a big as a cow, with dark wings on each side like a bat; that it had horns like a ram's, and as large round as a stovepipe, circling and curving like a spiral. Its feet were shaped like duck's feet, and measured a foot and a half across. Its body was covered with shells as big as quahaug shells, that made a noise by flopping up and down as the beast moved along. Jepp gave substantially the same description of the fire-breathing monster, but said it was not so large. He used to say, "By——, boys, as soon as I saw it, I flung down my shovel and run; I never was so scared in all my life. It had lights on its sides like those shining through the holes of an old tin lantern. The scales looked as large as clam shells and the light under them made them look like lattice work. The horns lopped down."

Jepp and Ben Cobb disagreed, apparently, about the presence of a tail on the "uncanny apparition" and "satanic beast." They all agreed on one point, however, "that the next day they could trace the course of the dreadful dragon for ten feet where the low huckleberry bushes, the ferns and the grass had been burned to the ground. They were all inclined to be reticent about the occurrence and would only mention it in times of festival and revelry, when the cider mug had gone around."

There is so much to unpack in this marvelous tale, which precedes two others in the essay concerning later treasure hunters, including Job Winslow, who pursued both Kidd and Blackbeard's gold that he thought awaited "beneath the brakes and the briars on the shores of Walton pond." To state the obvious, it is the source for the 1896 *New York World,* although that latter newspaper streamlined the narrative and placed the main description of the beast in the mouth of Albert Hicks—then an internationally infamous figure—rather than local men.[14] More importantly, it is one example of the copious tradition of Captain Kidd treasure tales that were extremely popular throughout New England during the nineteenth century, legends that instigated genuine treasure hunts throughout the region.[15] New England folklore is replete with variants, but the basic structure of each entails Kidd burying his treasure and placing a curse upon it so that it would dematerialize should a later discoverer make the slightest sound during its removal. In order to guarantee such an outcome, Kidd set a trap to frighten the gold-digger into screaming, often by murdering a crewmate to enlist his ghost to haunt the site, or the spectral remains of an animal or pack of animals (often aflame with supernatural fire), or a demonic being, or the Devil himself.

A comparable variant to the *Journal* tale, for example, appeared in the New Haven *Morning Journal Courier* on 25 July 1883, regarding Charles Island in Long Island Sound:

> Among the legends of the island is one regarding a search for Captain Kidd treasures, a part of which according to tradition was buried by the redoubtable chieftain on Charles Island. The story runs that two men assailed by an insatiable desire for

14. More precisely, the narrative in the *Journal* featured characters drawn from local references. As explained earlier, the family names of all these men existed in the Glocester area, but history and genealogy records only testify to Albert Hicks and Harris Bowen.
15. The real William Kidd was born in Scotland in the mid-1600s and emigrated to New York City. He undertook a career as a privateer for England in the 1680s but was declared a pirate in 1699. En route to clear his name in Boston, Kidd deposited some acquired riches on Gardiner's Island, just to the east of Long Island, presumably to have capital for negotiations. It was in vain. Kidd was arrested, imprisoned, and sent to London for trial. He was executed in 1701 and his body gibbetted for several years thereafter. Immediately following his death, Kidd became a subject of balladry, which fostered later folk narratives of his burying treasure elsewhere. New England became a hotbed for such tales in the 1800s and stories of his buried treasure reached deep inland.

shekels or gold laid their plans and visited the island under cover of night and commenced digging. They had a hole of some size dug, when suddenly they beheld a headless man descending from the upper air and bearing down upon them. In horror and affright they decamped suddenly for their boat and casting a glance behind saw a streak of blue flame in the air over where they had been digging. They came back the next morn to get their implements of labor, but could not find them nor any trace of the hole they dug. ("Poquahog")

It is impossible to ascertain if the *Journal* captured a local variant or simply devised one for the community, but another article published in the same newspaper on 8 June 1890, "Gold Mining in Glocester," lends credence to the former option:

That gold lies and has been discovered in that vicinity has long been the belief of people of Glocester. Stories of searches that have been made for it form some of the most weird and strange incidents in the history of this inland town, the favorite tales of its folk lore. Sometimes the delving has been for Kidd's hidden doubloons, again for nature's shining preciousness.

Independent support for this claim appears in an unexpected source: the confession of Albert Hicks. Therein he recalled his youth:

My only ambition was to be rich; but I had no desire to acquire riches in the plodding way in which our neighbors went through life; my dream was to become suddenly rich by some bold stroke, and then to give free reins to the passions and desires which governed me.

I never, even as a boy, hoarded money. I did not care for the mere possession of it. It was only valuable to me as the means of gratifying my passions.

I used to wish that I could find the pots of gold and silver which rumor said had been buried in our neighborhood by pirates and robbers, and used to listen with rapt attention to stories of pirates, robbers, highwaymen, etc., which my companions used sometimes to relate. (42)

Hicks left the Glocester area, he explains, at age fifteen, for Norwich, Connecticut, where he inaugurated his criminal livelihood with an act of theft. Arrested and convicted, he eventually escaped the Norwich jail and returned to "Lowerpart, Gloucester [*sic*]," where he undertook farm labor until his capture. Nowhere in his confession does Hicks mention the purported treasure hunt or any of the names of the men in the *Journal* tale, but his confession provides unequivocal evidence of a narrative tradition in the mid-1800s, a tradition to which his own name became associated in the decades following his death. The origin of the burning beast, then, probably lies as a guardian creature for a local Kidd tale.

It is also not apparent why John Walton became a nefarious character, but the evolution of his tales is fascinating. In the two earliest, those aforementioned from 1889, he transitioned from a cruel hostelry owner to a member of Kidd's crew and discoverer of the mine. He appeared again as the original gold mine owner in a brief article in the *Journal* on 8 June 1890. Within three years, however, stories recast Walton as a stranger to the community, an immigrant from England during the 1740s, and a "geologist and practical miner" who sought permission from Rhodes Page to mine on what would become known as Walton Pond and Durfee Hill, but his death and the impending American Revolution put an end to the experiment ("Gold in Rhode Island"). That tale of Walton the visiting English miner returned on 21 August the same year in an article on mining operations, whereas another essay published on 12 December 1897 identified him as "a member of the Madagascar band of pirates" ("Durfee Hill and the Gold Mine"), who discovered and worked the mine with a retinue of thirteen enslaved people.

John Walton, the actual man, appears in Perry's history only in a list of deputies to the General Assembly; he served as such in 1743 and 1756. A biographical sketch of Yale graduates published in 1885 provides much more detail. Born in 1684 near New London, Connecticut, he graduated in 1720 and became a minister in New Jersey. He was suspended, however, due to "lustful carriage to some young women" and related "contemptuous behavior" (Dexter 232), but he continued to preach in Rye and White Plains, New York. Considered a "bold, noisy fellow, of a voluble tongue" (232), Walton was the subject of a manifesto in 1726 that warned churches in Connecticut to beware of him. By 1728, Walton left for Providence, where he soon fell into controversy again for his religious views. He removed to Glocester by 1743, when he served as deputy. Walton died in 1764. He had a son, also named John. The Yale biography claims that this son became a minister and died in New Jersey in 1770, but two genealogies from the early 1900s (Greene; Ward) maintain that he served in the Revolution and died in 1778, having married Mercy Greene from Warwick, Rhode Island, and having a son also named John in 1751. None cites the hostelry, the mine, or the anecdote about an enslaved wife.

Although a contentious figure, Walton was not so abrasive as to become lasting in folk history through a continuous chain from the 1700s to the 1800s. It is far more probable that the stories of Walton the villainous hostel owner, gold mine proprietor, and pirate was born out of necessity, since the setting for those treasure tales in the nineteenth century was Walton Pond. Indeed, the 1897 article in the *Journal* relates that one of the camp miners provided the story about Walton. The rapid development of Walton as a folk character from 1889 to 1897 makes perfect sense, then, as a component of a thriving occupational folklore, entertaining narratives that mine workers shared with each other and with sightseers. That practice would also explain why records of the tales dropped sharply after the mine failed in the early twentieth century and the camp disbanded.

It is easy to miss, but the tale of the dreadful dragon reveals a different emphasis on the meaning of the Dark Swamp, one that wholly challenges the sense of foreboding enlisted by Lovecraft:

> Well might the natural situation of the little lake, its seclusion and the protection afforded by its encircling forests, have furnished a favorite living place for the dusky-skinned aborigines. Its mossy sloping banks would afford easy access to its surface for fishing when covered with ice. Clear and pure and bright as crystal came the bounding stream that flowed perennially down precipitous slopes into the basin, now obscuring the rock with a thin veil of water, then rushing on in a tiny torrent, swift and

resisting. The tops of the trees interarched and formed a forest roof that was almost impenetrable by snow, while the matted leaves underneath formed a carpet as soft as velvet, upon which the footsteps of the hunter fell noiselessly. It was a paradise for game, and happy was the Indian who selected "winter's camping pond" for his home. ("Glocester Gold Digging")

In other words, the same canopy that made the swamp dark also made it an ideal place for shelter and for hunting against the winter snows. It should also not be lost that this depiction suggests that the area around Walton Pond—that is, the Dark Swamp—was a "paradise for game." That is precisely what the ancient rustic of Lovecraft's letter to Baird said, "when one told the other that there were plenty left in the *Dark Swamp*."

In summary, there is no doubt that the area around the Dark Swamp (including Walton Pond, Page farm, and Durfee Hill) was the setting for a thriving tradition of folk narratives during the nineteenth century, a branch of the Kidd treasure tale cycles prevalent throughout the region. The existence of a mining operation and historical ties to the pirate Albert Hicks assisted the circulation, evolution, and extension of this folklore. If the "antient man with the flintlock" was indeed in southwestern Glocester in 1849 or anytime thereafter—and especially during the days of the mining camp, he surely would have heard those stories. This bodes well for those who wish to take Lovecraft's second letter at its word. There are, however, numerous marks against that possibility. The lack of recorded tales during the intermediary period of 1897 to 1923 is one, albeit more a sign of the *Providence Journal*'s interests than the collapse of a local tradition. More difficult are the particulars in Lovecraft's statements. None of them touches in any way upon any part of this rich webwork of tales. Neither letter invokes the elements of the treasure tales, the dreadful dragon, the treacherous Walton, or the pirate Hicks. Instead, Lovecraft's mention of IT entails a precolonial tradition of unnamed "Indians" who believed in a creature lurking in the potholes of the swamp. A survey of such beliefs is warranted before a conclusion about Lovecraft's claims can be made.

Swamps in the Lore of the Indigenous Peoples of Rhode Island

For the sake of argument, let us assume that Lovecraft's description of the "antient man with the flintlock" was accurate and that "he said his grandfather had told him in 1849, when he was a very little boy, that IT had been there when the first settlers came, and that the Indians believed IT had always been there." Some contemporary enthusiasts and legend trippers have assumed from that single line that the Indigenous people in the area believed in IT or at least that Lovecraft thought they did. D'Agostino, for example, speculated that the "Indians" rather than Lovecraft dubbed the creature IT and claimed "that IT resided in the muddy bowers of the swamp" (*Haunted Rhode Island* 69). Heather Moser, a blogger for the paranormal-themed series *Into the Fray,* frames the matter in a related manner:

> Why was H. P. Lovecraft interested in the Dark Swamp? According to his letter, Native American legend has it that this swamp is home to some sort of creature (he simply refers to the creature as IT) which has lived in the swamp since the beginning of time. It is because of this creature that small game, such as squirrels and rabbits, are nowhere to be found in the area. Lovecraft states that hunters have to travel to Connecticut in order to find those animals. The description of this creature is disturbing, and it certainly did not ease the mind of my friend who had already heard about people going missing in the swamp over the years. It is no wonder that Lovecraft would want to visit a place befitting a horror story!

Let us not overlook that Lovecraft was far removed from this purported source—from the Indigenous people to the "antient man's" grandfather to the "antient man" (in the letter to Long only) to Eddy to Lovecraft. That chain alone should command caution against quick acceptance, but for those who are intent on stirring a contemporary legend, such scant evidence is more than enough to proceed. This impulsive decision is vexing, however, for a more complete understanding of the claim and a consideration of the Dark Swamp. If authentic, it would suggest a tradition of folk narratives in the area that is older than buried treasure stories. Is there any corroborating evidence that the folklore of the Indigenous people might have conceptualized such a supernatural creature?

Traditionally, the area of Glocester was associated with the Nipmuc people, who themselves were often subject to or in alliance with the Narragansett people in southern Rhode Island and the Wampanoag to the east. In her history, Perry remarks that "some vestiges of these [tribes] still remain" in the town (6), so the grandfather of Lovecraft's "antient man" would have been able to interact with them. Furthermore, a prominent contemporaneous source underscores the presence of Indigenous people in those decades. It is a mock epic called *The Dorriad,* composed in 1843 by Henry Bowen Anthony, then editor of the *Providence Journal* and later governor of the state and a federal senator. *The Dorriad* satirizes the Dorr Rebellion, an unsuccessful uprising led by the political reformer Thomas Wilson Dorr in 1841 and 1842. After a disastrous defeat in Providence, the movement regrouped on Acote Hill in Chepachet. They disbanded when Governor Samuel King sent the state militia to combat them.

In an extended version of *The Dorriad,* in a section entitled "The Chepachet Campaign," Anthony sarcastically praises the throngs of Dorr's supporters who gather at "Chepi-Chuck." One stanza is revealing, although disturbing by today's standards for its overt racism against Indigenous people:

> And from those regions dark and hilly,
> In Glocester and "Burrillvilly,"
> Where old romance her charms hath thrown,
> And wonder claims the land her own;
> Where savage tribes are said to roam,
> And savage beasts still keep their home;
> Where, startling up from rock and glen,
> Fierce cannibals their faces show,
> And "Anthropphagi [*sic*], and men
> Whose heads beneath their shoulders grow." (18)

That final quote describing cannibals and monstrous beings derives from Shakespeare's *Othello*, not local lore, although in 1643 Roger Williams did record anxiety among the Indigenous people in Rhode Island concerning the Mohowaùgsuck—the Mohawks—as "man-eaters" living to the west (36). The greater point here is that Anthony's poetry, despite its unsettling xenophobia, testifies to the presence of Indigenous people in the region in the early and mid-1800s.

Anthony's endnotes to *The Dorriad* bring some of that romance into sharper focus. He claims that the original name of Chepachet was "Chepi-Chuck," meaning "the Devil's Bag," and cannot resist making a joke about the Devil missing an opportunity to join Dorr's ranks (23). He also explains that Acote Hill was named for a man who was murdered or committed suicide on the spot. "His ghost is said to haunt the place of his burial," Anthony continues, "and the wailings of his unquiet spirit are often heard, by the superstitious, on stormy nights" (24). Acote's ghost makes an appearance in *The Dorriad* as well, decrying Dorr and threatening to move his own bones so as not to be associated with the rebellion. The translation of Chepachet, however, became a point of contention.

In 1861, Usher Parsons published *Indian Names of Places in Rhode Island*. Parsons agreed with Anthony's translation of Chepachet (from Chepuck-chack) as the "Devil's Bag," and offered without further details a folkloric anecdote that some hunter must have dropped a bag or wallet there and when no one could identify the owner, "an Indian said it was the Devil," Chepuck being the word for the Devil (11). In 1881, James Hammond Trumbull reinterpreted Chepachet as "a place of separation" or a place where things divide, as in a river (10). The iconoclastic editor Sidney Rider found it difficult to understand how Chepachet could be a place of division given it was where two rivers united, but he found Anthony and Parson's offerings "silly" and "wretched" and "utter stupidity" and so agreed with Trumbull. Rider, drawing upon Roger William's compilation of Native American words, also dismissed the earlier translation since "no Indian knew the Englishman's Devil" and there was no such word "Chepuck" in the record to signify a diabolical being (136).

It is accurate that the pre-colonial Indigenous people of Rhode Island did not have a concept of a satanic being representing pure evil in the manner of the Christian colonialists. It is also true that "Chepuck" does not appear in Williams's dictionary as a word for the Devil. But "chèpeck" does appear, and it means "the dead" (161). It is cognate with "tcipai" and "djibai," words for a corpse and a specter in Wampanoag and Mohegan-Pequot dialectics, respectively. This term for the deceased has its origins in the word for separation—as in the separation of spirit from body—so this does not immediately solve the issue of whether Chepachet originally references separating rivers or the dead. Rider failed to recognize, further, an associated supernatural being called Cheepi, who was well established among the Indigenous people of Rhode Island, Massachusetts, and Connecticut. Cheepi represented the spirits of the dead—ghosts—and, as William Simmons noted, "the English and their Indian converts glossed it as the devil" (118). In brief, the pre-colonial people who may have named Chepachet did not believe in the European concept of the Devil, but they did believe in a being that the English later interpreted as the infernal lord.

There are copious surviving depictions of Cheepi across New England from the 1600s to the 1900s. He usually appears as a frightful being who takes the shape of horrible things, including large animals. He is associated with the restless dead, terrifying noises, the night, and disturbances in the weather. And Cheepi or similarly dire supernatural figures, as Simmons summarizes, "lingered around swamps" (128).[16] Comparable tales from the Narragansett in Rhode Island, the Mohegan in southeastern Connecticut, and the Wampanoag in Massachusetts from the late 1800s and early 1900s, for example, include swamp-dwelling supernatural beings that took the shape of spectral canines, fire-

---

16. Edward Johnson's statement from 1651 is typical: "It hath been a thing very frequent before the English came, for the Devil to appear unto to them in a bodily shape, sometimes very ugly and terrible, and sometimes like a white boy, and chiefly in the most hideous woods and swamps" (263).

breathing dogs, black horses, and a herd of pigs. In the 1920s, the Mashpee of Massachusetts still spoke of "tcipai wankas," a spirit fox, an omen of death that floated above the ground "like a light" and emitted weird cries (Simmons 138). Similar stories of will-o'-the-wisps in swamps (probably inspired by foxfire) abound in the lore of Indigenous people of the region, both historical and contemporaneous with Lovecraft's journey. On occasion, the Indigenous people narrated or adapted folklore of Kidd's treasure, and their supernatural lore equally influenced those of white storytellers.

All this means that it is *plausible* that the "antient man with the flintlock" may have invoked a tradition of supernatural beings in the swamps told by Indigenous peoples or a story cycle from whites that borrowed from it. But is it probable? And does it guarantee that Lovecraft's IT is a direct descendant of that folkloric tradition? An affirmative outcome is difficult to establish. Unlike the treasure tale cycle, there is no supporting evidence for an active tradition of storytelling concerning Cheepi or similar beings from Native American lore in western Glocester during the mid-1800s to early 1900s. This is not to suggest that Indigenous people were wholly absent—or that whites did not borrow their folk narratives—but that a trove of corroborating data remains nonexistent. Put bluntly, Lovecraft's assertions about IT have little substantiation and seem to have missed the actual folk narrative tradition that recently thrived in the area. That does not bode well for those who wish to take his second letter at its word.

IT: *Lovecraft's Coincidental Invention?*

Let us review the components of this analysis and consider the most reasonable conclusion to them. Six recollections concerning Lovecraft and Eddy's search for the Dark Swamp exist, albeit from different decades. All agree that the swamp was so called in reference to a canopy impenetrable to sunlight. Only Lovecraft's two narrations indulge a creature known as IT, and his depiction changes between both. Lovecraft further exhibits a dearth of knowledge—historical, geographical, and social—about the area

surrounding the Dark Swamp and most importantly an ignorance of a once flourishing storytelling tradition in the previous
generation. That folkloric tradition emerged from a Kidd treasure tale cycle that reigned throughout New England in the nineteenth century and that merged with local legends concerning a
gold mine and a celebrity criminal. Elements or remnants of that
tradition appear nowhere in Lovecraft's accounts. His invoca-
tion of a legend tradition concerning swamps among Indigenous
people is also suspect. Although comparable narrative practices
existed throughout New England, no substantiating and specific
evidence for the Dark Swamp is available. To the contrary, the
only commentary about Indigenous lore in the area—supplied
by white raconteurs—is of the benefits of the "winter camping
pond" where the snows were kept from reaching the ground due
to the thick canopy of trees and where game remained plentiful.

Those who wish to contend that Lovecraft tapped into a
folkloric tradition circulating around the Dark Swamp over-rely
on a passing comment by the "antient man with the flintlock." It
is plausible that such a man existed and spoke of IT (presumably
as a version of Cheepi) as a tradition passed along from the Indigenous people in the area to white settlers, but it is just as *implausible* that a local informant would not share the folk
narratives of the then recently closed mine. The simplest explanation, therefore, is that Lovecraft invented IT in his letter to
Baird and continued development in his letter to Long. In that
transition, Lovecraft began to fictionalize, transforming the "antient man" into a character in a horror tale, through whom the
author could project narrative elements that he had himself introduced.[17] Such sensational invention continues among a cadre
of Lovecraft enthusiasts, who have recently generated a proto-
legend about IT. In their fantasy to ennoble Lovecraft and Eddy's unsuccessful pursuit of the Dark Swamp and establish the
place as a worthy site for legend tripping, these fans are making

17. Evidence is lacking to make a firm case, but if HPL was the inventor of IT
and given the Eddys were insistent that he prodded the journey having learned
of the swamp, the possibility exists that HPL fabricated the entire origin story,
depicting Eddy as the impetus for dramatic purposes.

leaps that require correction. If a contemporary legend arises that proclaims IT and the burning beast to be the same, for example, such an application would be a development that is not historically established. Similar claims of IT's venerable origin in Indigenous lore are equally wanting without further evidence.

In conclusion, it appears that Lovecraft contrived IT as a manifestation of his desire to find inspiration for fictional tales—a desire that he himself recognized—from a location that coincidentally had been the site of an opulent folk narrative tradition. That tradition was dying out—if not nearly extinguished—by the time that Lovecraft visited the area, so his ignorance is understandable. Nevertheless, if this assessment is accurate, it is unfortunate. One could only speculate what echoes in the form of horror-tales Lovecraft and Eddy would have conjured had they discovered the rich folklore of the Dark Swamp.

Acknowledgements

I am grateful to Ray Huling, Davis Dunavin, Jim Dyer, and S. T. Joshi for support of this research. This essay is dedicated to the memory of my friend, Chris Hall. Perhaps someday we shall walk throughout Rhode Island again.

Works Cited

Anthony, Henry Bowen. *The Dorriad and the Great Slocum Dinner*. Providence: Sidney S. Rider & Brother, 1870.

"Cow, Monster or Ghost?" *New York World* (12 January 1896): 11.

D'Agostino, Thomas. "Dark Swamp's IT." *Smithfield Times* (July 2020): 20.

———. *Haunted Rhode Island*. Atglen, PA: Schiffer Publishing, 2006.

"Daring Explorer Scales State's Highest Peak." *Providence Sunday Journal* (9 July 1922): Fifth Section, p. 1+.

"The Dark Swamp." *The H. P. Lovecraft Wiki*. lovecraft.fandom.com/wiki/The_Dark_Swamp. Accessed 15 December 2021.

Dexter, Franklin Bowditch. *Biographical Sketches of the Graduates of Yale College*. New York: Henry Holt & Co., 1885.

"Durfee Hill and the Gold Mine." *Providence Sunday Journal* (12 December 1897): 18.

Eddy, Muriel. "H. P. Lovecraft among the Demons." *Providence Sunday Journal* (8 March 1970): *Rhode Islander* section, 23+.

———. *H. P. Lovecraft, Esquire, Gentleman.* Self-published, n.d.

———. "Howard Phillips Lovecraft." In Donald M. Grant and Thomas Hadley, ed. *Rhode Island on Lovecraft.* Providence: Grant-Hadley, 1945. 14–22.

———. *Howard Phillips Lovecraft: The Man and the Image.* Guild Studio Press, 1969.

———. *In the Gray of the Dusk: A Collection of Typewritten Treasures.* Ed. Jim Dyer. Narragansett, RI: Fenham Publishing, 2017.

———, and C. M. Eddy, Jr. *The Gentleman from Angell Street: Memories of H. P. Lovecraft.* Ed. Jim Dyer. Narragansett, RI: Fenham Publishing, 2019.

Faig, Kenneth W., Jr. *Lovecraftian Voyages.* New York: Hippocampus Press, 2017.

Girard, Michael. "The Glocester Ghoul." *Strange New England.* www.strange-new-england.com/2017/10/22/the-glocester-ghoul/. Accessed 15 December 2021.

"Ghosts and Witchcraft." *New York Times* (7 April 1889): 11.

"Glocester Gold Digging." *Providence Sunday Journal* (5 May 1889): 8.

"The Glocester Gold Mine." *Providence Sunday Journal* (16 August 1896): 4.

"Glocester Now Has Legal Names for 61 Roads, Highways in Town." *Providence Sunday Journal* (19 December 1948): 9.

"Gold in Rhode Island." *Providence Journal* (26 May 1893): 10.

"Gold Mining in Glocester." *Providence Sunday Journal* (8 June 1890): 8.

Greene, George. *The Greenes of Rhode Island.* New York: Knickerbocker Press, 1903.

"The Haunted Tale of the Dark Swamp." *The Rhode Show.* www.wpri.com/rhode-show/the-haunted-tale-of-the-dark-swamp/. Accessed 15 December 2021.

Hicks, Albert. *The Life, Trial, Confession and Execution of Albert W. Hicks, the Pirate and Murderer*. New York: De Witt Publishing House, 1860.

"History of the Hicks Family." *Providence Sunday Journal* (23 February 1890): 16.

"Hunting for Gold at Glocester, R.I." *Sun* (New York) (16 June 1890): 3.

Johnson, Edward. *Johnson's Wonder-Working Providence*. Ed. J. Franklin Jameson. New York: Charles Scribner's Sons, 1910.

"Jolly Old Ghost." *Red Lodge Picket* (29 February 1896): 3.

Joshi, S. T., and David Schultz. *An H. P. Lovecraft Encyclopedia*. Westport, CT: Greenwood Press, 2001.

Lovecraft, H. P. Letter to Edwin Baird. *Weird Tales* 3, No. 3 (March 1924): 89–92. In *Uncollected Letters*. Ed. S. T. Joshi. West Warwick, RI: Necronomicon Press, 1986. 7–10.

Moser, Heather. "The Dark Swamp." *Into the Fray Radio*. into thefrayradio.com/the-dark-swamp/. Accessed 15 December 2021.

Parsons, Usher. *Indian Names of Places in Rhode Island*. Providence: Knowles, Anthony & Co., 1861.

Perry, Elizabeth. *A Brief History of the Town of Glocester, Rhode Island*. Providence: Providence Press Co., 1886.

"Poquahog." *New Haven Morning Journal and Courier* (25 July 1883): 2.

"Rhode Island Criminals." *Providence Sunday Journal* (16 February 1890): 16.

Rider, Sidney. *The Lands of Rhode Island*. Providence: Published by the Author, 1904.

"Searching for Gold." *Providence Daily Journal* (21 August 1893): 1.

Simmons, William. *Spirit of the New England Tribes: Indian History and Folklore, 1620–1984*. Hanover, NH: University Press of New England, 1986.

Trumbull, John Hammond. *Indian Names of Places etc., in and on the Borders of Connecticut*. Hartford, CT: Press of the Case, Lockwood & Brainard Co., 1881.

"Up-Country Superstitions." *Providence Sunday Journal* (3 March 1889): 10.

Walling, Henry Francis. *Map of the State of Rhode Island, and Providence Plantations.* Boston: L. H. Bradford & Co's. Lith., 1855. Norman B. Leventhal Map & Education Center, collections. leventhalmap.org/search/commonwealth:cj82m786q

Ward, George. *Andrew Warde and His Descendants.* New York: A. T. De La Mare Printing & Publishing Co., 1910.

Wheeler, Robert. "With Necks Awry and Nails in Skulls." *Providence Sunday Journal* (21 October 1954): 16+.

Williams, Roger. *A Key into the Language of America.* Providence: John Miller, 1827.

Other maps of Glocester: 1831 (J. Stevens), 1851 (Walling), 1870 (J. H. Beers), 1895 (Everts and Richards).

The image on p. 93 is from the *Map of the State of Rhode Island and Providence-Plantations* (1855), reproduction courtesy of the Norman B. Leventhal Map & Education Center at the Boston Public Library

A Note on Nodens in Lovecraft's Mythos

Andrew Paul Wood

Nodens in Myth and Mythos

It is generally accepted that the entity Nodens in the Lovecraft Mythos was at least partly inspired by the reference in Arthur Machen's 1894 novella *The Great God Pan* to a fictional inscription:

DEMOMNODENi
PLAvISSENILSPOSSVit
PROPERNVPtias
quasVIDITSVBVMBra
To the great god Nodens (the god of the Great Deep or abyss) Flavius Senilis has erected this pillar on account of the marriage which he saw beneath the shade. (152)

In his 1922 autobiography, *Far Off Things*, Machen wrote that the basis for this was his childhood visits to the River Usk and the Roman-settled towns of Caerleon-on-Usk and Caerwent (Venta Silurum in Roman times) in Wales. He wrote that "strange relics" were found at Caerwent from the ruined temple of "Nodens, god of the depths" (19), though he was probably thinking of Lydney Park nine miles to the northeast. More specifically, however, Lovecraft first mentions Nodens in story "The Strange High House in the Mist," written in 1926, and again in the posthumously published novel *The Dream-Quest of Unknown Kadath*,[1] which he started in 1926 and finished in 1927.[2]

---

1. One of the few instances where the trope of the narrative turning out to be "just a dream" is not a trite cliché, being entirely subverted by the premise.

2. In a letter dated 26 November 1926, HPL writes to August Derleth: "Many tales I have destroyed as below even my most charitable standard, & I'm not

Lovecraft's describes Nodens thus:

And golden flames played about weedy locks,[3] so that Olney was dazzled as he did them homage. Trident-bearing Neptune was there, and sportive tritons and fantastic nereids, and upon dolphins' backs was balanced a vast crenulate shell wherein rode the grey and awful form of primal Nodens, Lord of the Great Abyss. And the conches of the tritons gave weird blasts, and the nereids made strange sounds by striking on the grotesque resonant shells of unknown lurkers in black sea-caves. Then hoary Nodens reached forth a wizened hand and helped Olney and his host into the vast shell, whereat the conches and the gongs set up a wild and awesome clamour. And out into the limitless aether reeled that fabulous train, the noise of whose shouting was lost in the echoes of thunder. (CF 2.94)

This "triumph" of Nodens, or to use Steven Lattimore's coinage, "marine *thiasos*," (*passim*) may have been influenced the passage in Pliny the Elder's *Naturalis Historia* describing the works of the Hellenistic sculptor Skopas:

But the most highly esteemed of all his works, are those in the Temple erected by Cneius Domitius, in the Flaminian Circus; a figure of Neptune himself, a Thetis and Achilles, Nereids seated upon dolphins, cetaceous fishes, and sea-horses, Tritons, the train of Phorcus, whales, and numerous other sea-monsters, all by the same hand; an admirable piece of workmanship, even if it had taken a whole life to complete it. (36.4)

---

sure but that this fate awaits the long fantasy I am concocting at this moment." A week later, in a letter dated 3 December 1926, HPL refers to being up to page 72 of his "dreamland fantasy" (*Essential Solitude* 52, 53). I am indebted to S. T. Joshi for drawing my attention to this and the dating of the handwritten ms. of "The Strange High House in the Mist" to 9 November 1926.

3. The description "golden flames played about weedy locks" perhaps suggests HPL was aware of Sir John Rhys's writings on Nodens outlined below. Rhys describes the god as depicted on the Lydney bronze headpiece as "a youthful deity crowned with rays like Phoebus: he stands in a chariot drawn by four horses, like the Roman Neptune" (127).

Such scenes, particularly in the Roman funerary context, have often been interpreted as a reference to a particularly notable soul being ferried across the sea to the Islands of the Blessed. There may also be a transmitted hint of the description of the battle between Dionysus and Poseidon in Nonnus of Pannopolis' *Dionysiaca*, a fifth-century epic in Greek and the longest surviving poem from antiquity (coinciding with the *floreat* of Lovecraft's fictional pun-author "Ibid," from the eponymous pseudohistory written c. 1927 and published in 1938), but it is uncertain how familiar Lovecraft would have been with it, though nineteenth-century editions were certainly in circulation. The *Dionysiaca* would be an intriguing parallel given that Nonnus was a Christian who ended up creating a repository of lost mythology, or according to Herbert Jennings Rose, "a faded and overcrowded tapestry, moving a little now and then as the breath of his sickly and unholy fancy stirs it" (xii). Will Murray in his essay "The Dunwich Chimera and Others" cogently demonstrates that Lovecraft's use and transmutation of classical and other mythologies in his work serves the specific function of tying his own creations to an ancient past by implying through the narrative that the standard versions are debased iterations of his fictional mythos.

As Marco Frenschkowski writes in "Nodens—Metamorphosis of a Deity," this apparent benignity of Nodens *helping* Olney—uniquely among Lovecraft deities—could not be applied to other of Lovecraft's oceanic deities such as Cthulhu or Dagon (3). Indeed, in Lovecraft's writings Nodens is the closest thing to an "Elder God" apparently on the side of humanity in the Derleth mold, though as Frenschkowski points out, there is no reason why the indifferent, amoral entities might not, on a whim, help the occasional mortal that catches their attention (7–8). That benignity is again on display in *The Dream-Quest of Unknown Kadath*, for the benefit of Randolph Carter: "Out of the void S'ngac the violet gas had pointed the way, and archaic Nodens was bellowing his guidance from unhinted deeps. . . . And hoary Nodens raised a howl of triumph when Nyarlathotep, close on his quarry, stopped baffled by a glare that seared his formless hunting-horrors to grey dust" (CF 2.213). There is here a suggestion of the Poseidon of the Orphic Hymns:

> Whose voice loud founding thro' the roaring deep,
> drives all its billows, in a raging heap;
> When fiercely riding thro' the boiling sea,
> thy hoarse command the trembling waves obey. (Taylor 51)

In *The Dream-Quest of Unknown Kadath* Lovecraft does rather seem to be setting up Nodens as an antagonist to Nyarlathotep, the Abyss versus the Chaos, complete with his own night-gaunts, and Derleth could be forgiven for reading too much into such sentences as "There were gods and presences and wills; beauty and evil, and the shrieking of noxious night robbed of its prey" (CF 2.212). Richard Huber in his "Nodens and the Elder Gods" draws attention to this sentence in his parsing of the Derlethian error, interpreting "beauty" to refer to Nodens and "evil" as Nyarlathotep (11), in which case Derleth's mistake was to understand "beauty" as a moral good rather than an arbitrary aesthetic abstraction.

There is a potential third outside and indirect mention of Nodens in "The Call of Cthulhu," written in the summer of 1926 and published in February 1928, placing it in the same timeframe as "The Strange High House in the Mist" and *The Dream-Quest of Unknown Kadath*:

> There were legends of a hidden lake unglimpsed by mortal sight, in which dwelt a huge, formless white polypous thing with luminous eyes; and squatters whispered that bat-winged devils flew up out of caverns in inner earth to worship it at midnight. They said it had been there before D'Iberville, before La Salle, before the Indians, and before even the wholesome beasts and birds of the woods. It was nightmare itself, and to see it was to die. But it made men dream, and so they knew enough to keep away. (CF 2.35)

This extremely unlikely attribution is based purely on the aquatic nature of the "polypous thing" and the "bat-winged devils" which, with interpretative largesse, resemble night-gaunts. The

thing's apparently malignity, and Nodens's otherwise anthropomorphic depictions in Lovecraft's writing, would seem to pre-
clude that possibility.

Nodens as Ocean God

The understanding of Nodens as an oceanic god first came
about with the excavation of a Romano-Briton temple of the deity at Lydney Park, Gloucestershire[4] by Charles Bathurst in
1805, the results being published by his son William Hiley Bathurst, illustrated with engravings by Samuel Lyson, in 1879.
Bathurst found fragments of a mosaic floor depicting dolphins,
fish, and other sea creatures, dedicated to Mars Nodens by a Titus Flavius Senilis (whence Machen presumably got the name)
and "Victorinus the Interpreter of the Governor's staff" (possibly
an interpreter of dreams (Fulford 26), which chimes with Lovecraft's association of Nodens with the Dreamlands), bronze stat-
uettes of hunting hounds, and a bronze object, possibly a
headdress or tiara worn by a priest, depicting a sea god wearing a
mural crown, in a chariot between torch-bearing putti and tritons (Bathurst; Wheeler and Wheeler 103).[5] As Frenschkowski

---

4. On the western bank of the Severn River, incidentally, putting it in Ramsey
Campbell territory. Nodens is occasionally hypothesized to be a deity of the
Severn.

5. Given that HPL wrote "Shadow over Innsmouth" at the end of 1931,
around the time of the first publication of the Wheelers' Lydney excavations
and the publication of "The Strange High House in the Mist," could not the
Lydney headpiece have inspired the tiara in the former? "It took no excessive
sensitiveness to beauty to make me literally gasp at the strange, unearthly
splendour of the alien, opulent phantasy that rested there on a purple velvet
cushion. Even now I can hardly describe what I saw, though it was clearly
enough a sort of tiara, as the description had said. It was tall in front, and with
a very large and curiously irregular periphery, as if designed for a head of almost freakishly elliptical outline. The material seemed to be predominantly
gold, though a weird lighter lustrousness hinted at some strange alloy with an
equally beautiful and scarcely identifiable metal. Its condition was almost perfect, and one could have spent hours in studying the striking and puzzlingly
untraditional designs—some simply geometrical, and some plainly marine—
chased or moulded in high relief on its surface with a craftsmanship of incredi-

observes, dogs are symbolic guardians of the underworld, linking Nodens with the realm of the dead (5), of which the classically minded Lovecraft, with his interest in English and Celtic folklore, was of course aware (cf. "The Hound" and the ghouls having canine features in "Pickman's Model" and *The Dream-Quest of Unknown Kadath*).

Figure 1: Engraving by Samuel Lyson, Bathurst 1879

If Lovecraft was not initially aware of Bathurst's work, his attention may well have been drawn to it by the second excavation undertaken at Lydney by Sir Mortimer and Tessa Wheeler in 1928–29 and not properly published until 1931 in the *Antiquaries Journal* (Casey). "The Strange High House in the Mist" was only first published in the October 1931 issue of *Weird Tales*, and the surviving handwritten manuscript and typescript, dated "Novr. 9, 1926" in the collection of Brown University Library,[6]

---

ble skill and grace" ("The Shadow over Innsmouth" [CF 3.167]).

6. "The Strange High House in the Mist," Howard P. Lovecraft collection, Ms. Lovecraft, Brown University Library, John Hay Library, University Archives and Manuscripts, Accession No. A32500 [583] (10). Available on the Brown Digital Repository (repository.library.brown.edu/studio/item/bdr:425278/).

appears to have been heavily revised and continued to be even
after the story was published; but the references to Nodens and
his entourage do not appear to have been changed. Certainly, as
Frenschkowski observes, Lovecraft was interested in Romano-
Britain, reading Weigall's popular *Wanderings in Roman Britain*
(1926) in the winter of 1933–34 (*SL* 5.374, 375ff.). This unfortunately places it too late to have been an influence on either
"The Strange High House in the Mist" or *The Dream-Quest of
Unknown Kadath*, unless this was a second reading, as it does
furnish the basics about the Nodens finds at Lydney Park (Wei-
gall 250). Most, if not all, of these details pertaining to Bathurst's discoveries were, however, available in a 1906 article by
British folklorist Arthur Bernard Cook, published in the journal
Folklore, which was available through Brown University Library.

Lovecraft was possibly also aware of the now lost sandstone
altar found at Vindolanda[7] near Hadrian's Wall, number 1694
in the standard *Roman Inscriptions of Britain*, engraved:

Deo
Neptuno
ara(m) [p]o-
s(uit) [ ] NO
To the god Neptune . . . set up the altar," though some have interpreted this as "To the god Nodens Neptune . . . set up the altar.

Lovecraft probably fleshed out his image of Nodens from Baroque and later art depicting the god Neptune in triumph, his
chariot drawn by dolphins, hippocamps, or icthyocentaurs. The
Greco-Roman mosaics depict Neptune's vehicle as an unexcep-
tional chariot. Depictions of Neptune riding in a sea shell are a
much later innovation, such as in Frans Franken's *The Triumph
of Neptune and Amphitrite* (1630s, Cleveland Museum of Art) or
the engravings made between 1717 and 1721 by Charles Dupuis

---

7. According to the *Roman Inscriptions of Britain* entry 1694, the nineteenth
century antiquarian Joseph Fairless placed the altar's finding at Hexham,
where he lived. HPL aficionados will of course recognise this as the probable
source of the Exham Priory of "The Rats in the Walls", written in 1923 and
published in *Weird Tales* the following year.

and Louis Desplaces of the lost *L'Eau: The Triumph of Neptune and Amphitrite* by Louis de Boullogne the Younger (1654–1733), Pietro Bracci's *Oceanus (Neptune)* completed for the Trevi Fountain in Rome sometime after 1759, and Jan van der Straet's drawing *Neptune in his Chariot* (c. 1859, Cooper Hewitt Museum, New York), to name but a few.

Nodens as Hunter God

As for Lovecraft's depiction of Nodens as a hunter, aside from the bronze hounds and the benign aspect of the god, we may potentially look to Sir John Rhys's remarks in his 1886 Hibbert Lecture "The Zeus of the Insular Celts," one of three in a series entitled *Lectures on the Origin and Growth of Religion, as Illustrated by Celtic Heathendom,* in which he links Nodens to the Irish god of hunting and fishing, Nuada of the Silver Hand, first king of the Tuatha dé Danann (Rhys 125), and states that the Romano-Britons saw Nodens, "the Silurian [the Silures, a powerful Celtic tribe of Wales] god as a Mars, most of the remains of antiquity connected with his temple make him a sort of Neptune" (126), and notes:

> Nor is it improbable that the name *Nodens* referred originally to that quality, though it would seem as if it were to be interpreted "the rich or wealthy" god; but I should prefer supposing it to have had the causative meaning of one who enabled others to enjoy riches and wealth, especially in the matter of cattle—one, in fact, who was supposed to be the giver of wealth, whence his traditional character for generosity. But all this must be considered highly conjectural until a related Celtic word is identified. (128)

It is worth noting that the Brown University Library holds a copy of the 1888 edition of Rhys's collected Hibbert lectures and therefore it is not out of the bounds of possibility Lovecraft had access to it. Although Lovecraft freely admitted ignorance of the Celtic languages (*SL* 5.181), he likely knew of Nuada, being knowledgeable about Irish history (de Camp 8) and mentioning the Irish epic *The Book of Invaders,* in which Nuada is a central figure, in the story "The Moon-Bog" (written 1921, published 1926). In *The Book of Invaders*, Nuada defends his people against the terrible Fomorians, the monstrous first inhabitants of Ireland—both a Machenian and a Lovecraftian theme. Rhys also connects Nodens to the mythical British king Lud, after whom the city of London was supposedly named, and that

> The probability is, that as a temple on a hill near the Severn associated him with that river in the west, so a still more ambitious temple on a hill connected him with the Thames in the east; and as an aggressive creed can hardly signalize its conquests more effectually than by appropriating the fanes of the retreating faith, no site could be guessed with more probability to have been sacred to the Celtic Zeus than the eminence on which the dome of St. Paul's now rears its magnificent form. (129)

Unfortunately for Lovecraft, the Wheelers' full report on Lydney would not be published until 1932, to which is attached a fascinating appendix on the etymology of the name Nodens by none other than J. R. R. Tolkien, Professor of Anglo-Saxon at the University of Oxford. Thus Nodens brings into conjunction two of the great fantasy mythopoeias of the twentieth century, Lovecraft's Mythos and Tolkien's Middle Earth legendarium. The current favored hypothesis of the origin of Tolkien's "One Ring" is not exclusively, as previously supposed, the Ring of the Nibelungen, but the so-called inscribed "Ring of Silvianus [or Senicianus]" (Anger; Kennedy) found in Hampshire in 1785, in conjunction with a lead curse tablet found by Bathurst at Lydney, which read:

DEVO NODENTI SILVIANVS ANILVM PERDEDIT DEMEDIAM PARTEM DONAVIT NODENTI INTER QVIBVS NOMEN SENICIANI NOLLIS PETMITTAS SANITATEM DONEC PERFERA VSQVE TEMPLVM DENTIS

For the god Nodens. Silvianus has lost a ring and has donated one half [its worth] to Nodens. Among those named Senicianus permit no good health until it is returned to the temple of Nodens. (National Trust Collections UK)

Nodens of the Great Abyss

But what did Nodens mean to Lovecraft? As seen above, Huber suggests that Nodens represents "beauty," which, given Lovecraft's transcendental imagination, might be better understood as combining the classical with the romantic elements of the Gothic and a sublime neither strictly Kantian nor Burkean. This in counterpoint to Nyarlathotep's "evil," the mercurial "crawling chaos" ("Nyarlathotep" [CF 1.202]), and perhaps, "It was the pit—the maelstrom—the ultimate abomination. . . . *it was the unnamable!*" ("The Unnamable" [CF 1.405]). Fritz Leiber interpreted the Lovecraftian Nodens as representing "the ultimate weakness of even mankind's traditions and dreams," suggesting that Nodens' apparent benignity is why humanity had not been overrun by eldritch abominations (35ff.), though this implies a Derlethian desire for tidy categories, structure, and order. To the contrary, though ancient and wizened, Lovecraft's Nodens clearly still possesses considerably potency. Frenschkowski asserts that for Lovecraft, Nodens represents a melancholy nostalgia for antiquity and fable (7) and "the enrichment and transformation prepared for him who seeks the depths of vision" (3). In other words, in the mythos he is a kind of psychopomp—a spiritual entity that leads the soul on vision journeys or to the afterlife.

This, interestingly, coincides with the astrological associations attached to the post-classical planet Neptune after its discovery in 1846—mystery, illusion, fluidity, transcendence—as typified by the composer Gustav Holst naming the Neptune movement of his 1914–16 suite *The Planets*, "Neptune the Mystic." Although Nodens has co-opted Neptune's trappings, the Roman sea god is present in his own right in Nodens' entourage in "The Strange High House in the Mist," though appears subservient to the Lord of the Abyss. The wildness and vivacity of Nodens' triumph, indirectly suggested by Machen's tale, perhaps indicates that Lovecraft imagined Nodens as a kind of oceanic Pan, particularly in the later Hellenistic syncretic sense of a god of *all* nature, or something in the manner of primaeval panpsychist

Oceanus[8] or a Super-Neptune. In that case, an oceanic meta-
phor extends itself pleasingly to the great ocean of the unconscious from which all archetypal images emerge and eventually
return to be forgotten. There is probably, too, a strong hint of
Proteus, the ancient, prophetic, mutable god of rivers and seas,
one of the deities described by Homer as "the Old Man of the
Sea" (*Odyssey*, Book 4) along with Nereus, Triton, Pontus,
Phorcys or Glaucus—who could all be said to share attributes
with Lovecraft's Nodens and the nameless "Terrible Old Man"
who lives in the Strange High House.[9]

Nodens' Lovecraftian-via-Machen epithet "Lord of the Great
Abyss" is, undoubtedly, our most fertile clue in understanding
Lovecraft's Nodens. In the Dreamlands the Great Abyss is a mysterious realm beneath even their lowest reaches, accessible from
an entrance among the fallen stones of Sarkomand,[10] guarded by
titanic twin winged lion or sphinx statues[11] carved in diorite.
Huber describes it as "a great tunnel or well that sinks into
dreamland" (11) Given that Lovecraft had at the very least a
superficial understanding of the theories of Freud, as evidenced

---

8. Homer refers to Oceanus as the "father of all things" (Iliad 14.246). There
are perhaps hints of this in HPL's 1918 poem "Oceanus" with its references to
"secrets that they dare not speak."

9. The Terrible Old Man first appears in the story "The Terrible Old Man"
(1920). He has an almost intercessory, priestlike role in "The Strange High
House in the Mist," a lesser divine guardian of the threshold to the mystical,
and the house a kind of temple. He reminds us somewhat of Erich Zann in
"The Music of Erich Zann" (1921), for just as the cliff-facing door of the
Strange High House opens on another realm, Zann's garret room overlooks
not Paris but "the blackness of space illimitable" (CF 1.289).

10. Perhaps suggested by the name of Samarkand in what is now Uzbekistan.

11. Dream symbols. In the Greek tradition the sphinx is a liminal creature that
guards the threshold with riddles. In Symbolist art and literature, the sphinx
represents power, strength, transformation, mystery, antiquity, and the anima.
It plays a prominent symbolic role in H. G. Wells's *The Time Machine* (1895).
Cf. Prince and Scafella. A winged lion is the first beast seen in the first vision
of the biblical prophet Daniel. Plutarch, in De Iside et Osiride, in the Moralia,
states that the Egyptians placed sphinxes before their temples to indicate their
religious mysteries.

in multiple letters mocking their psycho-sexual aspect, it is tempting to view the Great Abyss as the deepest, inchoate layer of the subconscious mind. Quite how this Great Abyss relates to the void of Azathoth—"the central void where the daemon-sultan Azathoth gnaws hungrily in the dark" (CF 2.112)—is not clear, but with the hint of the alchemical *Azoth*, the universal solvent (Price v–vi), in the daemon-sultan's name, perhaps that is where old dreams are permanently lost beyond retrieval.

In September 1866, Ralph Waldo Emerson wrote of the creative process in his journal, "There may be two or three or four steps, according to the genius of each, but for every seeing soul there are two absorbing facts,—*I and the Abyss*" (*Selections* 405; emphasis in original). Lovecraft writes approvingly of Emerson here and there, owning editions of his essays and lectures,[12] and this is a sentiment Lovecraft would have appreciated. The creative imagination is the only bastion against that Abyss, the Logos moving on the face of void in Genesis (*super faciem abyssi*). There is something distinctly Emersonian in "The Strange High House in the Mist" and *The Dream-Quest of Unknown Kadath,* particularly in Emerson's assertion that the individual can only create an illusion determined by that individual's own intrinsic qualities, granted the power to dwell within that illusion: "Dream delivers us to dream and there is no end to illusion," Emerson wrote, ". . . We animate what we can, and we see only what we animate" (*Essays* 50). And "Temperament also enters fully into the system of illusions and shuts us in a prison of glass we cannot see" (*Essays* 51–52). If Nodens is a god of the dream, perchance Nyarlathotep is the dream of the morbid imagination turned captor and prison. There are, I think, hints of, or even answers to, Poe's "The Domain of Arnheim" (1850), in the desire for a

---

12. The Emerson volumes known to be in HPL's personal library were: *Culture* (New York: Barse & Hopkins, 1910); *Emerson's Earlier Poems* (New York: Macmillan Co., 1908); *Essays: First Series* (Boston: Houghton Mifflin, 1889); *Essays: Second Series* (Boston: Houghton Mifflin, 1889); *Representative Men: Seven Lectures* (Boston: Houghton Mifflin, 1887)—items 313–17 in S. T. Joshi's *Lovecraft's Library: A Catalogue* (4th ed,, New York: Hippocampus Press, 2017).

world where reigns the "supreme majesty and dignity of the poetic sentiment," (298) and Percy Bysshe Shelley's *Alastor* (1815), in which a poet on a quest for poetic truth is ultimately led to supernatural transcendence at an "immeasurable void" (55).

Lovecraft's Great Abyss also carries with it echoes of Milton's "The dark unbottom'd infinite abyss" of *Paradise Lost*, which as Thomas Quayle notes in his essay "The Blind Idiot God" is a theme also picked up in Lovecraft's other stories, such as "The Whisperer in Darkness," where a devotee of the Mi-Go reveals the existence of "strangely organised abysses wholly beyond the utmost reach of any human imagination. The space-time globule which we recognise as the totality of all cosmic entity is only an atom in the genuine infinity which is theirs" (CF 2.503). Milton describes a similar conceptual abyss between Earth and other realms as:

> . . . a dark
> Illimitable Ocean without bound.
> Without dimension, where length, breadth, and heighth,
> And time and place are lost; where eldest Night
> And Chaos . . . hold Eternal Anarchy, amidst the noise
> Of endless wars, and by confusion stand . . . (90.891–97)

Milton, one of the last persons in history of whom it might reasonably be said without hyperbole that he had read *everything*, offers here one of the earliest articulations of an Enlightenment understanding of infinite space, theoretically inferred from mathematics and astronomy, but outside direct human experience, applied to the metaphysical. The period that followed Milton's, the eighteenth century "Age of Reason" that so fascinated Lovecraft's imagination, was characterized by the problem of rationalizing the material and metaphysical *aporia*, something that lasted well into the nineteenth century literature that also proved influential on Lovecraft.

Aaron Worth has written about Machen's tale as a late Victorian intellectual and Gothicized response to what historian David Lord Smail terms "deep history" opened up by archaeology, palaeontology, Darwin's evolutionary theories, and advances in geology (Smail *passim*). What this essentially entails is that the nineteenth century saw the realization of a new conceptual space representing "a powerful, collective act of integration"—John McPhee's "Deep Time" (77), which historians were obliged to marry with their "shallow time" humanistic historiography (Worth 218). Worth writes: "Smail's historians 'recoiling' in horror from 'the dark abyss of time,' sound uncannily like Machen's Clarke in *The Great God Pan*, 'who has peered over an abyss, and has drawn back in terror'" (Worth 217). This similarly echoes Scottish Enlightenment mathematician John Playfair, who on being confronted with the geological strata of Siccar Point in 1788 remarked, "the mind seemed to grow giddy by looking so far into the abyss of time" (73).

It would be redundant to remind the reader that Lovecraft ubiquitously explored this vertiginous abyss of forgotten and cosmic chronology in his own tales, but if Nodens must represent anything in the Lovecraftian imagination, it is that "deep history" and the complex, romantic *jouissance* of its contemplation. Whatever the case, Lovecraft's interest in Nodens was limited and ephemeral. There is no other obvious reference to the entity in Lovecraft's oeuvre other than these two texts, and as Frenschkowski notes, Nodens is not featured in the mock genealogy of Mythos entities Lovecraft sent to James F. Morton (18n24, citing *SL* 4.183). Perhaps this may be attributed to an increasing emphasis on cosmicism over romanticism in Lovecraft's literary philosophy.

Nodens, too, it seems, eventually fell victim to his own abyss.

Works Cited

Anger, Don N. "Report on the Excavation of the Prehistoric, Roman and Post-Roman Site in Lydney Park, Gloucestershire." In Michael D. C. Drout, ed. *The J. R. R. Tolkien Encyclopedia.* Abingdon-on-Thames, UK: Routledge, 2006. 563–64.

Bathurst, William Hiley. *Roman Antiquities at Lydney Park, Gloucestershire: Being a Posthumous Work of the Rev. William Hiley Bathurst, M.A.* With Notes by C. W. King. London: Longmans, Green, 1879.

Casey, D. A. "Lydney Castle." *Antiquaries Journal* 11 (1931): 240–61.

Cook, Arthur Bernard. "IV. The Celts." *Folklore* 17 (March 1906): 27–71.

de Camp, L. Sprague. "Young Man Lovecraft." *Xenophile* 2, No. 6 (October 1975): 8.

Emerson, Ralph Waldo. *Essays: Second Series.* Boston: Houghton, Mifflin, 1876.

———. *Selections from Ralph Waldo Emerson.* Ed. Stephen E. Whicher. Boston: Houghton Mifflin, 1960.

Frenschkowski, Marco. "Nodens—Metamorphosis of a Deity." *Crypt of Cthulhu* No. 87 (Lammas 1994): 3–8.

Fulford, Michael G. *The Second Augustan Legion in the West of Britain.* Ninth Annual Caerleon Lecture. Cardiff: National Museums and Galleries of Wales, 1996.

Huber, Richard. "Nodens and the Elder Gods." *Nyctalops* No. 14 (March 1978): 11.

Kennedy, Maev. "The Hobbit Ring That May Have Inspired Tolkien Put on Show." *Guardian* (2 April 2013), www.theguardian. com/books/2013/apr/02/hobbit-tolkien-ring-exhibition

Lattimore, Steven. *The Marine Thiasos in Greek Sculpture.* Los Angeles: Institute of Archaeology, University of California, Los Angeles, 1976.

Leiber, Fritz. "A Literary Copernicus." 1949. In S. T. Joshi, ed. *H. P. Lovecraft: Four Decades of Criticism.* Athens: Ohio University Press, 1980. 50–61.

Lovecraft, H. P., and August Derleth. *Essential Solitude: The Letters of H. P. Lovecraft and August Derleth.* Ed. David E. Schultz and S. T. Joshi. New York: Hippocampus Press, 2008. 2 vols.

Machen, Arthur. *The Great God Pan, and The Inmost Light.* Boston: Roberts Brothers, 1894.

———. *Far Off Things.* New York: Alfred A. Knopf, 1922.

McPhee, John. *Basin and Range: Annals of the Former World.* Volume 1. New York: Farrar, Straus & Giroux, 1981.

Milton, John. *Milton's Paradise Lost.* London: Dent and New York: Dutton, 1920.

Murray, Will. "The Dunwich Chimera and Others." *Lovecraft Studies* No. 8 (Spring 1984): 10–24.

Playfair, John. "Biographical account of the late Dr James Hutton, FRS, Edinburgh." *Earth and Environmental Science Transactions of the Royal Society of Edinburgh* 5 (1805): 39–99.

Pliny the Elder. *The Natural History of Pliny*. Tr. John Bostock and Henry Thomas Riley. London: Henry J. Bohn, 1855.

Poe, Edgar Allan. *The Works of Edgar Allan Poe*, Vol. 2. New York: P. F. Collier & Son, 1903.

Price, Robert M., ed. *The Azathoth Cycle*. Oakland, CA: Chaosium, 1995.

Prince, John S. "The 'True Riddle of the Sphinx' in *The Time Machine*." *Science Fiction Studies* 27, No. 3 (November 2000): 543–46.

Quayle, Thomas. "The Blind Idiot God: Miltonic Echoes in the Cthulhu Mythos." *Crypt of Cthulhu* No. 49 (Lammas 1987): 24–28.

Rhys, John. *Lectures on the Origin and Growth of Religion, as Illustrated by Celtic Heathendom*. London: Williams & Norgate, 1888.

"RIB 1694. Altar dedicated to Neptune." *Roman Inscriptions of Britain*, romaninscriptionsofbritain.org/inscriptions/1694#commentary-notes

"Ring of Senicianus." National Trust Collections UK, www.nationaltrustcollections.org.uk/object/719789

Rose, Herbert Jennings. "Introduction" to the Nonnus. *Dionysiaca*. With an English Translation by W. H. D. Rouse. London: Heinemann; Cambridge, MA: Harvard University Press (Loeb Classical Library), 1940.

Scafella, Frank. "The White Sphinx and *The Time Machine* (Le Sphynx blanc et la Machine à remonter le temps)." *Science-Fiction Studies* 8, No. 3 (November 1981): 255–65.

Shelley, Percy Bysshe. *Alastor; or, The spirit of solitude, and other poems*. London: Baldwin, Cradock, and Joy; and Carpenter and Son, 1816.

Smail, Daniel Lord. *On Deep History and the Brain*. Berkeley: University of California Press, 2007.

Taylor, Thomas, tr. *The Hymns of Orpheus.* 1792. Philadelphia: University of Pennsylvania Press, 1999.

Weigall, Arthur. *Wanderings in Roman Britain.* London: Butterworth, 1926.

Wheeler, R. E. M., and T. V. Wheeler. "Report on the Excavation of the Prehistoric, Roman, and Post-Roman Site in Lydney Park, Gloucestershire." *Reports of the Research Committee of the Society of Antiquaries London.* No. IX, Research Report No. 9. 1932.

Worth, Aaron. "Arthur Machen and the Horrors of Deep History." *Victorian Literature and Culture* 40 (2012): 215–27.

Briefly Noted

A vastly expanded edition of R. H. Barlow's *Eyes of the God* (first published in 2002) will appear shortly from Hippocampus Press. It is more than twice the size of the original volume and now contains nearly every scrap of Barlow's extant fiction (including numerous previously unpublished stories and story fragments), several additional poems, and his complete extant body of nonfiction (in English). In addition, a number of significant memoirs of Barlow by George T. Smisor (Barlow's literary executor), Rosalie Moore, Lawrence Hart, and Clare Mooser are included in an appendix.

Lovecraft's Garden: Heart's Blood at the Root

Jan B. W. Pedersen

In earlier writings[1] I have sought to establish a link between Howard Phillips Lovecraft and Romanticism, and this paper adds to that body of work. The essay begins with a preliminary sketch of the use of gardens in Romantic thought and the highlighting of six themes: contemplation, joy, the dramatic, the strange, the foreign, and the beautiful, that all underpins Romanticism. This is followed by an elucidation of Lovecraft's fascination with gardens, his dealings in Romantic themes, and what role they play in his short 1917 poem "A Garden." The essay concludes that, given Lovecraft's love of gardens and that his poem "A Garden" is imbued with Romantic themes and involves "wondrous contemplation" and "poetic knowledge," the case for his Romanticism has been strengthened.

Romantic Gardens and Their Themes: A Primer

Gardens can be wonderful places and are featured frequently in various kinds of literature, including poetry and indeed philosophy, where they work as metaphors and function as in-between places or vehicles of realisation and metamorphosis.

The famous twentieth-century American poet Robert Frost's short garden poem "Lodged," addressing vulnerability and hardships, is a prime example. The same goes for the stoic philosopher

---

1. "On Lovecraft's Lifelong Relationship with Wonder" (2017), "Howard Phillips Lovecraft: Romantic on the Nightside" (2018), and "Weird Fiction: A Catalyst for Wonder" (2020).

Seneca's passionate comments on the garden of Epicurus,[2] which had a sign above its entrance reading: "Stranger, here you will tarry; here our highest good is pleasure" (Seneca, *Epistle* 21). Gardens and indeed natural landscapes also play an important role in the Romantic movement to the extent that we today operate with a type of garden labelled "the Romantic garden."

The Romantic garden contrasts with the symmetrical Baroque garden associated with sixteenth-century Italy and the influential seventeenth-century French aristocracy.[3] Unlike the Baroque garden where every aspect is controlled, manipulated, and speaks of man's mastery over nature, the Romantic garden celebrates the unruliness of nature and enlarges the world of the person experiencing it. Thus, the Romantic garden symbolizes a particular outlook and functions as a catalyst for Romantic philosophy. Contrasting the Baroque garden, the Romantic garden is not to be observed from above or from a distance, so that an adequate appraisal of its symmetry may be produced. It is to be wandered through and wondered at because it is a place that aims to reposition humanity within the realm of Pan, within nature; unlike the Baroque garden, it is a place of asymmetry, where one is reminded of the marvels of the world, including things now distant and lost to us. Hence, Romantic gardens often include rare plants, ruins, and temples of all sorts dedicated to ancient and "forgotten" Gods (De Deulin 96–97).

Not far from where I am writing these lines, one finds Søndermarken (The Southern Field)—a public park in Frederiksberg, Denmark. Established in the early eighteenth century, this is by many considered to be the heart of Romanticism in Denmark because it was here the Danish poet and playwright Adam Oehlenschläger and his German friend, the philosopher, scientist, and poet Henrich Steffens, discussed new trends in German philosophy, including the thoughts of the German philosopher Friedrich Schelling. Schelling was one of the main driving forces

---

2. Epicurus (341–270 B.C.E.) founded "The Garden," which functioned both as a school and a circle of friends. Epicurus is known for a rational hedonistic ethics urging one to strive toward pleasure in order to achieve well-being.

3. Villa Borghese gardens in Rome is a prime example of a Baroque garden, and the same goes for the Gardens of Versailles in France.

in German Romanticism and had a profound influence on the English Romantic poet Samuel Taylor Coleridge. This becomes evident upon reading Coleridge's 1802 poem "Dejection: An Ode," which is concerned with the loss of the shaping spirit of imagination and the joy that follows upon the use of this faculty (Pedersen, *Balanced Wonder* 100–101).

Furthermore, Coleridge, whom Lovecraft very much admired, is the author of the poem *The Rime of the Ancient Mariner* and he is important to Romantics as well as students of supernatural horror (CE 2.87): to the former because the infamous traveling Romantic Lord Byron identified himself with the ancient mariner (Thomson 60); to the latter because M. R. James, the twentieth-century English medievalist and ghost story writer, whom Lovecraft also admired, used it to great effect in his 1911 short story "Casting the Runes" (Berlin 97–98; CE 2.123–24, 145; James 160; SL 2.334).

Originally a Baroque garden, Søndermarken was changed into a Romantic garden in the years 1780–1805. Back then, as today, it offered the visitor a glimpse into the Romantic fascination with themes including the dramatic, the strange, the foreign, and the beautiful. There is for example a grotto, with a natural spring inside hinting at the Romantics' fascination with ancient Greece and Rome and the promise of insight into mysteries that such animated places supposedly offered. One can also locate a memorial mound harboring a statue of "Mother Denmark" holding a baby. Surrounded by beautiful tall trees, it commemorates the Danes who long ago emigrated to America; chiseled above the entrance of the mound one finds the dramatic inscription: "They who set out, never to return." Additionally, one may also find a strange Norwegian cabin, a Chinese pagoda, and the mysterious Cisterns—an early underground water reservoir now turned into a contemporary museum.

As an arboreal breathing space contrasting the artificiality of the surrounding city, Søndermarken serves as a refuge for the local fauna, including different kinds of birds, rodents, and insects, as well as the frequent and all too human flaneur. All in all, Søndermarken is a precious and beneficial place as it caters to the contemplative mind and brings joy to many.

Now contemplation and joy are both complicated labels that deserve attention because both are—aside from the dramatic, the strange, the foreign, and the beautiful—important Romantic themes.

Contemplation is difficult to understand and has been deliberated and celebrated since the ancient Peripatetic philosopher Aristotle taught at the Lyceum.[4] Furthermore, it has a close connection with the peculiar state of mind we call wonder, which was particularly important not only to the ancient Greek philosophers but also to the Romantics, and Lovecraft (Pedersen, "Relationship with Wonder" 26–34; "Romantic on the Nightside" 165–67; *Balanced Wonder* 4, 32–34; "Weird Fiction" 318–31). To elaborate, let us take a brief look at philosopher Anders Schinkel's notion of "contemplative wonder," which he understands as:

> A mode of consciousness in which we experience that which we perceive or are contemplating as strange, deeply other or mysterious, fundamentally beyond the limits of our understanding, yet worthy of attention for its own sake, in which our attention takes the form of an open receptive stance, and an attunement towards mystery. (Schinkel 54)

The term is insightful and praiseworthy because it makes clear that there could well be different kinds of wonderment. One might wonder how a combustion engine works, or what makes a helicopter fly, and such kinds of wonder correspond to what Schinkel labels "inquisitive wonder." Since both objects of wonder qualify as mechanical inventions, one could in principle find out how they work.

Another kind of wonder is, as mentioned, contemplative wonder, and this sort of wonderment Schinkel describes as "silent response to mystery not immediately accompanied by an active search for answers; and at any rate there are no answers here, nothing that will dissolve the mystery or the wonder" (54). The state of mind Schinkel is referring to could occur when pondering the concept of "eternity": can we truly understand what it is for something to be eternal? Some would point out

---

4. The Lyceum was originally a sanctuary dedicated to Apollo but also a gymnasium. Book 10 of Aristotle's *Nicomachean Ethics* is concerned with contemplation.

that what is eternal is merely that which is not finite, but do we really know what it means to be finite or what it means for something to go out of existence? Naturally, philosophical advancement or sophistication can be made, but ultimately it seems Schinkel is right that no matter what we do our action will not solve the mystery at hand.

Moving on, contemplative wonder is useful for our present purpose. If we flip it around and put "wonder" before "contemplation" we end up with another fusion, i.e., "wondrous contemplation."

This is important because wondrous contemplation is the type of contemplation the Romantics and indeed Lovecraft advocated, experienced, and sought. If we focus solely on the Romantic movement, we could also say that wondrous contemplation served as the starting point of the movement because it is by means of such deeply reflective, introspective mental activity that Romanticism, viewed as an attack on the Enlightenment, came about in the first place. Furthermore, one could also hold that it is by means of contemplation that Romanticism arose as a rebellion against eighteenth-century philosopher Adam Smith's proclamation that human beings are laboring animals above and before all else (Berlin21; Adelman).

Now the critical reader could attempt a rebuke by interjecting that all this is merely superfluous sophistry or gratuitous conjunction and that "wondrous contemplation," "contemplative wonder," "contemplation," and indeed "wonder" merely refers to the same thing or mental phenomenon. I am sympathetic to such a stance, but insofar there is such a thing as "wondrous contemplation" it is important to realize that by distinguishing the term we are engaged in the most praiseworthy art of taxonomy. A rock is never "just" a rock, because there are different kinds of rocks, and so if we wish to advance our knowledge and understanding of rocks we are forced to taxonomize and define them as igneous, sedimentary, and so on. The same applies when we address mental activities such as wonder and contemplation: although they may look the same, they are not necessarily so. Having said that, the key to understand what wondrous contemplation is or what sets it apart from similar designations is introspection: as we shall see later in connection with Lovecraft's

poem "A Garden," wondrous contemplation, unlike contemplative wonder, does lead to something. It leads to self-realisation
and poetic knowledge.

Now joy is equally particular and important to the Romantics
because, as Coleridge claims, it is synonymous with the soul—it
is the very power that animates us or gives us life as it transforms
perception into feeling (Pedersen, *Balanced Wonder* 101). Paraphrasing the eminent philosopher Mary Warnock, one might say
that without joy we only see, and regardless of whether we see
an object as beautiful or not, we do so without feeling that it is
one or the other (Warnock 78).

To exemplify, imagine beholding the face of Leonardo da
Vinci's most famous painting, *Mona Lisa*. Realizing that her face
is beautiful is one thing, but feeling that it is so, including that
one can stare at her without grasping why she is so beautiful, is
another. Naturally the critic could put forth that the reason why
one feels this way is purely because Leonardo cleverly incorpo-
rated the Fibonacci sequence in the painting. However, this
does not take away the feeling at all. If anything, it encourages it
because upon, realizing that the golden ratio plays a part in Mona Lisa's beauty, we are left to wonder and contemplate the curious fact that since the sequence can be found in many a
natural object including roses, ocean waves, and spiral galaxies,
Mona Lisa incorporates an aspect of the natural world that human beings are highly susceptible to and have an affinity for
classifying as beautiful. We must now consider if there is an objective ring to the notion of beauty and, by extension, ugliness
that goes beyond mere matters of taste.

We are now at liberty to say that the Romantic traveler who
saunters around in places such as Søndermarken, observing the
sights, in doing so becomes an honorable figure because his or
her very activity, including the search for the dramatic, the
strange, the foreign, and the beautiful is closely connected to the
complex workings of contemplation and joy.

Lovecraft's Romantic Bent: An Advance

The gentleman of Providence was no stranger to the abovemen-
tioned Romantic themes, including contemplation and the

search for joy that fueled many valuable adventures to places outside his beloved Providence, among them Cape Cod, Charleston, Key West, Marblehead, New Orleans, Quebec, Salem, and Vermont (CE 4.7, 261; SL 1.117, 3.447).[5]

Despite his reputation as a recluse, Lovecraft was quite outgoing and held the woodlands of New England in October in high esteem. Likewise, he had an affinity for Wade Park in Cleveland and the Japanese garden located in Brooklyn (SL 2.334, 3.412). In 1930 he found his ideal garden at Maymont—a Victorian estate in Richmond, Virginia—and in a most joyous and enthusiastic letter[6] to Alfred Galpin dated May 15 he writes:

> Gad, Sir, I swoon! I swoon with the conscious contemplation of complete and culminant beauty [. . .] This is something to see and dream about all the rest of one's life. I am sure I shall think of very little else during my few remaining days! It is Poe's "Domain of Arnheim" and "Island of the Fay" all rolled into one—with my own Cathuria and gardens of Yin added for good measure. (SL 3.412)

Besides revealing his love for Poe's work and flashing elements of his own creations, including the wondrous "Cathuria" (the land of hope from the short dreamland story "The White Ship," 1919) and "The gardens of Yin" (sonnet XVIII from his curious collection of poetry entitled Fungi from Yuggoth), the letter discloses Lovecraft's appreciation of gardens and attention to contemplation and joy. Additionally, his enthusiastic confessions concerning the beauty of Maymont reveal his Romanticism and rich emotional life. Lovecraft held the experience of walking through gardens as one of the supreme incarnations of what he calls "utter perfect beauty" (SL 3.412, 413), and this singular deep-felt focus on the notion of beauty ties him to the Romantics, to whom beauty was

---

5. Naturally, not all such adventures were successful, and one noteworthy and exhausting misadventure is the mysterious 1923 trip to "Dark Swamp," a blighted wild area close to Chepachet, Rhode Island (Eddy 67–68; SL 1.149).

6. HPL's enthusiasm in relation to Maymont was so intense that he more or less repeated his wording in a letter sent to James Ferdinand Morton on the same day (SL 3.413).

to be treasured.[7] In the same letter to Galpin he elaborates:

> The experience of walking (or, as in most of my dreams, aerially floating) through aethereal and enchanted gardens of exotic delicacy and opulence, with carved stone, bridges, labyrinthine paths, marble fountains, terraces and staircases, strange pagodas, hillside grottos, curious statues, termini, sundials, benches, basins and lanthorns, lily'd pools of swans and streams with tiers of waterfalls, spreading gingko-trees and dropping, feathery willows, and sun- touch'd flowers of bizarre, Klarkash-Tonick pattern never beheld on land or beneath the sea. . . . (SL 3.412)

The Romantic notion of walking though gardens engaging in contemplation and the enjoyment of beauty was clearly important to Lovecraft and a recurring leitmotif in his literary work.

Consider his early prose poem "Ex Oblivione" (1921). In the story, the narrator finds in the dreamlands some of the beauty he vainly sought in life, as he wanders through old gardens and enchanted woods.

Lovecraft's last story, "The Haunter of the Dark" (1935), features a protagonist, upon returning to Providence, takes up the upper floor of a respected house in a grassy court of College Street. Lovecraft describes it as "a cosy and fascinating place, in a little garden oasis of village-like antiquity where huge, friendly cats sunned themselves atop on a convenient shed" (CF 3.453). Of course, one might say that there is not much going on in terms of wandering through beautiful gardens in "The Haunter of the Dark," but the point is that the notion of being situated in a "life-giving" place was something Lovecraft contemplated and found important as much in 1935, two years before his passing, as he did in 1921 when he wrote "Ex Oblivione." Lovecraft

---

7. Lord Byron's lyrical and most celebrated poem "She Walks in Beauty" is a testimony of the importance of beauty in Romantic thought. The same goes for German Romantic philosopher par excellence Immanuel Kant's distinction between beauty and the sublime as found in his *The Critique of Judgment*. In §23 he notes that beauty is connected with the form of the object. The sublime is different in the sense that it is represented by boundlessness—something we cannot quantify like the misty surroundings of the lonely wanderer in Caspar Friedrich's famous 1818 painting *Der Wanderer über dem Nebelmeer*.

comes across as an enduring Romantic, which is important to our understanding of him as a person.[8]

Romantic Qualities in Lovecraft's Short Stories and Poetry: A Précis

Several of Lovecraft's stories have a Romantic ring to them, because they are centered on contemplative characters searching for joy. One such story is "The Strange High House in the Mist" (1926), which focuses on the restless philosopher Thomas Olney, who taught ponderous things in a college by Narragansett Bay and one summer found unexpected joy in the ancient house mentioned in the title of the story. Another story is "The Quest of Iranon" (1921), which tracks the exploits of Iranon—the traveling protagonist who questions the ways of the god(s)-fearing hardworking men of Teloth. Iranon asks:

> "Wherefore do ye toil; is it not that ye may live and be happy? And if ye toil only that ye may toil more, when shall happiness find you? Ye toil to live, but is not life made of beauty and song? And if ye suffer no singers among you, where shall be the fruits of your toil? Toil without song is like a weary journey without an end. Were not death more pleasing?" (CF 1.250)

Both Olney and Iranon are thoughtful seekers who question the ways of people around them, and through both we become

---

8. We find some of the same thoughts and feelings in 1921 short story "The Moon-Bog," where HPL reveals the details of a wonderful dream experienced by the narrator centred around a stately city in a green valley where, "marble streets and statues, villas and temples, carvings and inscriptions, all spoke in certain tones the glory that was Greece" (CF 1.259). Greece or the idea that is Greece is a pivotal point for the great poets of the Romantic movement as well as for HPL. Lord Byron's narrative poem *Childe Harold's Pilgrimage*, published in the beginning of the nineteenth century, reveals the melancholic thoughts and feelings of a disillusioned traveler and points out the grandeur of Greece (canto II). John Keats likewise celebrated Greece in his 1819 poem "Ode on a Grecian Urn," which influenced both HPL and Anna Helen Crofts, who incorporated its ending "beauty is truth, truth beauty,—that is all / Ye know on earth, and all ye need to know" into their 1920 short story "Poetry of the Gods" (Keats 50; CF 4.27).

acquainted with some of Lovecraft's innermost Romantic senti-
ments and longings.

As mouthpieces of Lovecraft, both characters are in a sense
philosopher kings or Romantics par excellence, although they
enjoy/suffer radically different fates. Both have fathomed the
"enslaving" machinery we call culture and have in a sense broken free. However, where Olney finds the contentment and joy
he seeks,[9] Iranon ultimately fails in doing so and ceases to exist
following a moment of devastating self-understanding. This does
not make him less of a Romantic, because discomfort, suffering,
and failure are fully fledged Romantic trappings as they make for
a tragic hero (Thomson 58).

Let us now turn attention to an even earlier work by Lovecraft, the poem "A Garden" (1917), while keeping in mind the
above-mentioned Romantic themes. The poem read as follows:

There's an ancient, ancient garden that I see sometimes in
   dreams,
Where the very Maytime sunlight plays and glows with spectral
   gleams;

---

9. The fate of Olney is mysterious as he in a sense gets split in two. "Olney 1"
stays at the strange high house in the mist and indulges in joys beyond earth's
joys; "Olney 2," who walks into Kingsport the next day, is something else entirely because he is utterly complacent, and one wonders if this phantom dop-
pelgänger indeed is the real Olney. This question becomes more pressing as the
story moves forward, because we learn that "Olney 2" simply became whatever
society and his family wanted him to be; he no longer sought secrets or the
magic of farther hills. Furthermore, HPL reveals that "Olney 2" bore the
sameness of his days without complaint and that his well-disciplined thoughts,
which bored him before he ascended the crag and came face to face with the
entity dwelling in the strange high house in the mist, became enough for him.
At the end of the story, we likewise learn that "Olney 2" eventually moves
with his family to a bungalow at Bristol Highlands where everything is urban
and modern and is never heard of again. This is an important detail, and the
keyword here is "modern," because already in 1919 HPL thought himself an
antique personality and not a modern one (SL 1.50). Thus, through the fate of
Olney, we get glimpse into HPL's Romanticism—his longing for something
more. In their entry on "The Strange High House in the Mist" Lovecraft
scholars S. T. Joshi and David E. Schultz pinpoint that Olney realizes while in
the house that he belongs in realm of "nebulous wonder." I think that this corresponds to HPL himself as well (Joshi and Schultz 253).

Where the gaudy-tinted blossoms seem to wither into grey,
And the crumbling walls and pillars waken thoughts of yesterday.
There are vines in nooks and crannies, and there's moss about
    the pool,
And the tangled weedy thicket chokes the arbour dark and cool:
In the silent sunken pathways springs an herbage sparse and spare,
While the musty scent of dead things dulls the fragrance of the air.
There is not a living creature in the lonely space around,
And the hedge-encompass'd quiet never echoes to a sound.
As I walk, and wait, and listen, I will often seek to find
When it was I knew that garden in an age long left behind;
I will oft conjure a vision of a day that is no more,
As I gaze upon the grey, grey scenes I feel I knew before.
Then a sadness settles o'er me, and a tremor seems to start:
For I know the flow'rs are shrivell'd hopes—the garden is my
    heart! (AT 278)

The poem stands as evidence of Lovecraft's Romanticism because it deals in all the Romantic themes mentioned thus far. In the following analysis, I shall elaborate on each theme in turn, saving contemplation and joy for last.

The poem is dramatic primarily because of the lamentation and loss it conveys. Furthermore, it stages a gloomy and most dramatic atmosphere much like the beginning of Edgar Allan Poe's Gothic tale "The Fall of the House of Usher," where the protagonist during a dull, dark, and soundless autumn day passes alone through a dreary track of the country only to end up at the melancholy House of Usher (Poe 244).

This dramatic poem shares a confessional tone with the opening stanza of Wordsworth's Romantic poem "Ode: Intimations of Immortality," which reads:

There was a time when meadow, grove, and stream,
The earth, and every common sight,
                To me did seem
        Apparelled in celestial light,
The glory and the freshness of a dream.
It is not now as it has been of yore;—
        Turn wheresoe'er I may,

By night or day,
The things which I have seen I now can see no more. (297)

Lovecraft's "A Garden" and Wordsworth "Ode: Intimations of
Immortality" both express the same mood; the same intense notion of a paradise lost or the drama surrounding the pain of lost
things. Wordsworth's poem, given the framework of this essay, is
much too lengthy for adequate treatment, but it ends, after a
roller-coaster ride filled with melancholy realizations and enthusiastic appreciations, on a positive and wise note. Lovecraft's "A
Garden" is dramatic, but very different. It is short in comparison
and resembles in its message merely the first stanza of "Ode: Intimations of Immortality," which thoroughly communicates the
gloomy disposition of the poetic confessor.

Lovecraft's poem also differs from Wordsworth's in the sense
that where Wordsworth's melancholy and gradual change of
perspective seem conceived amidst beautiful scenery, Lovecraft's
poem comes across as a perplexing introspective ramble though
a desolate dream-country culminating[10] in an upsetting moment
of stark self-realization where it is revealed that the garden metaphorically speaking is in fact Lovecraft's own heart.

Adding to the drama, one can say that the last line represents a truly remarkable moment in Lovecraft's authorship, because it shows a Lovecraft far removed from the supposedly
"supremely unemotional" character that he later claimed to be
—a character that does "not weep or indulge in lugubrious
demonstrations of the vulgar" (SL 1.76). The closing line un-
veils a tenderness and a Romantic quality to Lovecraft that is
generally unsung. It speaks of the inner dramatic workings of
Lovecraft's mind and the intense feelings he harbored, and a
longing for something that once was or had never been.

"A Garden" is Romantic because it deals in the strange and
the foreign, and there are three reasons this. First, the garden is
strange and foreign because it is idiosyncratic to Lovecraft in the

---

10. HPL also put the mechanism to use in the short story "The Outsider"
(1921), where the narrator after much wandering through bleak and austere
environments at the end faces a most unwelcome truth in the form of a mirror
and the realisation that he is indeed a monster.

sense that it is not a garden the reader can readily visit and form an opinion about independently of Lovecraft's description. Thus "A Garden" is not a clear-cut case of topographical poetry like John Dyers's 1726 poem *Grongar Hill,* but a piece of poetry twice removed from our common experiential world: it takes the reader on a voyage into both Lovecraft's dreamworld and lifeworld as only he conceives and experiences it. In turn, this promotes alienation; it makes us think of the poem as strange and foreign at least until the closing line, where author and reader come together in a fellowship of understanding about the fragility of the heart.

Secondly, the lines "There is not a living creature in the lonely space around, / And the hedge-encompassed'd quiet never echoes to a sound" speaks of a place strange and foreign to us. Most people live out their lives in environments rich in life and sound. Human beings are social creatures and thus we are drawn to lively places such as bars, cafés, clubs, markets, and public houses because here we meet with others of our kind, which is important for our flourishing as human beings.

Thirdly, the line describing the crumbling walls and pillars that waken thoughts of yesterday deals in the strange and the foreign because what Lovecraft is talking about is ruins. As mentioned earlier, ruins and the appreciation of such are an established theme within Romanticism, because ruins speak of bygone things and cater to the contemplative, reflective, and wundersüchtig[11] mind. Lovecraft uses the ruins to help us connect to the notion of the distant past, and to build an atmosphere of strangeness and alienation that in turn drives the poem toward its painful and surprising conclusion.

Upon realizing that the garden represents Lovecraft's very own heart, the ruins take on a strange new dimension and make us think of them not as remnants from the past external to Lovecraft, but as representations of Lovecraft's personal ruin and tragedy, which, qua their idiosyncrasy, come across as truly foreign indeed.

---

11. L. Sprague de Camp is using this German word term to describe HPL in his biography, and it roughly refers to someone who has an affinity for the supernatural or that which lies just beyond our senses (de Camp 20; Pedersen, "Weird Fiction" 321).

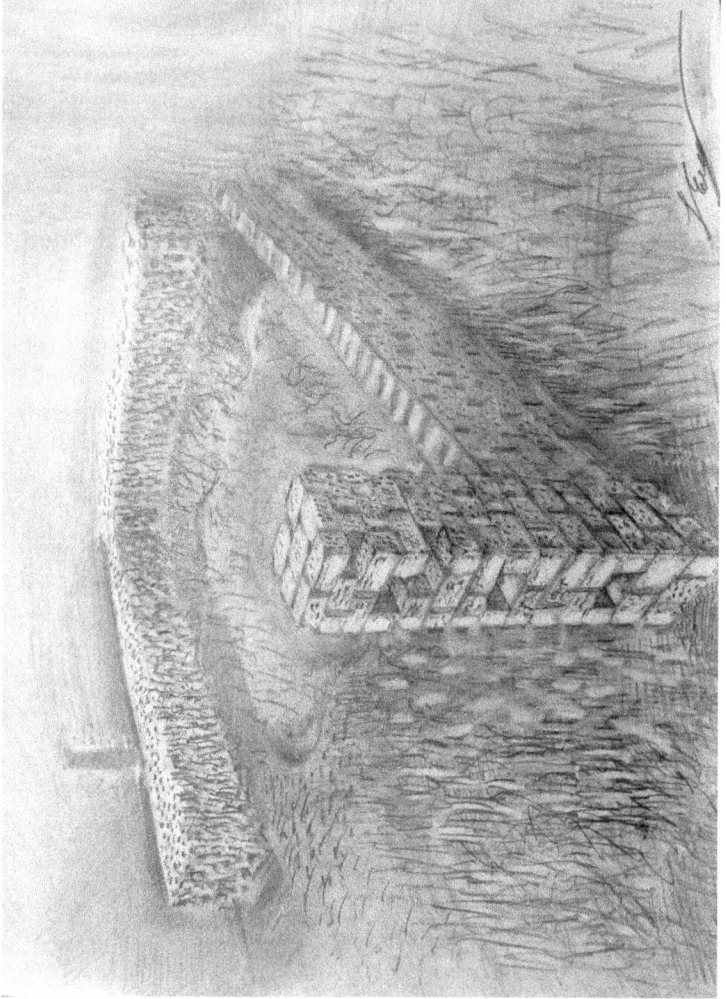

Harry Evans, *Withered*. 2022. Courtesy of Harry Evans.

Because Lovecraft's "A Garden" incorporates the notion of beauty it can also be classified as Romantic, but Romantic beauty is something special as it is interwoven with ugliness (Eco, *On Ugliness* 8). In this regard it is important to understand that Romanticism is littered with dichotomies, meaning that the Romantic vision tends to pendulate between two poles in which each not only informs the other but also conveys a unique philosophy or vision aiming at resolving antithesis (Eco, *On Beauty* 299). This is the reason why Romantic works often contain contrasts or direct opposites such as life and death, heart and reason, misery and happiness, and indeed beauty and ugliness.

To illustrate, consider Charles-Auguste Mengin's 1867 painting *Sappho*, which depicts the radiant beauty of the ancient Greek poet Sappho against an ugly threatening background. What makes the painting alluring and Romantic is partly that the threatening background highlights Sappho's beauty, which in turn lends an extra offensive dimension to the background. To illustrate this further, suppose we were to change the background and set Sappho against a lush and peaceful backdrop; one could then rightly wonder if her beauty would not somehow change in quality—perhaps even fade a little.

The same can be said of the gloomy background. Imagine if Sappho was depicted with a hideous face like the plague in Arnold Böcklin's 1898 eponymous painting or after a fashion resembling the uncanny white malformed ape or anthropomorphic fiend from Lovecraft's "Reanimator." Would it not change the aesthetic quality of the background? Would it not diminish some of the ugliness, leaving us with an entirely different experience or aesthetic judgment?

Why bring all this up? Well, Lovecraft's "A Garden" plays with beauty and ugliness the same way Mengin's *Sappho* does.[12]

---

12. In his lifework HPL often dealt with beauty and ugliness separately, and earlier we saw how he used the word beauty in connection with his report to Alfred Galpin concerning the garden in Maymont. He also focused on beauty in "Ex Oblivione," where the narrator found some of the beauty he vainly sought in life in the mysterious dreamlands. In terms of HPL's dealings in ugliness the predicate appears in his campaign against alcohol, where he simply labels drink "ugly." For more on this subject, see Pedersen, "'Now Will You be

In "A Garden" ugliness is used first to make us aware of the quality the garden lacks, i.e., beauty. This takes up most of the poem and is quite overwhelming as we are guided from one ugliness to another and hear about everything from how the May-time sunlight glows with spectral gleams to how the musty scent of dead things dulls the fragrance of the air and how the narrator often conjures up a vision of a day that is no more.

Secondly, the focus on ugliness in the poem serves the purpose of strengthening the impact and beauty of the closing line, where we learn that the ruined garden corresponds to Lovecraft's heart. As a whole "A Garden" conjures up an awareness akin to Mengin's *Sappho* in the sense that, as much as we can acknowledge that Sappho's beauty is enhanced by the ugly background, we can acknowledge that the beauty of the last sentence in "A Garden" is enhanced by the overwhelming ugliness described beforehand.

One might even say that the ugliness of the garden contrasting the beauty of the last sentence helps us recognize that Lovecraft the poet harbors a most sensitive and beautiful mind despite his melancholy. It helps us to see that the gentleman of Providence is indeed a Romantic.

"A Garden" likewise portrays Lovecraft as a Romantic because it deals in contemplation and joy. That the poem is contemplative in nature is clear for at least two reasons. The first and most obvious one is linked to the passage reading: "As I walk, and wait, and listen, I will often seek to find / When it was I knew that garden in an age long left behind." The narrator is perplexed by the uncanny yet strangely familiar location and he is trying his best to find out where he is by observing the surrounding dreamscape, which inspires nothing but a strange sense familiarity. The second reason is due to its powerful closing line, because this line induces a focus-shift from the curious dreamscape to the narrator himself, whose unknown past and plans for life suddenly become of immense importance to the reader and the key to understanding what or who the poem is all about.

Good?"' Likewise, he uses the word ugly in his signature piece of fiction "The Call of Cthulhu" to describe the roots and malignant hanging nooses of Spanish moss the police faced during their search for the Louisiana swamp worshippers.

Charles Auguste Mengin, *Sappho*. 1877.

At first it may seem an overstatement of Cyclopean proportion to categorize the poem as joyful: how can ugliness and deso-
lation even remotely communicate joy? The answer is twofold
and connected to the remarkable closing line, the state of mind
we call "wonder" and indeed "wondrous contemplation."

The poem is joyful because of the utter surprise of the closing
line. This does not mean that we must draw enjoyment from
Lovecraft's broken heart, nor am I referring to schadenfreude.
What makes the line joyful is the fact that it is an anomaly to
hear Lovecraft speak of his heart in such a manner, and consequently it makes the heart of the reader leap up in the same
fashion as Wordsworth's did when he beheld a rainbow in the
sky (246). Like the rainbow, it is a wonder to behold Lovecraft
speak in this manner, and it inflicts a crack in our conception of
Lovecraft, leaving the gentleman of Providence mysterious and
undefined. The closing line makes us realize that our knowledge
of him is broken—that our understanding of him is incomplete—and that instigates wonder, which in turn evokes joy
(Pedersen, *Balanced Wonder*).

Additionally, one can argue that the closing line is joyful because it is a testimony of Lovecraft's wondrous contemplation in
action. Unlike Schinkel's "contemplative wonder," which does
not produce anything new, "wondrous contemplation" indeed
does produce something new in terms of self-realization and poetic knowledge, which literary scholar James S. Taylor defines as
"A spontaneous act of external and internal senses with the in-
tellect, integrated and whole, rather than an act associated with
the power of analytic reasoning" (6).

Since the bleak garden is a returning dream, and given that
the narrator is Lovecraft himself, the realization at the end of
the poem is the result of Lovecraft's observations and analysis of
the dreamscape in conjunction with introspection, an active
search though his own memory palace. The purpose of this sophisticated engagement is simply to grasp what the garden is;
and the terrific revelation or self-realization at the end of the
poem is, although seemingly surprising to Lovecraft, not exclusively a horrifying one. Indeed, it is also wonderful and even
therapeutic because it moves Lovecraft forward, in that he now

understands an important point about himself and his life. In this sense, the ending of the poem converges into a moment of truth—a moment of poetic knowledge where what is good, what is beautiful, and what is true all come together. This is a truly wonderful point in Lovecraft's work—a joyful high point signifying the importance of the learned statement by Professor Parkins from M. R. James's short story "'Oh, Whistle, and I'll Come to You, My Lad'" that truth is never offensive (76).

Summary: A Closure

Gardens play a significant role in Romanticism. Lovecraft's love of gardens, together with his dealings in the dramatic, the strange, the foreign, the beautiful, as well as contemplation and joy, all underpins his Romanticism. Boldly stated, all the above culminates in his short poem "A Garden"—a poem imbued with Romantic themes that until now have been somewhat unnoticed by Lovecraft scholars.

In earlier writing I have argued that Lovecraft was a Romantic "on the nightside" given his enormous contribution to weird fiction, and that Lovecraft is best viewed as a man of letters dealing in dark wonder but with a defiantly Romantic twist. With this essay now coming to as close, it is evident that the view of Lovecraft as a Romantic has been strengthened, especially when we consider his dealings in wondrous contemplation and poetic knowledge. To end the present essay, I should think it fitting to echo Keats and say that wondrous contemplation is poetic knowledge, poetic knowledge wondrous contemplation— that is all ye know on earth, and all ye need to know.

Works Cited

Adelman, Richard. *Idleness, Contemplation and the Aesthetic, 1750–1830*. Cambridge: Cambridge University Press, 2011.

Berlin, Isaiah. *The Roots of Romanticism*. Ed. Henry Hardy. Princeton, NJ: Princeton University Press, 2001.

Byron, Lord. *The Complete Poetical Works*. Ed. Jerome J. McGann. Oxford: Clarendon Press 1980. 3 vols.

de Camp, Sprague. L. *Lovecraft: A Biography*. Garden City, NY: Doubleday, 1975.

De Deulin, Nathalie de Harlez. "The Influence of England on the First English Gardens in the Southern Low Countries and the Principality of Liege." *Garden History* 44, Supplement 44 (Autumn 2016): 87–100.

Eco, Umberto. *On Beauty*. London: Secker & Warburg, 2004.

———. *On Ugliness*. New York: Rizzoli, 2007.

Eddy, Jr., C. M. "Walks with H. P. Lovecraft." 1966. In Peter Cannon, ed. *Lovecraft Remembered*. Sauk City, WI: Arkham House Publishers, 1998. 65–68.

James, M. R. *Collected Ghost Stories*. Ed. Darryl Jones. London: Oxford University Press, 2011.

Joshi, S. T., and David E. Schultz. *An H. P. Lovecraft Encyclopedia*. 2001. New York: Hippocampus Press, 2004.

Keats, John. *The Complete Poetry and Selected Prose of John Keats*. Ed. Harold E. Briggs. New York: Random House, 1951.

Kant, Immanuel. *Critique of Judgment*. Tr. W. S. Pluhar. New York: Hackett Publishing Co., 1987.

Pedersen, Jan B. W. *Balanced Wonder: Experiential Sources of Imagination, Virtue and Human Flourishing*. Lanham, MD: Lexington Books, 2019.

———. "Howard Phillips Lovecraft: Romantic on the Nightside." *Lovecraft Annual* No. 12 (2018): 165–73.

———. "'Now Will You Be Good?': Lovecraft, Teetotalism, and Philosophy." *Lovecraft Annual* No 13 (2019): 119–44.

———. "On Lovecraft's Lifelong Relationship with Wonder." *Lovecraft Annual* No. 11 (2017): 23–36.

———. "Weird Fiction: A Catalyst for Wonder." In Anders Schinkel, ed. *Wonder, Education and Human Flourishing: Theoretical, Empirical and Practical Perspectives*. Amsterdam: VU University Press 2020. 318–31.

Poe, Edgar Allan. *The Portable Poe*. Ed. Philip Van Doren Stern. New York: Penguin, 1977.

Schinkel, Anders. *Wonder and Education: On the Educational Importance of Contemplative Wonder*. London: Bloomsbury Academic London, 2021.

Seneca the Younger. *Epistles 1–65*. Tr. Richard Cummere. Cambridge, MA: Harvard University Press (Loeb Classical Library), 1917.

Taylor, James S. *Poetic Knowledge: The Recovery of Education.* Albany: State University of New York Press, 1998.

Thomson, Carl. *The Sufferings Traveller and the Romantic Imagination.* Oxford: Clarendon Press, 2007.

Warnock, Mary. *Imagination and Time.* Oxford: Basil Blackwell, 1994.

Wordsworth, William. *The Major Works.* Oxford: Oxford University Press, 2008.

The Authorship of *The Cancer of Superstition* and Lovecraft's Late Readings on Folklore

César Guarde-Paz

In recent years, *The Cancer of Superstition,* an unfinished book ghostwritten by Lovecraft and C. M. Eddy, Jr. for the magician Harry Houdini, has attracted considerable attention due to the resurfacing of two extended copies, one typescript and one manuscript, both sold on auction and now in private hands. The handwritten manuscript, clearly on Eddy's hand, has served to complicate further the question of authorship and textual integrity of this particular work, and has tipped the scales of craftsmanship in his favor. My main contention in this paper is twofold: on the one hand, I shall show that *The Cancer of Superstition* not only draws upon Fiske's *Myths and Myth-Makers* and Frazer's *The Golden Bough*, as S. T. Joshi had already suspected (*IAP* 651), but it is, in almost its entirety, a shameless verbatim plagiarizing of these and other texts on folklore that Lovecraft had excerpted for Eddy's research. Secondly, I trace the influence of these readings in one of Lovecraft's most popular stories, "The Call of Cthulhu," written in the course of his groundwork for Houdini.

Lovecraft's Didactic Collaborations with Eddy and Houdini

Lovecraft probably became acquainted with Clifford Martin Eddy, Jr. (1896–1967) in the summer or autumn of 1923. Although in one of the two memoirs written by the latter's wife Muriel Eddy, *The Gentleman from Angell Street* (1961), she claimed that the

Lovecrafts and the Eddys had already met before (presumably in 1918), most scholars are skeptical regarding this early encounter (*IAP* 464–65), which is not supported by Lovecraft's own testimony and epistolary.[1] C. M. Eddy had already published a number of stories, including "Sign of the Dragon" (*Mystery Magazine*, September 1919), "A Little Bit of Good Luck" (*Munsey's Magazine*, November 1920), "Moonshine" (*Action Stories*, May 1922), and "The Unshorn Lamb" (*Snappy Stories*, 3 September 1922) (Eddy iii), and although their literary quality was generally slight, Lovecraft seems to have been rather fond of his enthusiastic fellow Providentian or, as he called him, his "adopted son." For instance, he revised his stories without charge, asking Eddy to type in return one of his approved manuscripts for every story successfully "jazzed up" (*JFM* 57; *MWM* 139). They also met periodically for long walks of antiquarian exploration (*MWM* 135–36), casting away the myth of Lovecraft's reclusiveness; and most famously, they engaged in their own legend tripping on 4 November 1923, setting out in search for the Dark Swamp, a mysterious area located about 7 miles from Chepachet, Rhode Island. (They never reach the actual location, for it was already late and the pair had to head back.)

During these years (1923–24), Lovecraft intensively revised for Eddy at least four stories: "Ashes," "The Ghost-Eater" (both previously rejected by *Weird Tales*), "Deaf, Dumb, and Blind" (for which he wrote the first part; see *DS* 74), and the celebrated "The Loved Dead." The extension of Lovecraft's revisionary work in these tales has always been a matter of controversy, especially in relation to the last, as the issue of *Weird Tales* in which it appeared was banned from the stands in Indiana following Senate action (*IAP* 1.501; *FF* 1.507). As S. T. Joshi has noted, this tale "certainly reads as if Lovecraft had written the entire thing" (*IAP* 466), and from Lovecraft's letters we can conclude that, despite modern computer analysis claiming otherwise (Look, Gladwin, and Lavin), his role was indeed significant:

---

1. HPL to Frank Belknap Long, 7 October 1923 (*SL* 1.254); HPL to Edwin Baird, *Weird Tales* 3, No. 3 (March 1924): 91.

> He [Howard Wolf] is wrong in saying that it was a tale of *mine* which caused an issue of *Weird Tales* to be barred from the stands in Indiana. The story in question was Eddy's "Loved Dead"—which, however, had much of my work in it. (*FF* 652–53)

> I revised the now-notorious "Loved Dead" myself—practically re-writing the latter half. Eddy is a Providence man, & I was in fairly close touch in '23. I did not, though, devise the necrophilic portion which so ruffled the tranquillity of parents & pedagogues on the banks of the Wabash. (*RB* 132; cf. *DS* 594)

This, given Lovecraft's modest remarks about his own work, probably meant that his responsibility in "The Loved Dead" was considerable, and it may account for the otherwise excessively ornate prose absent in other Eddy's tales. In fact, a reading of Eddy's earlier stories, as well as other non-Lovecraftian stories published in *Weird Tales* immediately after ("With Weapons of Stone" [*WT*, December 1924; "Arhl-a of the Caves" [*WT*, January 1925; "The Better Choice" [*WT*, March 1925), seems to indicate that the prose of "The Loved Dead" owes more to Lovecraft than it has been recognized.[2]

At this time, Lovecraft also received an invitation to ghost-write a story for the famous escapist Harry Houdini (1874–1926), who had been enlisted by J. C. Henneberger (1890–1969), owner of *Weird Tales*, to write an "Ask Houdini" column in the magazine. The result was "Imprisoned with the Pharaohs," originally entitled "Under the Pyramids" by Lovecraft, and Henneberger traveled all the way to Tennessee to show it to Houdini, who expressed great admiration and immediately wrote a note to Lovecraft (*FF* 115). Lovecraft and Houdini, however, seem to have been in contact at least since February for reasons not necessarily related to the writing of this story, as a letter to James F. Morton seems to indicate: "Henny says that Houdini wants to get in touch with me about some books or other when he gets back from a lecture tour" (*JFM* 67).[3] These

---

2. It is then not strange that Donald Wandrei referred to HPL as my "Dear Necrophilist and Ghost-Eater" (*DW* 169).

3. By 25 February HPL had not yet started to write "Under the Pyramids" (*IAP*

tours were a series of twenty-four lectures organized by the Coit-Alber Lyceum Bureau, with which Houdini had signed a contract in February, that took him across the Midwest and southern U.S. Approaching his fiftieth birthday, Houdini had planned to retire as an escapist and dedicate his efforts to debunk fraud and educate people about the falsehood of mediums and spiritualism. These lectures were an immediate success: the theatrical magazine *Billboard* reported that he had become "Houdini, the educator,"[4] and he started collaborating on an investigation conducted by the *Scientific American* on spiritualism.[5] A new tour of eight weeks with lectures on spiritualistic fraud was scheduled by the bureau in October (Silverman 298–300), to be followed by another twenty-week tour the next year.[6]

All these activities explain the hiatus between "Under the Pyramids" and his later collaborations with Lovecraft and Eddy, which Houdini may have had in mind as early as February 1924. Lovecraft, who was living in Brooklyn at the time, mentions the escapist and magician again in September 1924, when Houdini visited Providence just before restarting his second conference tour:

> On this day [20 September 1924] I received a letter from Houdini—who was playing at the Albee [Theater in Providence] and

498), but he had already received from Henneberger the specifics of Houdini's story, "a strange narrative which the magician Houdini related orally to Henneberger" (SL 1.311–12), so Houdini's letter to HPL would not be related to this project.

4. "Magic and Magicians," *Billboard*, 36 (23 February 1924): 49.

5. *Scientific American* offered a prize of $2,500 to whoever could produce any genuine psychic phenomena. Houdini was appointed to assist scientists in exposing fraudulent contesters. See "Round the Rialto," *Billboard* 36 (3 May 1924): 23; "Vaudeville Magician Solves Problem That Baffled Pundits," *Billboard* 36 (25 October 1924): 18, as well as the advertising note for his book *Houdini Exposes the Tricks Used by the Boston Medium "Margery"* (New York: Adams Press, 1924).

6. The second tour covered Texas, Colorado, California, and Illinois (see the reports in *The Billboard*, 36/43 (25 October 1924), 78; 36/45 (8 November 1924), 45; 36/46 (15 November 1924), 16; and 36/47 (22 November 1924), 56). For the second tour, which reportedly featured escapist tricks, see "Houdini to Resume Vaude.," *The Billboard*, 36/47 (22 November 1924), 13.

stopping at the Crown—offering to assist me in finding a position on his return to N. Y. I had given Eddy a letter of introduction to him, and the two had had some very exhaustive discussions, during which the magician expressed much eagerness to be of assistance to us both. I enclose the letter—which I answered, and to which I have just received a reply, asking me to telephone Houdini next Sunday or Monday, when he will be here before leaving for a vaudeville tour of the Pacific Coast. (FF 173)

This job offer came to nothing (FF 192), but it seems that Houdini may have had something in mind for Eddy as well. They both met in New York on 2 February 1925 for literary business—Lovecraft didn't join any of the meetings, but accompanied Eddy to Houdini's residence a couple of times (FF 249)—and at some point Lovecraft noticed that Eddy may have been doing some revision for the former magician (FF 501). The nature of these revisions is not clear: Muriel reports that Eddy also worked on Houdini's unpublished novel, *Thoughts and Feelings of a Head Cut Off* (M. Eddy 20) and, given Houdini's busy agenda at the time, it is possible that Eddy was also involved in ghostwriting some articles for him, probably for the *Popular Science Monthly*, where he had five pieces published between October 1925 and February 1926 (Moses 75).

Whereas Eddy and Houdini seem to have been in contact henceforth, Lovecraft appears to have drifted into ennui and aloofness, distancing himself from "the daily dropping-in and cafeteria loafing" deathly "to any personal intellectual life or creative accomplishment" (FF 290; IAP 585), as well as from some of his former acquaintances:

As for me, I'm sick of Bohemians, odds & ends, freaks, & plebeians—C. M. Eddys & satellites & miscellany &c. They amuse me for a while, but begin after a time to get frightfully on one's nerves. People get on one's nerves when they harbor different kinds of memories & live by different kinds of standards & cherish different kinds of goals & ideals. (FF 536)

This unnerving feeling of unrelatedness, intensified by the alien pinnacles of New York's modern architecture and its equally alien denizens, along with the increasingly overwhelming nostalgia for his ancestral Providence, probably accounts for the distancing between Lovecraft and Eddy during his final months in New York, as well as upon his return to Providence in April 1926 and thereafter. Lovecraft appears to have spent the rest of spring and summer sightseeing unknown parts of Providence and expanding his readings (*IAP* 635).

We don't know when Houdini contacted Lovecraft again, but in October 1926 Lovecraft mentions the magician requesting his presence in Detroit for a week for some personal collaboration on a daily basis (*ES* 45). This was part of "a whole series of exposés of the different branches of occultism" (*RK* 351), the first of which was an "anti-astrological article to be finished before his departure—a matter of five days," for which he would receive a remuneration of $75 (*JFM* 114–15). Houdini had performed in Providence on 20 September and again on 4 to 9 October,[7] and he reportedly had dinner with Lovecraft and Eddy on the 20th at midnight (M. Eddy 21). He then proceeded to Albany, where he had scheduled performances on 11–13 October, Schenectady (14–16 October), and Montreal (18–23 October), before arriving in Detroit on 24th (Silverman 406).[8] This places the anecdote on 4 or 5 October, and Lovecraft describes the hasty writing of this article as "beastly laborious, & forced me to work continuously till night before last [October 9] with very little sleep" (*WBT* 46). A fifteen-page manuscript of this text resurfaced on April 2009 on eBay (Item 120404416969) and, apparently, it was resold on August 2013 on the same platform (Item 370716061710). The quality of the images supplied therein

---

7. L. E. M., "Providence Opera House. The Gay Deceiver," *Providence Journal* (5 October 1926): 9. A window card featuring the announcement of Houdini's show on 20 September was discovered recently in Warwick and is now in the personal collection of John Cox, author at *Wild About Houdini* (www.wildabout houdini.com), to whom I owe the aforementioned reference.

8. Dates can be reconstructed from the reports in "Houdini, Magician, Hurt When Weight Is Dropped," *Evening News* (Harrisburg, PA) (12 October 1926): 1; Silverman 406–7; as well as from the numerous advertisements of his shows, for instance in *Schenectady Gazette* (11 October 1926): 10; and *Gazette* (Montreal) (18–19 October 1926): 13.

was extremely poor and only a few words can be easily identified, but it bears Houdini's name at the very end of the manuscript and it seems to match other examples of Lovecraftiana.

Lovecraft's next assignment was an article on witchcraft, which he mentions simultaneously with another project originally entrusted to Eddy by Houdini:

> At present I'm loaded down with a lot of books he's lent me for research, & a weighty list of subjects—beginning with witchcraft—which he wants tackled. Once I receive orders to go ahead on the witchcraft article, it's goodbye to the sunny world outside my scholastic cell—for it sure does take digging to satisfy that bozo! Meanwhile I am breathing while breathing is good, & am also helping honest C. M. Eddy Jr. a bit on some work he's doing for our magical taskmaster. The necromantic neo-Bush is inclined to be dissatisfied with Eddy's unaided performances, yet poor E. can't afford to lose so important a client. (*JFM* 115; cf. *SL* 2.79 and *WBT* 46)

A typescript of what appears to be the first item, entitled "Witchcraft," was auctioned by Swann Auction on October 2002 (Lot 179) and resold by Potter & Potter Auction (Lot 67) on August 2014 for $15,000, together with an unsigned letter dated 16 July 1926. A similar manuscript appears in an early catalogue of Houdiniana collected right after the magician's demise (Dunninger 43). The auctioned piece consisted of sixty-two numbered pages with corrections on Houdini's hand and, according to the auctioneer's description, "hundreds of corrections" with a "tendency toward misspellings and awkward phrases,"[9] which could be the work of an unqualified ghostwriter. An examination of the opening paragraphs of the typescript clearly shows that Lovecraft himself could hardly have written this article:

> Why embarrass the mind of the present generation with the superstitions and vagaries of past ages?

---

9. See the description at www.liveauctioneers.com/item/28862178_houdini-harry-witchcraft-an-unpublished-manuscript (retrieved on 11 March 2022). References to the text of the article follow the images and data published therein.

The question might be asked with propriety. But the answer comes back with equal force.

Because, superstition with its baneful results are [*sic!*] not altogether a thing of the past—it still exists far more than is realized by millions of intelligent people who flatter themselves that they live in an age beyond the pale of such ignorance.

This is certainly a dull and comparatively simple, unimpressive prose that retains nothing of the vibrant style and carefully constructed phrases of other Lovecraftian essays (including those not intended for publication, such as the unpolished "A Layman Looks at the Government" [*CE* 5.96–111]). Literary style is of course highly subjective, but the tempo and the embarrassing misspellings are consistent with the typescript of other Eddy creations, such as "The Red Cap of the Mara" (with Lovecraft's corrections in JHL). Furthermore, Lovecraft's letter to Morton states that he was still awaiting Houdini's approval to start writing this article, something that most likely never came considering that almost the same information is reproduced in a letter to Frank Belknap Long written on 26 October, two days after Houdini's collapse in Detroit. Unlike "Astrology," this was a rather long paper—sixty-two pages in the auctioned item—and, even in the hypothetical case that Lovecraft had received authorization from Houdini to proceed, it is extremely doubtful that he could finish it before the magician passed away.

The second job mentioned in his letter to Morton was, most likely, *The Cancer of Superstition* (referred to herein as *CoS*), a text whose authorship has been a matter of scholarly discussion, especially after Eddy's clearly stated that "THE CANCER OF SUPERSTITION was mine" (Eddy to August Derleth, 23 October 1944).[10] According to Derleth's introduction to the first

---

10. Letter preserved among the August W. Derleth Papers, Wisconsin Historical Society, call number Wis Mss WO, Box 16, Folder 5. In another letter in private hands, Eddy still maintains that "I wrote the first three chapters of the proposed book. The first two were read and approved by Houdini, and the third was in the mail, addressed to him in Detroit, when he was stricken with the appendicitis attack which resulted in his death" (9 June 1962). This letter

chapter, published in *The Dark Brotherhood,* Houdini sketched a book on the origins, growth, and falsity of superstition and suggested that Eddy and Lovecraft could work together: the latter "could put the notes [from Houdini] into shape so that Eddy could work from the outline Lovecraft prepared" (246). Just a few days later, on 31 October, Houdini died of peritonitis and his wife decided to abandon the project given that Houdini did not grant his final *nihil obstat* (JFM 122).

The main problem with Eddy's recollection is that, as it was the case with "The Loved Dead," the prose style and rich vocabulary of *CoS* are vastly different in terms of depth and technique from anything produced by him. Although S. T. Joshi originally considered that the surviving chapter was "clearly by Eddy" (*IAP* 651), a recent re-examining of the text has led him to conclude that "Eddy was not capable of writing the *Cancer* chapters, even if the raw data for those chapters came from elsewhere [. . .] We can consider both the chapters and the synopsis as largely the work of Lovecraft" (www.stjoshi.org, blog entry, 30 March 2016). Nevertheless, the recent resurfacing of a nineteen-page handwritten manuscript of the text clearly written by Eddy and copiously annotated and corrected by Lovecraft himself seems to have settled the question of authorship in favor of Eddy.[11]

In what follows, I shall contest Eddy's assertion that he wrote *CoS* by showing that almost the totality of the Arkham House's published text is, in fact, a collection of fragments from books on folklore that Lovecraft supplied him with for research. These excerpts were not expanded or rewritten: they were shamelessly copied verbatim and connected together with excerpts from Lovecraft's draft (preserved in JHL and published in CE 3.320–22). Eddy's contribution to *CoS*, if any, amounts to less than 15% of the published text, that is, barely one page (and mainly the first page) of the eleven published by Arkham House.

---

was auditioned online on July 2016, together with the 19 manuscript pages of the three chapters mentioned therein.

11. The manuscript was listed online at AbeBooks.com on July 2016 for $65,000.

Dissecting *The Cancer of Superstition*

The *CoS* opens with the following lines:

> [Superstition maintains a far reaching] <The> influence <of
> superstition is far> more powerful and widespread than the ma-
> jority are willing to believe. Its roots planted <before history>
> in the mind of mankind, [in the dim, incalculable ages before
> the dawn of written records,] superstition has become a malig-
> nant growth which persist with a tenacity little suspected. [. . .]
> It seems almost incredible in this age of <general> [knowledge,
> literature, scientific] <intellectual> advancement [and pro-
> found mental capacity] that mankind should still be fettered by
> [the bounds of] such <a type of> prehistoric [lack of erudition]
> <ignorance>. Yet after a century of [scientific attainment and
> more than] <unpredictable rapid scientific progress & nearly>
> five hundred years of modern civilization the vast majority of us
> are heathens in the innermost recesses of our hearts and minds,
> doggedly maintaining a grim hold on our faith in <ghosts,>
> magic numbers, [spooks,] witchcraft, incantations, mews, and
> signs the [valid] <validity> of which has long since been indis-
> putably refuted.[12]

And a paragraph later, in the same page:

> Superstition has always swayed the mind of the masses[. We]
> <, and we> can find its imprint on the earliest known <hu-
> man> writings. [As we] Follow<ing> it down [through] the
> ages, we find <can never escape> its indelible traces in the
> [contemporary literature] <literature of any period>. The
> [weird] folk-lore of Shakespeare fills a volume of more than five
> hundred pages, while the works of Chaucer are even more re-
> plete with such allusions. [Just as,] <And> in the present day,
> we find [countless] <just as many> proofs of the [grip] <te-
> nacity> with which superstition [has] <is> fastened [to]
> <on> the mind of mankind.

---

12. Eddy's original text, crossed out by HPL, appears within brackets, whereas
HPL's corrections have been supplemented within angle brackets.

This is probably the most original page of the whole *CoS*; and yet, when we discard Lovecraft's corrections, what emerges is a partial rewriting of two texts. The first and last lines are borrowed from *Kentucky Superstitions*:

> Superstitious beliefs are more persistent and more widespread than most people would suspect. We have all been fully aware that they swayed the minds of people in earlier centuries. We know, also, that they are sprinkled through our earlier literature; for example, the folk superstitions of Shakespeare fill a volume of generous size, and instances are no less common in the writings of his contemporaries and perhaps even more common in the works of Chaucer. Their potent presence, however, in the minds of people of our time may reasonably cause surprise. (Thomas and Thomas 1)

The middle part, however, is an almost literal excerpt from "The Curse of Superstition," published in Leon Carroll Marshall's *Readings in the Story of Human Progress:*

> The phenomenon is familiar to everybody, tho, says the Brawley *News*, a newspaper published in the Imperial Valley, California, it seems impossible that in this age of enlightenment, books, scientific progress and general intellectuality American people should be bound in chains of medieval ignorance. [...] After 2,000 years of Christianity, and after 500 years of modern civilization, and after 100 years of scientific achievement, it still appears that in America we have a large class who, at heart, are pagans, believing in spooks, incantations, magic numbers, signs, mews and witchcraft. (Marshall 367)

The specificity of the remarks contained in this brief column, taking into account the subtleties of vocabulary and tone once we dispose of Lovecraft's improvements to Eddy's text, testify against the originality of the text. That being said, quotations have been integrated to a certain degree and there is at least one full paragraph in between that, to the best of my knowledge, cannot be traced back to any other source. Unfortunately, the same cannot be asserted about the remaining pages of the first chapter published by Arkham House. They are, plainly and simply, a clear example of indolence and plagiarism. In order to prove this point, I would like to reproduce word by word and without any omission the totality of the second page of the *CoS* (Lovecraft et al. 252) and compare every single paragraph with the original text from which it has been excerpted:

> It is true that civilized communities no longer stand collectively in awe of superstitious fallacies[. It is] <, but> equally true that individuals in every community retain a lively faith.

We find almost the exact text in H. Addington Bruce's "Our Superstitions," and article mentioned in a footnote to the text copied before from *Kentucky Superstitions* (1, note 2):

> It may be a demonstrable fact that civilized communities no longer collectively stand in awe of the evil eye, hang witches, or tremble before practitioners of magic. It is equally demonstrable, however, that large numbers of individuals in such communities—men and women who pass as people of education—retain a lively faith in even the most absurd among the superstitions of their ancestors. (Bruce 999)

Eddy continues providing a few examples of superstitions in Western communities:

> No class or creed is free from such bugbears and the more unlikely they are, the more staunchly they seem to have intrenched themselves. In Germany, the old sun-worship is recalled in the pretzel, once an offering for the temples, while human sacrifice is held to be suggested in the red sugar on holiday gingerbread which is baked in the shape of men. Canada and South America still keep their jeweled snakes, their werewolves, their healing statues and their sacred springs.

Compare this to Skinner's "Every-day Superstitions":

> No class or creed is free from bugaboos, and the more impossible they are the more firmly they are believed. [. . .] In Germany the old sun-worship is recalled in the shape of the pretzel, once an offering for the temples, while human sacrifice is held to be suggested in the red sugar on holiday gingerbread which is

> baked in the shape of men. [. . .] Canada and South America
> keep their jeweled snakes, their were-wolves, their healing stat-
> ues, and their sacred springs. (613 and 616)

And immediately after, compare Eddy's:

> The people of Devon, until recent years, consulted the White
> Witch, while Irish lasses still visit the wishing wells and keep up
> the glamour of Hallowe'en. The official records of the Motor
> Vehicle Department of California were loaded, in 1924, with
> requests for auto license plates in which the number thirteen or
> any combinations of that number did not appear.
>
> According to Lewis Edwin Theiss, in the state of Pennsylva-
> nia, as late as 1916, not only do the country-folk believe in signs,
> portents, and omens, but investigations of alleged witchcraft are
> not infrequent! A recent book lists 2,083 separate superstitions of
> the Pennsylvania Germans, while another offers a compilation
> of nearly four thousand superstitions still given credence in Ken-
> tucky! Indeed, one of the most remarkable classes of folk-lore
> survivals in the mountainous regions of Kentucky is that of witch-
> lore. There is no other place in the English-speaking world where
> witch-superstition receives such whole-hearted belief.

to the following cuttings from contemporary articles:

> The people of Devon until recent years consulted the White
> Witch, the girls of the Green Isle of Erin still visit the wishing
> wells and keep up the glamour of hallowe'en. ("Wishbone" 701)

> Yet, we are told, the official records of the Motor Vehicle De-
> partment of California are loaded with requests for auto license
> plates in which the number "13," or any combination of that
> number, will not appear. (Marshall 367)

> Not only do our country folk believe in signs and portents and
> omens, but trials for witchcraft are of not infrequent occurrence
> in this same State of Pennsylvania. (Theiss 924)

And, again, in Kentucky Superstitions:

> Professor Edwin M. Fogel, whose volume of superstitions con-
> tains the largest collection hitherto published in America, has

listed 2,083 separate superstitions that are current among Pennsylvania Germans. The authors of the present volume have found almost 4,000 superstitions in Kentucky. [. . .] One of the most remarkable classes of folk-lore survivals in the mountains of Kentucky is that of witch lore. Perhaps there is at this time no other place in the English-speaking parts of the world where superstitions concerning witches receive so much credence. (Thomas and Thomas 2 and 6)

The use of this book extends to the next page, where the second paragraph—a total of sixteen lines—has also been reproduced from *Kentucky Superstitions* (1–3). Finally, compare Eddy's last paragraph in the second page:

Nor is any big city free from the yoke of superstition. New York is veritably honeycombed with fallacious fancies! Ghosts stalk through the crowded regions about Grand Street. Italians fear the evil eye, have faith in the magic of the amulet. Folkmedicine is widely studied and practiced in Teutonic tenements. The denizens of Hell's Kitchen contribute their quota of tales in which the leading characters are spirits, banshees and fays, Chinatown is filled with tales of demonology, & Harlem abounds in rabbits' feet & voodoo charms. And far down along the waterfront, marvelous yarns are spun of ancient sailor's lore.

to Shackleton's account of New York superstitions:

Ghosts are told of in the crowded regions north of Grand Street. There are tales of demonology in Chinatown. Almshouse dwellers, sitting in the sun, watching the surging tide and the glistening water, tell of spirits and banshees and fays. Italians dread the devil eye, but have faith in amulets. [. . .] Superstition is seen, luminous in its ineradicability, in a little book of necromancy, especially for the sick, which is widely studied in Teutonic tenements. [. . .] And far down the East River, where great bowsprits stretch far over South Street, where there are casks and bales and endless rope and chain, you may hear, in ancient taverns nodding dreamily toward the water, marvelous tales from them that go down to the sea in ships, for these weather-beaten men retain belief in ancient sailor's lore. (265–66, 268)

I do not wish to numb readers with more needlessly lengthy and repetitive citations. In light of the fact that this problem with the text of the *CoS* involves more than just a few appropriations and is not isolated to a couple of bibliographical materials, I will sum up Eddy's remaining sources with references to the Arkham House edition.

The *CoS* continues with a familiar reference to the Angels of Mons (*CoS* reads "Mars") in Arthur Machen's "The Bowmen." Machen had insisted that the tale was purely imaginary, but many readers believed that angelic forces did actually shield British soldiers in the battlefield. There are indeed many sources for this account in *CoS*, including Lovecraft's essay "Merlinus Redivivus" (*CE* 5.31), but the paragraph has been directly extracted, verbatim, from the opening lines of "Twentieth-Century Superstition" (845), a brief column in the *Literary Digest*. Appropriation of many different literary materials continues in the next page, which constitutes a veritable jigsaw of quotations from multiples sources: The first two sentences are directly borrowed from either William Harris's account of the Scottish kings James I and Charles I (Harris 2.61, note 15), or from John Brand's quotation of the same paragraph in his British *Antiquities* (1.ix, note 2). These are followed by a few lines from historian Henry Charles Lea's "Judicial Ordeals" (97–98) on witchcraft and the Inquisition, Bruce's "Our Superstitions" (999), and a column edited by Edward J. Wheeler, a prominent prohibitionist, on the perils of the underground intellectual culture of spiritualism and mediumnity (44). All these fragments are unsteadily connected through two brief excerpts from the first point in Lovecraft's draft, again, reproduced verbatim (*CE* 3.320).

Such considerable structural similarities cannot not be justified by any didactic requirement to convey identical information. They exhibit, at the very least, an effort to integrate and concatenate knowledge extracted—or rather copied—from a variety of materials. However, imitators are proverbially seduced by the principle of indolence, and hence it is not by chance that Eddy turns to two unique sources for the next six pages: Fiske's *Myths and Myth-Makers* and Frazer's *The Golden Bough*. Lovecraft encountered Fiske at least two years previous, when he in-corporated a passage from the chapter "Werewolves and Swan-Maidens" into "The Shunned House" (*LL* 317; *CF* 1.466). Cu-riously enough, Eddy did exactly the same with another passage from the same chapter, in this case on the relation between werewolves and the Mara, a female demon, which he incorpo-rated to the core of his short story "The Red Cap of the Mara" (mss., JHL; cf. Fiske 93–100). In the *CoS*, Eddy's discussion on the origins of superstition in primitive man, volition, and the per-sonification of the forces of Nature, specifically in the cosmogony of the Indian and Scandinavian peoples (255), is a direct repro-duction of scattered passages from Fiske (116, 143, 209, 47, 134–35, 17, and 21). Frazer's excerpts follow immediately for two pages (*CoS* 256–57; cf. Frazer 8–14, 18–22, and 25–28), combined with a few lines from Knowlson's *The Origins of Popu-lar Superstitions and Customs* (1–3) on the "tempest, the blight which spoiled the harvest, the mysteries of disease and death," and the second and third points in Lovecraft's draft (*CE* 3.320).

Finally, the remaining pages (258–61) are comprised of long paragraphs reproduced from Tylor's *Primitive Culture,* discussing animism (*CoS* 258; Tylor 21, 425–32, and 479), fetishism and tree spirits (*CoS* 259; Tylor 157, 205, and 215), the Soul of the Universe (*CoS* 260; Tylor 354), the spirits of nature (*CoS* 260; Tylor 287–88), and the cosmogony of Egyptians, Mesoameri-cans, and other civilizations (*CoS* 261; Tylor 288–93). In be-tween, the text is interrupted by some quotations from Frazer on the correlation between the soul and volition in natural phe-nomena, the tree spirits in East Africa and Borneo, and the dif-ference between spirits and gods (*CoS* 258–60; Frazer 59–62, 121, and 348). There are, additionally, very brief quotations bor-rowed from different articles from the *Encyclopedia Britannica:* Auguste Comte's religious consciousness (*CoS* 258; Carpenter 62); a comparison between animism and fetishism (*CoS* 259; "Idolatry" 288; Cana 327); a brief mention of the sacred stone or Bethel (*CoS* 259; Conybeare 329); and the tree worship among the Somrai and Gaberi tribes (*CoS* 260; "Bagirmi" 201). A con-cise account of Chinese's ancestor worship (*CoS* 260), copied from Groot's *Religion of the Chinese* (87), completes the puzzle.

There are, nonetheless, two paragraphs at the end of pages 253 and 254 that, to the extent of my observations, do not seems to have been borrowed or reproduced from any available source. They look, however, distinctly Lovecraftian in their prose and tone, and were probably corrected based on Eddy's original text. For instance, consider these lines:

> From the viewpoint of the believer, the scientific marvels of modernity only afford an opportunity to create new and often ludicrous delusions to add to the already overwhelming store. The average devotee of superstition believes because he wants to believe, and more often than not resents any attempt to expose his reasoning as irrational. (*CoS* 253)

In any case, these two paragraphs amount to the only original content in the first chapter of the *CoS* published by Arkham House, and given the indolence exhibited in its second half, we must remain skeptical about the contents of the remaining chapters.

Concluding Remarks: Superstition and Lovecraft's Mythos

Although Fritz Leiber characterized Lovecraft as a "Literary Copernicus" who "shifted the focus of supernatural dread from man and his little world and his gods, to the stars and the black and unplumbed gulfs of intergalactic space" (290), the presence of superstitious motives in his narrative has been noted a number of times, from "certain special formulae and incantations" to either conjure or hinder Yog-Sothoth's coming in the "The Dunwich Horror" (*CF* 2.449; Salonia 70) to the necromancy and witchcraft in *The Case of Charles Dexter Ward* (Joshi 189). Many of these themes were transformed and updated within the framework of our mechanized and scientific modern world (Salonia 53), and although their origins have been traced elsewhere (Joshi and Schultz 33–34 and 80), it is possible that Lovecraft's readings on astrology, witchcraft, and other superstitions in 1926 inspired some of the contents of these and other stories. As he himself notes:

Back in 1914 I conducted a heavy newspaper campaign against a local defender of astrology, and in 1926 I read quite a few astrological books (since largely forgotten) in order to ghost-write a thorough and systematic exposé of the fake science for no less notable a client than the late Houdini. (*EHP* 62)

In fact, Houdini and Lovecraft were already in contact as early as February 1924, and it is not entirely impossible that the magician had already recommended him some readings on superstition for future collaborations, "some books or other," as he explained to Morton at the time (*JFM* 67), that would constitute the core of their future collaborations. This could account for the verbatim quotation from Fiske's *Myths and Myth-Makers* in "The Shunned House," written in mid-October 1924, as well as for Eddy's almost serendipitous use of the same chapter in "The Red Cap of the Mara."[13]

There is one short story in particular, however, where the impact of these readings seems to be most noticeable: "The Call of Cthulhu." Although the plot was already developed a year earlier, Lovecraft did not write this story until August or September 1926 (Joshi and Schultz 27), when he was already in contact with Houdini and just one month before the magician requested his presence in Detroit, in October of that year. The story comprises a collection of strange facts assembled by Francis Wayland Thurston on a mysterious secret cult that seeks to unleash the extraterrestrial, godlike entity Cthulhu onto the world.

One significant part of the story features a "statuette, idol, fetish, or whatever it was" of the mentioned entity that was "brought in dim aeras from dark stars" (*CF* 2.31 and 2.39). This surely resonates with Lovecraft/Eddy's description of the animistic cults in the *CoS*, extracted from the entries on "Idolatry" and "Image Worship" in the *Encyclopaedia Britannica*:

---

13. The typescript of this story is undated, and the description for *The Loved Dead and Other Tales* (2008) in Fenham Publishing's website, established by Eddy's grandson Jim Dyer, dates it to 1922. However, HPL's corrections cannot be earlier than summer or autumn 1923. In the corner of the first page HPL has added a note: "Revise Mail Dec. to Feb.," later crossed out and updated to "Jan. to Mar.," so the corrections must date from early 1924 or 1925.

> Perhaps the most primitive or degraded form of Animism is that
> which is known as Fetishism, which is usually the direct anteced-
> ent of idolatry. A fetish is adorned not for itself but for the spirit
> that dwells in it and works through it. [. . .] In the forests of the
> Congo and among the many lagoons and estuaries of the Guin-
> ea Coast region is a primitive form of Fetishism with the belief
> that death is due to witchcraft, secret societies, or the use of
> masked anthropomorphic figures and wooden gongs. (*CoS* 259)

Notice that Cthulhu worked through the dreams of the young
sculptor Henry Anthony Wilcox to create, in his sleep, a bas-
relief identical to the idol unearthed by Inspector John Raymond
Legrasse, and that it was around these idols that secret cults
worshipping the Great Old Ones were formed, waiting for their
ultimate return (*CF* 2.39). According to the devotees of this ancient faith, their gods would be able to enter our world "when
the stars were right," when the celestial bodies "had come round
again to the right positions in the cycle of eternity." This is by
no means unimportant, for the idea is repeated not fewer than
six times in the story (*CF* 2.38–40, and 53), and although it has
become a most celebrated cliché among fans of the Mythos, it is
nonetheless a rather embarrassing piece of astrological lore.
Lovecraft had already written against astrology in his notorious
controversy with the local astrologer Joachim Friedrich Hartmann in 1914, noting that there is no such thing as a "right" position of the stars:

> In this age of enlightenment it ought not to be necessary to
> shew the utter absurdity of the idea that our daily affairs can be
> governed by the mere apparent motions of infinitely distant
> bodies whose seeming arrangements and configurations, on
> which the calculations of judicial astrology are based, arise only
> from perspective as seen from our particular place in the uni-
> verse. (*CE* 3.260–61)

> Indeed, astrology is based wholly upon apparent celestial mo-
> tions, which, as I pointed out in my previous letter, are merely
> the result of perspective as viewed from this one puny planet
> which we call Earth. (*CE* 3.263)

The use of astrology in "The Call of Cthulhu" is not limited to the ignorant cultists, who may have resorted to superstition due to their inability to understand the true nature of the future coming of the Great Old Ones. The narrator, at the end of the story, seems to give credence to these beliefs:

> The Thing of the idols, the green, sticky spawn of the stars, had awaked to claim his own. The stars were right again, and what an age-old cult had failed to do by design, a band of innocent sailors had done by accident. After vigintillions of years great Cthulhu was loose again, and ravening for delight. (CF 2.53)

A third central element in the story is the earthquake that liberates Cthulhu, famously adapted to match the real Charlevoix-Kamouraska earthquake that struck northeastern North America on 28 February 1925:

> There had been a slight earthquake tremor the night before, the most considerable felt in New England for some years; and Wilcox's imagination had been keenly affected. Upon retiring, he had had an unprecedented dream of great Cyclopean cities of titan blocks and sky-flung monoliths, all dripping with green ooze and sinister with latent horror. Hieroglyphics had covered the walls and pillars, and from some undetermined point below had come a voice that was not a voice; a chaotic sensation which only fancy could transmute into sound, but which he attempted to render by the almost unpronounceable jumble of letters, "*Cthulhu fhtagn.*" (CF 2.25–26)

The earthquake itself is not only connected with dreams and nightmares, but it is also followed by a tremendous storm:

> March 1st—our February 28th according to the International Date Line—the earthquake and storm had come. From Dunedin the *Alert* and her noisome crew had darted eagerly forth as if imperiously summoned, and on the other side of the earth poets and artists had begun to dream of a strange, dank Cyclopean city whilst a young sculptor had moulded in his sleep the form of the dreaded Cthulhu. (CF 2.47)

> The *Emma*, in ballast, had cleared Auckland on February 20th, and had felt the full force of that earthquake-born tempest which must have heaved up from the sea-bottom the horrors that filled men's dreams. (CF 2.50)

This is again reminiscent of Lovecraft's reading of Fiske and his description of how physical phenomena operated according to the mythology of the primitive men, that is, how earthquakes and tempests were attributed to the actions of gods:

> Grinim propounded the tenable theory that all superstition and mythology sprang from certain common primitive originals which in themselves were a mere description of physical phenomena—marvels imputed to the direct workings of such a volition of the observers recognized within their own minds. [. . .] Earthquakes, floods and similar cataclysms of Nature are terrible enough even to us in this age when the forces behind such phenomena can be catalogued and analyzed. (CoS 255)

These three elements represent an important challenge to the fundamental principles of cosmicism that we usually recognize in Lovecraft's late stories—the insignificance of human existence when the vastness of the universe is confronted from the perspective of the materialist and the atheist, untrammeled by the theological and teleological trivialities bequeathed to us by local and ephemeral traditions. Ironically enough, the essence of this thought was advanced in a letter to Farnsworth Wright following the resubmittal of "The Call of Cthulhu":

> Now all my tales are based on the fundamental premise that common human laws and interests and emotions have no validity or significance in the vast cosmos-at-large. [. . .] Only the human scenes and characters must have human qualities. *These* must be handled with unsparing *realism*, (*not* catch-penny *romanticism*) but when we cross the line to the boundless and hideous unknown—the shadow-haunted *Outside*—we must remember to leave our humanity and terrestrialism at the threshold. (*Letters to Woodburn Harris* 48)

As Salonia notes at the end of his study on Lovecraft's witch-craft, it could be hardly believable to use scientific means to depict the effects of incantations or instances of sorcery (73). After all, Lovecraft's fiction rests upon the assumption that there is *some* truth (or some misinterpreted factuality) behind the religious experiences of humanity (Geeraert 128)—a truth, perhaps, whose disturbing hideousness lies not in those aspects that we got right, but in those where we failed to unshroud the veil of superstition. Degenerate cultists, ghastly idols, proscribed grimoires, sunken temples, and other "hyperphysical" gadgets work better as instruments of storytelling, and the potent effectiveness of these narrative devices, even when they bestow astrological absurdities such as "when the stars are right," can hardly be dismissed in order to avoid any instance of terrestrialism.

Works Cited

"Bagirmi." In *The Encyclopaedia Britannica*. Cambridge: Cambridge University Press, 1911. 3.201.

Brand, John. *Observations on the Popular Antiquities of Great Britain*. London, 1848.

Bruce, H. Addington. "Our Superstitions." *Outlook* 98 (26 August 1911): 999–1006.

Cana, Frank R. "Africa." In *The Encyclopaedia Britannica*. Cambridge: Cambridge University Press, 1911. 1.320–58.

Carpenter, Joseph Estlin. "Religion." In *The Encyclopaedia Britannica*. Cambridge: Cambridge University Press, 1911. 23.61–76.

Conybeare, Frederick Cornwallis. "Image Worship." In *The Encyclopaedia Britannica*. Cambridge: Cambridge University Press, 1911. 14.329–30.

Dunninger, Joseph. *Houdini's Spirit: Exposés from Houdini's Own Manuscripts, Records and Photographs*. New York: Experimenter Publisher, 1928.

Eddy, C. M., Jr. *Exit into Eternity. Tales of the Bizarre and Supernatural*. Warwick, RI: Fenham Publishing, 1973.

Eddy, Muriel, and C. M. Eddy, Jr. *The Gentleman from Angell Street: Memories of H. P. Lovecraft*. Narragansett, RI: Fenham Publishing, 2001.

Fiske, John. *Myths and Myth-Makers*. Boston: Houghton Mifflin, 1872.

Frazer, James George. *The Golden Bough*. New York: Macmillan, 1890.

Geeraert, Dustin. "Sanity, Subjectivity, and the Supernatural: Dreams of the Devil in Existentialism and the Weird Tale." *Lovecraft Annual* No. 8 (2014): 111–30.

Groot, Jakob Maria. *The Religion of the Chinese*. New York. Macmillan, 1912.

Harris, William. *An Historical and Critical Account of the Lives and Writings of James I. and Charles I*. London, 1814.

"Idolatry." In *The Encyclopaedia Britannica*. Cambridge: Cambridge University Press, 1911. 14.288.

Joshi, S. T. "Time, Space, and Natural Law: Science and Pseudo-Science in Lovecraft." *Lovecraft Annual* No. 4 (2010): 171–201.

———, and David E. Schultz. *An H. P. Encyclopedia*. Westport, CT: Greenwood Press, 2001.

Knowlson, Thomas Sharper. *The Origins of Popular Superstitions and Customs*. London: T. Werner Laurie, 1910.

Lea, Henry Charles. "Judicial Ordeals." *North American Review* 89 (1859): 97–98. Rpt. as "The Ordeal." In Lea's *Superstition and Force*. Philadelphia, 1878. 369.

Leiber, Fritz. "A Literary Copernicus." In *Something about Cats and Other Pieces*. By H. P. Lovecraft and Others. Ed. August Derleth. Sauk City, WI: Arkham House, 1949. 290–303.

Look, Daniel; Gladwin, Alex; and Lavin, Matt. "Stylometry and Collaborative Authorship: Eddy, Lovecraft, and 'The Loved Dead.'" *Digital Scholarship in the Humanities* 32 (2017): 123–40.

Lovecraft, H. P. *Letters to E. Hoffmann Price and Richard F. Searight*. Ed. David E. Schultz and S. T. Joshi. New York: Hippocampus Press, 2021. [Abbreviated in the text as *EHP*.]

———. *Letters to Family and Family Friends*. Ed. S. T. Joshi and David E. Schultz. New York: Hippocampus Press, 2020. [Abbreviated in the text as *FF*.]

———. *Letters to James F. Morton*. Ed. David E. Schultz and S. T. Joshi. New York: Hippocampus Press, 2011. [Abbreviated in the text as *JFM*.]

———. *Letters to Maurice W. Moe and Others*. Ed. David E. Schultz and S. T. Joshi. New York: Hippocampus Press, 2018. [Abbreviated in the text as *MWM*.]

———. *Letters to Rheinhart Kleiner and Others*. Ed. S. T. Joshi and David E. Schultz. New York: Hippocampus Press, 2020. [Abbreviated in the text as *RK*.]

———. *Letters to Robert Bloch and Others*. Ed. David E. Schultz and S. T. Joshi. New York: Hippocampus Press, 2015. [Abbreviated in the text as *RB*.]

———. *Letters to Wilfred B. Talman and Helen V. and Genevieve Sully*. Ed. David E. Schultz and S. T. Joshi. New York: Hippocampus Press, 2019. [Abbreviated in the text as *WBT*.]

———. *Letters to Woodburn Harris and Others*. Ed. S. T. Joshi and David E. Schultz. New York: Hippocampus Press, 2022. [Abbreviated in the text as *WH*.]

———. *Letters with Donald and Howard Wandrei and to Emil Petaja*. Ed. S. T. Joshi and David E. Schultz. New York: Hippocampus Press, 2019. [Abbreviated in the text as *DW*.]

———, and August Derleth. *Essential Solitude. The Letters of H. P. Lovecraft and August Derleth*. Ed. David E. Schultz and S. T. Joshi. New York: Hippocampus Press, 2008. [Abbreviated in the text as *ES*.]

———, and Clark Ashton Smith. *Dawnward Spire, Lonely Hill. The Letters of H. P. Lovecraft and Clark Ashton Smith*. Ed. David E. Schultz and S. T. Joshi. New York: Hippocampus Press, 2017. [Abbreviated in the text as *DS*.]

———, et al. *The Dark Brotherhood and Other Pieces*. Ed. August Derleth. Sauk City, WI: Arkham House, 1966.

Marshall, Leon Carroll. *Readings in the Story of Human Progress*. New York: Macmillan, 1926.

Moses, Arthur. *Houdini: Periodical Bibliography*. Humble, TX: H & R Magic Books, 2006.

Salonia, John. "Essential Saltes: Lovecraft's Witchcraft." *Lovecraft Annual* No. 10 (2016): 53–74.

Shackleton, Robert. "Superstitions of a Cosmopolitan City." *Harper's Monthly Magazine* 110 (January 1905): 265–68.

Silverman, Kenneth. *Houdini!!! The Career of Ehrich Weiss*. New York: HarperCollins, 1996.

Skinner, Charles M. "Every-day Superstitions." *Lippincott's Monthly Magazine* 67 (1901): 613–16.

"The Wishbone." *Living Age* 283 (12 December 1914): 700–702.

Theiss, Lewis Edwin. "The Moon and the High Cost of Living." *Outlook* 113 (16 August 1916): 924–28.

Thomas, David Lindsay, and Lucy Blayney Thomas. *Kentucky Superstitions*. Princeton, NJ: Princeton University Press, 1920.

"Twentieth-Century Superstition." *Literary Digest* 52 (25 March 1916): 845–46.

Tylor, Edward Burnett. *Primitive Culture*. London: John Murray, 1871.

Wheeler, Edward J. "The Menace of the Intellectual Underworld." *Current Opinion* 56 (January 1914): 44.

Painting in Word Shadows: The Role of the Hidden and Unknown to the Reader in Lovecraft

Duncan Norris

In acclaimed horror director John Carpenter's distinct Lovecraftian homage, *In the Mouth of Madness* (1994), the protagonist John Trent is discussing the works of the ersatz H. P. Lovecraft of the tale, author Sutter Kane. Of Kane, Trent states;

> Pulp horror novels. They're all pretty familiar. They all seem to have the same plot. Slimy things in the dark, people go mad . . . they turn into monsters. The funny thing is that they're kind of better written . . . than you'd expect. They sort of get to you in a way. I don't know if it's his style of writing . . . or his use of description or whatever, but—

It is in part the (oxymoronic) exact ineffableness of this sentiment that helps define horror master Howard Phillips Lovecraft's works. Critics, both strongly for and vitriolically against him, frequently struggle to explain in concrete terms the precise reasons for his longevity and popularity, while pastichists, acolytes, imitators, and the merely influenced attempt—with varying degrees of success—in their own writings to attain at least some soupçon of his power. Yet the attempted dissection of his works in order to duplicate them is invariably a failure. The truth is that, like other masters in their fields, Lovecraft's genius, by its very nature, ultimately defies understanding despite all the genuine and valid analyses that attempt to do so. To quote from the autobiography of Margaret Murray, whose *Witch-Cult in Western Europe* is the genuine work Lovecraft most referenced in his fiction, "genius is not the same thing as talent. There are degrees of talent, but there are no degrees in genius, either it is there complete, or it is not there" (107). As with all true genius, Lovecraft's creation is inevitably far more than the sum of its parts. For all the myriad of influences upon him, Lovecraft is very much sui generis in his creation; it is not for nothing that Lovecraftian has become a recognized adjective.

This is not to say that we should all throw our hands into the air and cry "Unknowable!" Yet this very idea of the unknown, the unknowable, the hidden, obscured, hinted at, half-glimpsed, inchoate, unfinished, or incomplete is paradoxically one of the key understandings that invest so much power into Lovecraft's work. The following is an examination of the importance of the indirectly unseen in Lovecraft's writings, not just to the characters in the stories, but to the reader. Proceeding in chronological fashion, it will demonstrate that in the entire body of his original horror fiction that is generally categorized as being under the umbrella of the Cthulhu Mythos, the ultimate horror is not shown directly to the reader. Lovecraft *never* directly reveals the true monster. This of course defies the well-known dictum of horror fiction—albeit primarily film—that one shouldn't reveal the monster too soon, but not withhold it too long. This diktat can be ignored far more in writing than in film, as many excellent examples attest. However, a body of work that consistently does this should bring with it a certain amount of opprobrium and dissatisfaction. Yet in Lovecraft's case it has created a mythology and interest spanning a number of generations, with an exponential growth. An examination of how Lovecraft stokes engagement and imagination by means of obscurement throughout the course of his work can perhaps allow a little bit more of the ineffable to become a little less opaque.

Before we begin, it is important to understand what is meant in this context by the words *show* and *monster*. The latter can be literal, or it can be the implications of the horrific that events and understandings imply. This focus upon the monster solely as entity, and its revelation, is one of the reason for the failings in so many Cthulhu Mythos pastiches. It is the combination of both physical being and underpinning ideas that creates the monster as a whole, unshadowed. By way of illustration of the point, in a story wherein there is a vampire, one can have the deaths of the villagers drained of blood and the insinuations of the unnatural, which is a partial revelation—by implication and inferences—of the monster. One can then have a confrontation at the end of the tale with the vampire, which is a true revelation of the monster. Alternatively, the monster can be explained away or die or vanish outside of the reader's direct knowledge, which is a contained obscurement of the monster, or perhaps in this context an unrevelation. But it could also end with the vampire met and confronted, then revealed to have been only a desperate escapee from an unseen but vaguely exposited-upon hidden crypt realm of a nightmare society of vampire masters and a hell of their farmed and subjugated prey. This recontextualizes the monster of the tale as but a lesser monster, the real monster now being this darker vision, which is to an extent unseen.

Unseen is also a key component in his examination, in the usage of the term *show*. It must be the reader who never directly sees the monster. This can be by means of simply not showing it at all, or merely in part. But often it is about layering and distance; information coming at a lack of the personal, at a distance from those in the tale experiencing it, even if only slightly, to give a different experiential connection to the reader. Again, as an example, seeing an event personally gives a different interaction from watching it live on a screen, and we have a different level of engagement the further a remove we are at. We interact with information differently hearing the description of an events from a friend who is an eyewitness from one who is relating an event that he himself was told of by someone else. This layering of distance of information is another key factor in how Lovecraft gains narrative power across his tales. The two in conjunction are undoubtedly a foundational element and key to what makes his writings so resonant so many years after his own death, and after so many attempts to replicate his authenticity.

As a final caveat concerning terminology, the always controversial topic of which Lovecraft stories belong in the Cthulhu Mythos naturally comes to the fore. What follows is not designed to be definitive, but merely one person's opinion germane to the topic at hand. It is with a specific eye to excluding those tales which seem less naturally a part of the artificial mythology both thematically and via direct commonalities despite some connections, although casting a wide net to include some tales whose Mythos connection is perhaps more dubious textually but deeply allied thematically. Importantly, this marginalization of the majority of Lovecraft's tales for a (far from canonical) list does not even exclude them from the general principles of not showing the monster. It is more that this aspect in stories not as germane to the Mythos does not add greatly to the underpinning of Lovecraft's greater, more cohesive body of work, and would become tedious for the reader via repetition. "The Tree," for example, very much follows the patterning of not showing the monster—what actually happens with the transmogrification of Kalos and especially the fate of Musides is not at all clear—yet it is very much more homage to Greek myth admixed with a Gothic revenge tale than anything connected with Lovecraft's later works.

"Dagon" (1917) is an obvious starting point for our survey, its archeological horrors of the deep past and hidden places combined with the idea of the inhumanly intelligent and ancient creatures being in many ways the prototype of the Lovecraftian oeuvre. The immediate argument against my hypothesis is that the tale does show the monster, literally:

> Then suddenly I saw it. With only a slight churning to mark its rise to the surface, the thing slid into view above the dark waters. Vast, Polyphemus-like, and loathsome, it darted like a stupendous monster of nightmares to the monolith, about which it flung its gigantic scaly arms, the while it bowed its hideous head and gave vent to certain measured sounds. (CF 1.57)

Thus some might claim, at a shallow and superficial reading, that the entire premise of Lovecraft never showing the monster to the reader collapses. But, as will be the case throughout Lovecraft's writings, and what gives it much of its power, the terror of the tale is not the actual monster. The protagonist had been awed and perplexed by the ancient monolith thrown up from the bottom of the ocean with its grotesque and frightening carving, but this had been rationalized by the narrator as but figments of the imagination of some long-dead human peoples. The appearance of the monster shatters the illusion and lays starkly bare the horrors of the unknown:

> I cannot think of the deep sea without shuddering at the nameless things that may at this very moment be crawling and floundering on its slimy bed, worshipping their ancient stone idols and carving their own detestable likenesses on submarine obelisks of water-soaked granite. I dream of a day when they may rise above the billows to drag down in their reeking talons the remnants of puny, war-exhausted mankind—of a day when the land shall sink, and the dark ocean floor shall ascend amidst universal pandemonium. (CF 1.58)

The true horror is not known, but rather it is in the thoughts of the unknown that lies beneath the waves and of the normal, recognized earth which, now slightly glimpsed, cannot be denied. What is truly happening, what is the truth of the horrors the narrator has witnessed, is not in any way understood. This is a perspective the narrator himself even acknowledges, as he sought unfound answers in orthodox science via his "peculiar questions" to the "celebrated ethnologist" (CF 1.58). Important too is the enormous under-description of the monster. In art it is almost universally portrayed as a humanoid fish-man, and this is almost certainly Lovecraft's intent. He spent the preceding paragraph creating and describing such imagery depicted upon the monolith. Yet the actual description of the monster is sparse, almost absent. In terms of tangible characteristics, it has only immense size, a head, scaly arms, and (presumably) a mouth. "Polyphemus-like" reinforces first the impression of size (vast, gigantic, and, to a lesser degree by connected association, stupendous) and horror (loathsome, monster of nightmares, hideous head). Polyphemus, the Cyclops of the *Odyssey*, is an anthropophagous monster, yet one possessing many traits specific to humanity, such as artifice and language. The almost-naming of Polyphemus also conveys the idea of the human form at unnatural scale, Cyclopses being fundamentally anthropoid save for their single eye. All this is conveyed in a single sentence. Yet immediately beforehand it is called a thing, clearly differentiating it from humanity. It is the very existence of it that is opening the lid of the true horror. Even as Lovecraft has literally shown the monster and guided the reader to consider by implication and association more about its appearance than is ever actually said, he keeps it under-described to almost absurd degree even as the real horror is the mere consequence of its existence and all that can be inferred thereby. Every time Lovecraft reveals a monster, or a specific horror, it is almost always a gateway to the next horror or greater revelation. Also important in "Dagon" is that the narrator is not telling the story to the reader. Rather we are reading their account after he has committed suicide. This subtle distancing is of relatively minor significance to this specific tale, but the idea will assume ever greater importance in the larger body of Lovecraft's work to come.

"The Nameless City" (1921) is another archeological tale—the appearance of such in the core tales of the Cthulhu Mythos is not coincidental. Archaeology intrinsically involves the reconstruction of the past as a story absent its authors, and which inevitably has missing pieces. In this instance, the story follows the template Lovecraft has laid out for himself in terms of not showing the monster, but in giving exposition that elaborates on the monster via the reading and the decipherment of images. It is important to emphasize that this template is not literal. Like the artist with a specific look to his paintings or the musician whose work has a distinctive sound, Lovecraft as a writer has certain motifs, tropes, ideas, structures, themes, and patterns that recur in his work when viewed as a whole. Indeed, this is one of many aspects that increase the vitality of the Cthulhu Mythos Lovecraft is creating even as he writes largely independent tales. His uniqueness of prose style is also one of the aspects that make Lovecraft's work so easy to copy superficially, or to recognize. In his own time numerous people saw his hand in the revisions appears in *Weird Tales* under the names of the authors he ghostwrote for, or thought he had a hand in tales by others wherein his style was being overtly copied. There are certainly trends in Lovecraft's language—Cyclopean is a particularly famous example—and in his writings. A number of later tales in particular seem to be recrudescences of key ides in early ones, done far bet-ter: "The Moon-Bog" into "The Rats in the Walls," "Dagon" in-to "The Call of Cthulhu," "The Nameless City" into *At the Mountains of Madness,* "The Horror at Red Hook" into "The Thing on the Doorstep." But crucially Lovecraft is not, like so many of his pulp contemporaries, consciously following a pat-tern. Rather he is creating a pattern, to a large degree uncon-sciously, by the naturally expression of his own unique style, perspective and approach.

Venturing like the narrator back into "The Nameless City," he, and thus the reader, gets the horrific story of the inhabitants of the Nameless City largely via interpreting their history laid out upon the subterranean walls. This leads us, the reader, to understand to some degree what has occurred and ultimately what is occurring in the final demoniacal attack. That the tale is less deftly written—the end scene is muddled in a manner that is more than the obfuscation of the monster—doesn't detract from the intention, which is once again to suggest that the hor-ror is that the remnants of the malign reptiles who predate hu-manity are not entirely gone. Exactly what they are, where they have gone into, and what vestiges lurk therein is unclear but de-cidedly of a malicious and inimical disposition. We have literally encountered the monster, but we do not comprehend the mon-ster. All the information we have about it comes at second hand via the quotation from the *Necronomicon* and the interpretation of the friezes and frescos. The narrator has a far more extensive exposure and understanding of the history of the Nameless City by his direct access to this primal source. We the reader are merely obtaining his surmise, interpretation, and impressions of it. The importance of this distancing, the layering of the story, is essential to Lovecraft's power as an author. It is very rare that we the reader get most of our direct exposition from an omnisci-ent narrator. Everything is channeled to us via the obfuscating and distancing of different parties and methods. It adds veraci-ty—we are being told something by an authority—and also al-lows for a lack of specific detail while simultaneously conveying enough information to set a framework for impressions and spe-cific modes and directions of thought.

"The Music of Erich Zann" (1921) is a far more straightforward example of not showing the monster. We the reader come face to face with many horrors directly with the protagonist—the missing address, the view into the unknown from the garret window, and the corpse continuing to play its frantic music in the dark—but only gain glimpses of the greater terror from Outside that Zann was so frantically trying to hold back. The explanation is glimpsed, literally, in the form of Zann's written explanation, which is tantalizingly produced and then snatched away. The reader is given enough of a taste of the nightmarish reality of Zann and the Rue d'Auseil to form a satisfying weird tale, but the greater wonder that remains unexplained is what gives a deeper resonance to the tale, which Lovecraft himself consistently ranked as one of his favorites. This writing technique, of there clearly being further information available inside the tale that we as the reader never obtain, will be constantly revisited in both Lovecraft's Mythos fiction and elsewhere; his letters, for example, abound with allusion to greater wholes, mysteries, unknown aspects and ideas upon which he never expanded.

"The Call of Cthulhu" (1926), being Lovecraft's masterpiece, is naturally filled with many layers and shades of the aspects of the unseen monster which is such a powerful undercurrent to his work. Again the reader might cry foul and point out, rightly, that Cthulhu itself[1] appears in the tale. Or so it would seem. Yet a closer examination reveals a slightly different reality. Our narrator does not in fact see Cthulhu. Rather he obtains the diary of Johansen and reads his account of seeing Cthulhu. This distancing, as noted earlier, gives a very different perspective for us the reader. We are further removed from the event, so less is revealed to us. It would be an entirely different experience for us

---

1. The gender of Cthulhu is a curious topic. It is gendered in the tale itself, but by the cultists whose understanding may certainly be called into question, and who may just be using a default "he." As such I choose, like many, to think of it as outside such humanocentric and earthly terms, although others interpret Cthulhu specifically as female, such as in Cradle of Filth's song "Mother of Abominations." HPL himself specifically stated in letters that Cthulhu was male. Then again, in such a medium HPL made all sorts of jests about it that are clearly not germane to the being as portrayed so horrifically in the tale.

to go with the narrator as he located the hideous corpse-city of risen R'lyeh. And there are deeper subtleties here too. Our diarist Johansen, it is specifically noted, "thank God, did not know quite all, even though he saw the city and the Thing" and admits in the account there is deliberate self-censorship, including at least "a sound that the chronicler would not put on paper" (CF 2.54). His account is thus at least slightly tainted, and becomes more so when it is considered further. When he describes the unknown it is less clear and detailed, more prone to error, than something we understand. There is the further fact that Jorgensen is unlettered—that is to say, without a university level education—and thus without the formal training that comes from being such or the experience of having written masses of documentation for the scrutiny of others. The narrator specifically calls the diary "a simple, rambling thing" (CF 2.49). Furthermore, Johansen is writing in English, which is clearly not his native language. All this adds to the ideas of obscuration inherent in the fact that we the reader are given a précis of his diary as filtered through the narrator. We are not seeing Cthulhu. We are seeing the narrator's highly condensed version of Johansen's diary, which in turn is his censored version of something he did not truly understand written long after the events occurred in a language other than the writer's mother tongue.

This distancing is a factor throughout the tale. It is to be remembered that, when originally published, "The Call of Cthulhu" was presented as the papers of the late Francis Wayland Thurston, and that Thurston hints at his own impending death coming shortly after the end of the narrative. We, the reader, are thus at an additional distance from the events by the mere mechanism of reading a dead man's papers, rather than hearing a narrative from Thurston himself. Everything we hear is at various layers of remove, and very little of the action is exposited. In fact, most of the action that occurs in the story is glossed over; the actual raid on the cult in the swamps takes up three sentences, the fight between the crews of the *Emma* and the *Vigilant* only two. All the key events of the story occur without any participation by the narrator at all. Consider how we, the reader, discover information of the Cthulhu cult. We learn of it from the papers of the (probably murdered) dead Thurston, who is reading the papers of his (undoubtedly murdered) dead great-uncle, who is relating the experiences of Inspector Legrasse, who is relating the experiences cultist Castro, himself "immensely aged," "mentally aberrant" (CF 2.38, 37), and probably clinically insane—it is unclear if Castro is one of the two "found sane enough to be hanged" (CF 2.38)—while Castro was himself apparently told such by the "undying leaders of the cult in the mountains of China" (CF 2.38).[2] Everything is filtered, and as such there are missing aspects throughout the narrative, speculations and glimpses of bigger things. Every time we gather more information we are immediately confronted with a deeper layer of obscurity. "The Call of Cthulhu" is a natural building upon of the ideas in "The Music of Erich Zann," with the entirely hidden story of Zann being given, in part, in the account of the narrator.

Yet it is not all subtle clues and deeper readings that show the greater distance from Cthulhu for the reader. Because of Lovecraft's skill in set-up and composition, is is rarely noticed. Yet Cthulhu, when it appears, is not at all described—in fact, Lovecraft specifically has the narrator state after Cthulhu's advent "The Thing cannot be described" (CF 2.53). In terms of physical portrayal this is the entirety of that offered by the reader's meeting with Cthulhu: "It lumbered slobberingly into sight and gropingly squeezed Its gelatinous green immensity through the black doorway"; "The Thing of the idols, the green, sticky spawn of the stars"; "ravening for delight" (although one could argue this is not a description of Cthulhu in any meaningful way that produces an image rather than a feeling); "swept up by the flabby claws"; "mountainous monstrosity flopped down the slimy stones"; "titan Thing from the stars slavered and gibbered like Polypheme"; "great Cthulhu slid greasily into the water and began to pursue with vast wave-raising strokes of cosmic potency"; "The awful squid-head with writhing feelers came nearly up to the bowsprit of the sturdy yacht" (CF 2.54); and finally,

---

2. To belabor the point, it does seem likely that Castro is also not a native speaker of any Chinese languages, but then again there is no guarantee the leaders are themselves Chinese.

bursting as of an exploding bladder, a slushy nastiness as of a cloven sunfish, a stench as of a thousand opened graves, and a sound that the chronicler would not put on paper. For an instant the ship was befouled by an acrid and blinding green cloud, and then there was only a venomous seething astern; where—God in heaven!—the scattered plasticity of that nameless sky-spawn was nebulously *recombining* in its hateful original form. (CF 2.54)

Note how the most distinctive image created and the only one to give any idea of shape and visage—"awful squid-head with writhing feelers"—is given second-to-last, and immediately prior to the statement that the "nameless sky-spawn was nebulously recombining in its hateful original form." This original form, you will note, is not directly stated in the preceding events. Cthulhu is not at all shown to us, the reader, in this scene. Rather we are given a detailed description back in "The Tale of Inspector Legrasse" via the medium of the idol, and given a condensation and recapitulation of the description in the narrator's examination of the *Alert's* idol at the Museum in Sydney—"The crouching image with its cuttlefish head, dragon body, scaly wings" (CF 2.48)—as refresher while we draw closer to encountering the reality. We do not see Cthulhu. Rather we encounter Cthulhu at the removes and distances discussed, and graft onto that our previous knowledge from the idols to create a mental image of the very alien being seen by the sailors landing upon R'lyeh. Despite encountering Cthulhu we in truth are not actually shown the monster. This is crucial to the story. An excessive descriptive examination of Cthulhu would only take away from the horror. The remote, forensic, calm, and clinical examination of the original idol creates the mental image. This gives the reader enough information to fill in the blanks spaces mentally when we come across the reality, reinforced by the brief discussion of the second idol, yet ultimately without showing Cthulhu to us as such. It is the two presentations in conjunction that gives the story its power.

To elaborate further upon this, Lovecraft famously wrote of planning his tales with the verisimilitude of well-planned hoax (*Dawnward Spire* 244). This is often taken, correctly, to mean

that he made a genuine effort to make his outré facts and experiences seem plausible by surrounding them with absolute truth
and genuine, if obscure, knowledge. Yet to consider only this is
to miss the deeper levels to this ideological statement. Lovecraft
also speaks of things on a more primal level, talking about the importance of following the "natural myth-making tendencies" (*Letters to C. L. Moore* 268) of humanity to create this appearance and
illusion of truth. Another aspect of this hoax mentality is that it is
vital not to show that which will break the reader's belief.

To divert for a moment, consider the modern myth of Bigfoot. It has a tenacious hold on the popular psyche, despite its
status as a relative newcomer—the Wildman mythology present
in various cultures has been read back into the narrative as
much as being the genesis of Bigfoot—and the almost overwhelming lack of credible evidences. The search for Bigfoot has
been particularly hampered by the abundance of pranks, hoaxes,
frauds, and fakes that form the undercurrents about which the
stories accrete. Yet this has not stopped belief. The most credible signs of Bigfoot, other than strange noises, half-seen glimpses, feelings of being watched, etc., that cluster with ubiquity
around any paranormal or preternatural creature, site, or event
without any other evidences, are of course the giant footprints
that give the creature its moniker. Photographs and casts of
such can be pointed to as proof that there may be something to
the stories, despite the abundance of cases that are acknowledged pranks or exposed hoaxes. They provide just enough evidence to the willing to open the possibility of there being a
creature such as Bigfoot. Yet the (in)famous Patterson–Gimlin
film allegedly showing a Bigfoot—if you have seen film or an image of Bigfoot looking back over a log from a distance as it walks
away, this is Patterson–Gimlin footage—rather than increasing
belief to the skeptical or interested, tends instead to harden
viewers of it against the idea. Whether or not the footage is a
hoax is ultimately irrelevant. Seeing Bigfoot paradoxically makes
it seem less believable, and the footage is widely dismissed.

Lovecraft as a writer instinctively understands this idea, of
knowing how to show just enough to create believability, not to
display the unbelievable past a certain point but rather to have

the readers fill in the gaps for themselves. His execution as if a well-planned hoax has gone on to fool generations of readers into believing in his fictional creations, sometimes quite literally, albeit unintentionally in that particular instance in terms of the creator's intent. This process takes on an additional import and layering when the reader considers one of the few close to direct contacts with events in "The Call of Cthulhu" the narrator relates, this being his interview with a member of the raiding party to the cult in the swamp;

> This man, Joseph D. Galvez, I later met and questioned; and he proved distractingly imaginative. He indeed went so far as to hint of the faint beating of great wings, and of a glimpse of shining eyes and a mountainous white bulk beyond the remotest trees—but I suppose he had been hearing too much native superstition. (CF 2.36–7)

Note how the eyewitness to events deemed impossible by the interviewer is twice subtly dismissed, and it is implied that he is the victim of an over-active imagination combined with a tendency to superstition. The information is thus relayed to us the reader, but in a suitably sensible and cautious manner that does not strain their credulity of the narrator.

This is particularly important in "The Call of Cthulhu" as there are actually three distinct, and two indistinct, classes of monsters in the tale. Cthulhu is obvious, but there are other Great Old Ones, about whom "none might say whether or not the others were precisely like him" (CF 2.38). This sets up a much wider idea that places Cthulhu inside a framework of mythology that makes its existence more plausible. There is the "huge, formless white polypous thing with luminous eyes" (CF 2.35) dwelling in a hidden lake spoken of in legends, and the Black Winged Ones who committed the mutilating murders attributed to the cult "but of those mysterious allies no coherent account could ever be gained" (CF 2.38). That "mankind was not absolutely alone among the conscious things of earth, for shapes came out of the dark to visit the faithful few" (CF 2.38), which are the explicitly stated to be different from the Great Old Ones, adds to the shadows; it is unclear if this refers to the previously mentioned beings or something different again. All this sets up atmosphere and, with the proof of Cthulhu as seen through the extended series of proxies the reader uncovers, seems retroactively to be all true.

The Case of Charles Dexter Ward (1927) is another prime example of the deliberate obscuring of the events from the reader. The key participants in the events of both timelines never tell their own story. Instead, from colonial New England we get the account of Eleazar Smith, companion to Erza Weeden, who was obviously neither as literate nor as deeply invested as the jilted fiancé of the necromancer Curwen's wife. Most vitally, Weeden is not part of the final raiding party to Curwen's home. Even then we do not get to read Weeden's unabridged account, nor do we obtain more than a glimpse of Curwen's discovered diary that ultimately draws Charles Dexter Ward more fully to his doom. Likewise, Ward himself is killed before he can deliver his tale, and everything is put together in smaller glimpses and limited expositions. Curwen is of course unmasked and unmade at the conclusion of the tale, but this is not revealing the monster, who is after all merely a man, albeit one who had no right to exist in a sane and natural world. The monster is what Curwen and his evil cronies have done, and what they are planning to do, which is deliberately kept horrific but vague.

Again, we as the reader do not truly know what it is the trio (Cuwen, Orne, and Hutchinson) has done and further plan to do; instead, we get glimpses and hints via their letters that raise more questions than offer tangible answers. The two more classical monsters encountered under Curwen's Pawtuxet locale both get the same treatment. We get some ideas about the shape and nature of the mewling starving thing in the pit well, but even then it is described in a series of feelings it creates in evocative but non-specific phrases. As readers we are well aware that "there was Noth'g butt ye liveliest Awfulness" (CF 2.251) in those called back from imperfect salts, and have had plenty of time to internalize and digest this information, to create a mental template of how such might appear, before we come across the reality in the well. Then immediately after not physically describing the thing in the well Lovecraft has Willett recall that very line, now drawing back that template as a description. Even then these pits are clearly but part of an antechamber and a gateway to deeper horrors. As with "The Rats in the Walls," these horrors of the upper levels clearly pale in comparison to the implications of what occurs further below. Likewise, the summoned being from the essential saltes is not shown, named, or described outside of Willett's questions as he awoke "crying out, *'That beard . . . those eyes . . . God, who are you?'*" (CF 2.348).

The entire novel is a master class in walking the line between too much information and infuriating the reader with insufficient facts; everything is loaded with menace and meaning, and every time some new information is offered it obfuscates as much as it clarifies. Consider this sentence: "Of the citizen leaders, Capt. Whipple and Moses Brown were most severely hurt, and letters of their wives testify the bewilderment which their reticence and close guarding of their bandages produced" (CF 2.262). In combination with various hints and suggestions about what went on in the Curwen raid, there is a multitude of possibilities that add to the aura of menace and danger concerning the events which exposition would not be able to achieve. That they, like many of the individuals named in the story, are genuine historic figures also subtly adds to the air of verisimilitude. One could indeed look up more information about them, and this frequent implication of more information is one of the underpinning strengths of the story. Equally, in a maneuver that adds to the determined sense of reality of the tale, there are present-day newspaper accounts of "the revolting cases of vampirism which the press so sensationally reported at the time" (CF 2.300). Continuing this theme, it is added that "these cases, too recent and celebrated to need detailed mention" (CF 2.300), which manages to convey a sense of authenticity and missing narrative, even as it then gives but two additional sentences—admittedly the typical extended Lovecraftian sentences—to cover the details. That we the reader have previously been given multiple newspaper extracts to read that hint superficially at nightmarish events further fuels the effectiveness of the technique. The idea subtly conveyed through the entire story is that there is so much more happening than the reader has direct access to, and adds further credibility to the narratives of the other epistolary forms of address frequently scattered throughout the work; yet it is all ultimately done without further exposition or extensive revelation.

"The Colour out of Space" (1927), another of Lovecraft's favorites among his own writings, again utilizes the distancing effect of the distinct layering of the narration. The story comes to the reader largely from the surveyor's recitation of the account of old Ammi Pierce, telling of what happened to his friend Nahum Gardner more than four decades ago and of which he is at times only a partial witness. This is added to greatly by the fact that there is no monster, in the more traditional sense. It is a completely alien order of being, literally just a color out of space. We can behold its effects and glimpse aspects of it without any true understanding, because it is beyond our understanding—"it was only by analogy that they called it colour at all" (CF 2.373). Scientific testing is thoroughly and meticulously applied and the results unambiguously given, a process that ultimately gives no revelation. The key is that Lovecraft delivers the tale in such a way as to make that lack of knowledge generate tension and excitement, rather than disappointment or dissatisfaction. As we draw toward the hideous conclusion we gain more conjecture rather than facts—"But whatever daemon hatchling is there, it must be tethered to something or else it would quickly spread. Is it fastened to the roots of those trees that claw the air? One of the current Arkham tales is about fat oaks that shine and move as they ought not to do at night" (CF 2.399). Even the very final lines, which add such a dread to the entire episode—"Ammi is such a good old man—when the reservoir gang gets to work I must write the chief engineer to keep a sharp watch on him. I would hate to think of him as the grey, twisted, brittle monstrosity which persists more and more in troubling my sleep" (CF 2.399)—refer not to something witnessed but to something feared yet to happen.

"The Dunwich Horror" (1928) is, unlike many of the stories under discussion, in the main told by the omniscient narrator rather than the voice of a character in the tale. This of course creates a foreshortening of the distance between the reader and the events. Yet despite this Lovecraft manages to prevent the reader from observing the monster, in this case quite literally, with Wilbur's even more malign sibling being invisible. Again the classic dictum cited earlier about not showing the monster at first but ultimately revealing it lest reader dissatisfaction ensue is particularly apparent here, in a story leading authority S. T. Joshi persuasively considers was unconsciously molded to the requirements of Lovecraft's primary publisher, *Weird Tales,* which had begun a run of rejections of his work (*Rise and Fall* 77). Yet Lovecraft manages to maintain a cumulative suspense and ultimate integrity by ultimately revealing the fullest glimpse of the creature *after* the climactic battle and banishment of it has been accomplished, and even then via the medium of a single glimpse from a distant figure via a telescope to further occlude its appearance.

Despite an omniscient narrator we constantly return to the perspective of those inside the tale and obtain only the information, understanding, and experience they possess, sometimes at third hand. For example, we hear about the destruction of Seth Bishop's household via the account of several unnamed persons in a crowd of Dunwich men as they relay what they have heard of events from other, more direct witnesses. We the reader do not get the narrative of "the three men from Arkham" (CF 2.460) who actually climb the hill and confront the blasphemy, just the distant, fragmentary account of the men of Dunwich observing incompletely from at a physical, and comprehending, remove. Yet even then the deeper horror, the true monster of the tale is what the Whateleys had been up to and what their plans were for using this evil sibling, which had all been forestalled by the death of Wilbur in the library. Importantly, that information has not simply died with Wilbur. It is still extant and available, in the form of Wilbur's diary, which Armitage has read and which we, the reader, are aware of but only gain the most tantalizing glimpses therein. As is frequently the case in a Lovecraft story, we the readers are not given the primary information and sources, but rather a summation, extract, and interpretation of them. It is clear there is much more information available, but we are never given the full story, even when the full story is laid out before us to read.

The italicized revelation at the end of the story is not the monster's appearance or actions, but his origins. Equally, the key piece of exposition in the tale, the extract from the *Necronomicon,* is not presented to us by the omniscient narrator, but rather from the text of the book itself being read by Armitage in the story. Furthermore, it is not merely reading a proffered text. Armitage is reading a copy in Latin that we the readers of the story are not given approach to, but rather indirectly access it via his own translation as he reads it. Lovecraft as narrator does this throughout the story, diving directly into the viewpoints of people in the tale itself, which adds to the verisimilitude and also adds a layer of obfuscation. We the readers often only get to know specifically what certain characters or groups of people know, and this keeps the air of the unknown even after the tale is completed.

"The Whisperer in Darkness" (1930) is back to the in-story narrator, with many of the events being related by Wilmarth's recollection of Akeley's correspondence. Such is occasionally reproduced in full, yet as per Lovecraft's favored technique most of it is known to exist yet is not seen by the reader. This fact is even highlighted and lamented by Wilmarth in the tale itself, particularly concerning Akeley's clandestine recording made in the woods: "Those to whom I have since described the record profess to find nothing but cheap imposture or madness in it; but could they have heard the accursed thing itself, or read the bulk of Akeley's correspondence (especially that terrible and encyclopaedic second letter), I know they would think differently" (CF 2.488). Yet despite the in-story narrator the monster is doubly unrevealed in the tale. The Mi-Go, the fungi from Yuggoth who are the central antagonists of the tale and who loom menacingly over the events in the Vermont hills, are never observed directly by our protagonist Wilmarth. They are only—like the aforementioned Bigfoot—read of in newspaper accounts, heard via a strange recording in the woods, known by tales told by a lone rustic, and seen tangibly only through the medium of prints left in the earth. Equally, the truth of exactly who or what is sitting in the chair in place of Akeley, something

Lovecraftians have been arguing about since the story was first published in 1931, remains opaque within the information available in the tale itself. Behind the scenes it is worth noting that Lovecraft originally had additional material, about six pages worth, in his first competed draft of the tale. On the advice of early readers he revised it, notably changing the ending to make it implied but without proof that Akeley's brain is in the device on the shelf rather than displaying it explicitly, and removing text from Akeley's letters in the beginning of the tale. That these changes add power to the tale yet obfuscate details is of course a microcosm of the wider body of Lovecraft's Mythos writings.

At the Mountains of Madness (1931) has our narrator Dyer completely removed from almost all the key action of the tale in which he is theoretically the central protagonist. He is not present for the finding of the Old Ones in the ice, absent for the attack at the camp, comes late to the scene of the killing of the Old Ones by the shoggoths, and does not see the final thing that Danforth sees and which sends the latter to a deeper trauma and perhaps madness. As in "The Whisperer in Darkness," no living version of the alien beings with their bizarre biological form is seen, which increases their sense of verisimilitude. As a reader we are constantly engaged at deeper and deeper levels with them—bodies to revivified monsters to intelligent beings taking sleds with specimens to decapitated victims of their own creations—yet this is not ever done via glimpses of them as living creatures. Importantly, Dyer discusses the evidences he will be using to give credibility to his tale, photographs, notes, and sketches, to which we the reader of course are not privy. The information gained about the Old Ones and their civilization and history is given to us by the surmise of Dyer, who has read a version of it on the walls of the city that he himself admits he only shallowly understands. Furthermore, he states that there were certain aspects of the sculptures that could not be grasped by those lacking certain "mental and emotional background, and a fuller or different sensory equipment" (CF 3.88) and that whole sections were passed by entirely.

There are, moreover, references in these frescos to other aspects of Lovecraft's prehuman history that has by now truly become the Cthulhu Mythos—but, paradoxically, the information herein demythologizes it substantially. These connections add weight to the narrative, regardless of whether or not the reader is familiar with the other stories; they do no more than add greater mystery outside of the slight information in the extremely broad terms presented. Equally important is the line "It is significant that their annals failed to mention many advanced and potent races of beings whose mighty cultures and towering cities figure persistently in certain obscure legends" (CF 3.105). There is clearly more to the story of these ancient civilizations of might and horror than even the Old Ones willingly tell of, a particularly germane point to be addressed presently. In terms of showing the monster, Dyer does see a shoggoth, but that is only a portion of the horror of the tale; the history of earth and true origins of the humanity ("a shambling primitive mammal, used sometimes for food and sometimes as an amusing buffoon" [CF 3.100]) are far more disturbing. It is also clear in the tale that the shoggoths are but a lesser evil; the true source of fear lies in the further mountains and their unknown inhabitants. No matter what darkness and malignity is uncovered in a Lovecraft tale, there are always at least hints of a deeper well of further threat and malfeasant alienage lurking behind it. Cthulhu after all, while it might be as a god to us, is specifically described as but a priest, obviously itself serving a higher power.

"The Shadow over Innsmouth" (1931) follows in the same pattern. There is a long build-up, with many hints so that the reader will understand the nature of the horrors that inhabit the town. The reader is then offered a glimpse, literally, of the horde of Deep Ones, hybrids and perhaps other monstrosities as the narrator hides in the dark after escaping the Gilman House but never truly comes to see them. Note how even in the description the narrator uses the qualifier "I think" before describing their color. Even in the eyewitness account there is uncertainty. More importantly, the true horror of the tale is twofold and has nothing to do with the monsters as pursuers or as beings. The narrator's discovery of his own blood ties to them and his acceptance is the obvious one. But one of the subtleties with which

Lovecraft intersperses his tales, and which add immeasurably in this case to the dread underpinning the rotting town, comes in the final ravings of Zadok Allen: "Them haouses north o' the river betwixt Water an' Main Streets is full of 'em—them devils *an' what they brung*—an' when they git ready . . . I say, *when they git ready* . . . ever hear tell of a *shoggoth?*" (CF 3.200). The Deep Ones have plans that go beyond miscegenation in a small New England seaport to which we the reader are not privy, yet equally feel their menace. Again, though it is not as obvious, the constant allusions to various newspaper accounts of the events of the raid on Innsmouth that occurred after the narrator's visit add an air of verisimilitude and of paradoxically available yet missing information for the reader.

"The Dreams in the Witch House" (1932), for all the complaints of some about the fusion of real-world religion and witch-lore that undergird the tale, is another excellent example of how Lovecraft mixes in enough facts and experiences to create a compelling tale yet occludes the horrors. Keziah Mason is, for all her malignity, merely a human, while Brown Jenkin is described just enough for an image to be formed—"witnesses said it had long hair and the shape of a rat, but that its sharp-toothed, bearded face was evilly human while its paws were like tiny human hands" (CF 3.236). Note as ever that Lovecraft takes us at a remove from merely seeing Brown Jenkin at this juncture, despite having an omniscient narrator for the story, and gives the reader instead an (at least) second-hand description from the nebulous "witnesses." Likewise, other than fangs and hair Brown Jenkin's having a face as "evilly human" is at once highly evocative yet open to a wide interpretation; the word in constant juxtaposition in the depiction of Brown Jenkin's visage is "bearded," but "evilly" is appended as description to Keziah twice more, tying the two together in appearance subconsciously before Lovecraft makes the connection explicit in the later line "the accursed little face which he at last realised bore such a shocking, mocking resemblance to old Keziah's" (CF 3.266).

Throughout the tale there is a lack of concrete detail and open exposition, but the layering of hints and fragments creates a full image, in the same manner as ruins of an antique temple convey its fallen grandeur and dimensions despite largely being absent and deficient in many crucial details. The Black Man of the tale is described enough to convey menace and sense of the inhuman, despite a mostly human form, but he is not the horror of the tale, which is a mix of the centuries of ritual murder of infants, knowledge of the darker things that lurk outside the normal world in the unexpectedly malign word of higher mathematics, and the "primal evil too horrible for description" that is—poignantly—"mercifully cloaked under the name of Azathoth" (CF 3.244, 2.521) in the *Necronomicon*. With Walter Gilman we travel to strange dimensions and unknown worlds, but to what end or purpose is entirely unexplored. The experienced Lovecraftian reader will immediately connect the Old Ones of *At the Mountains of Madness* with the starfish aliens visited in Gilman's dream excursion that resulted in his curious sunburn, but this would not have been possible to a contemporary public audience when it appeared in *Weird Tales* in July 1933. *At the Mountains of Madness*, rejected by *Weird Tales*, would not see publication in *Astounding Stories* until 1936. Yet this knowledge to the modern reader who commonly has access to both in a single volume in no way explains what is occurring.

In the same manner that Lovecraft manages throughout his individual stories, whether there is a more concrete explanation or not, such small moments just add further tantalizing hints of detail to create greater depth but no elucidation, and raise more questions. Likewise it appears that Azathoth, or his proxies, claims some rulership of the higher dimensions and that these dimensions have a sort of rhythm or patterning that requires tribute. Yet this is one possible explanation; any number of other possible explanations as to what is actually occurring can be presented with equal validity based upon the slim evidence. No matter what the cause and effect—or lack thereof—why does this require the blood of murdered children? The monster and the monstrous are on exhibition yet simultaneously inexplicable. This is displayed, quite literally, in Gilman's travel in the twilight abysses wherein he sees the forms of other travelers and (possibly) locales in forms that are described but wherein it is specifically noted that "physical organisation and faculties were somehow marvellously transmuted and obliquely projected—though not without a certain grotesque relationship to his normal proportions and properties" (CF 3.237), We can see them, they are described after a fashion, but this is not their hideous reality as would be in the more material world.

"The Thing on the Doorstep" (1933) is a return to the first-person narrator, a technique that is perfectly suited to Lovecraft's presentation of horror and the weird. Again, like many of the tales under discussion, the horror has a very human aspect, and the revelation of the monster as such is thus the revelation of what is occurring, rather than the appearance of a physical being. This is the deeper undercurrent that flows beneath all Lovecraft's tales, and what contributes to their enduring power. Yet even with that caveat the tale is filled with endless allusions to dark events and supernatural battles and evils of which he the reader only gain the merest glimpse. Edward Derby's frenzied confession in the car epitomizes this propensity toward (paradoxically) exposition lacking crucial information:

> "Dan—for God's sake! The pit of the shoggoths! Down the six thousand steps . . . the abomination of abominations . . . I never would let her take me, and then I found myself there . . . Iä! Shub-Niggurath! . . . The shape rose up from the altar, and there were 500 that howled . . . The Hooded Thing bleated 'Kamog! Kamog!'—that was old Ephraim's secret name in the coven . . . I was there, where she promised she wouldn't take me . . . A minute before I was locked in the library, and then I was there where she had gone with my body—in the place of utter blasphemy, the unholy pit where the black realm begins and the watcher guards the gate . . . I saw a shoggoth—it changed shape . . . I can't stand it . . . I won't stand it . . . I'll kill her if she ever sends me there again . . . I'll kill that entity . . . her, him, it . . . I'll kill it! I'll kill it with my own hands!" (CF 3.197–98)

It is patently clear what has occurred to Derby, yet there is a scarcity of detail that is not readily apparent as the construction creates in the mind of the reader the necessary circumstances to envisage something that is in reality not described at all. Again, to the contemporary *Weird Tales* reader, this was probably even more obscure. The work in which the shoggoths are a central feature, *At the Mountains of Madness,* was by now published, having appeared the year before over two issues of the afore-mentioned *Astounding.* Yet while there was much cross-over in audience—the same letter writers appear in print in both maga-zines—there was equally a common prejudice shared between both sets of primary readerships between *Weird Tales* and *Astounding* that the others sort of fantastic material was the less-er and unworthy of them, causing much antagonism between the two fandoms that (sadly) continues in mutated forms to the present day. Yet it is in the minor as much as the major aspects of the tale that Lovecraft brings his delicate balance of obscured information: "Meanwhile the Derbys almost dropped out of the gay college circle—not through their own disgust, we heard, but because something about their present studies shocked even the most callous of the other decadents" (CF 3.334), or "I made her promise to stop preying on me. Of course I had certain—certain occult defences I never told you about" (CF 3.345). It is not merely that Lovecraft withholds information. Rather it is that he gives an abundance of information but without any finalizing de-tail that creates more questions even as it illuminates.

"The Shadow out of Time" (1934–35), again with an inter-nal narrator, follows both the general pattern of Lovecraft's writ-ings and the more specific formulae he concocted in *At the Mountains of Madness.* We the reader do get to understand the hideous change that has occurred to Nathaniel Wingate Pea-slee, but we get only fragments of the authentic events; the ac-tual transcripts of his dreams and the series of articles he wrote in the *Journal of the American Psychological Society* that contain the true data are of course not available to the reader, much as Dyer's notes resulting from his nightmare excursion and the photographs he took to back it up are not in evidence. Lovecraft offers a fantastic—in both senses so the word—account of Pea-slee's interactions while inhabiting the body of a sojourning Great Race member that bears repeating in full:

> I seemed to talk, in some odd language of claw-clickings, with exiled intellects from every corner of the solar system. [. . .]
>
> There was a mind from the planet we know as Venus, which would live incalculable epochs to come, and one from an outer

moon of Jupiter six million years in the past. Of earthly minds there were some from the winged, star-headed, half-vegetable race of palaeogean Antarctica; one from the reptile people of fabled Valusia; three from the furry pre-human Hyperborean worshippers of Tsathoggua; one from the wholly abominable Tcho-Tchos; two from the arachnid denizens of earth's last age; five from the hardy coleopterous species immediately following mankind, to which the Great Race was some day to transfer its keenest minds en masse in the face of horrible peril; and several from different branches of humanity.

I talked with the mind of Yiang-Li, a philosopher from the cruel empire of Tsan-Chan, which is to come in A.D. 5000; with that of a general of the great-headed brown people who held South Africa in B.C. 50,000; with that of a twelfth-century Florentine monk named Bartolomeo Corsi; with that of a king of Lomar who had ruled that terrible polar land 100,000 years before the squat, yellow Inutos came from the west to engulf it; with that of Nug-Soth, a magician of the dark conquerors of A.D. 16,000; with that of a Roman named Titus Sempronius Blaesus, who had been a quaestor in Sulla's time; with that of Khephnes, an Egyptian of the 14th Dynasty who told me the hideous secret of Nyarlathotep; with that of a priest of Atlantis' middle kingdom; with that of a Suffolk gentleman of Cromwell's day, James Woodville; with that of a court astronomer of pre-Inca Peru; with that of the Australian physicist Nevil Kingston-Brown, who will die in A.D. 2518; with that of an archimage of vanished Yhe in the Pacific; with that of Theodotides, a Graeco-Bactrian official of B.C. 200; with that of an aged Frenchman of Louis XIII's time named Pierre-Louis Montmagny; with that of Crom-Ya, a Cimmerian chieftain of B.C. 15,000; and with so many others that my brain cannot hold the shocking secrets and dizzying marvels I learned from them. (CF 3.397–99)

There is a depth of knowledge and implications in those paragraphs that is without any natural cessation, and which creates a sense of time and history even as it fails to elucidate beyond that which it presents, creating yet greater mysteries. Implications in mere fractions of lines are staggering; the forthcoming extinction of the human race is glossed over in a mere nine words, while the existence of an alternative humanity to our own is dealt with in an even fewer six. In common with the Old Ones in *At the Mountains of Madness*, the Great Race, while they are clearly alien and somewhat inimical to humanity—and indeed other sentient races—are not shown as ravening monsters, but intelligent, at least partially comprehendible beings. This of course is somewhat showing the monster, and this knowledge of necessity dilutes the terror of them, breaking it would seem with Lovecraft's own dictum that "the oldest and strongest kind of fear is fear of the unknown" (CE 2.82). Yet Lovecraft obviously understands this, and it is why in both tales he has a secondary, obscured source of fear, something of which the beings of their respective tales themselves are fearful. The "half-polypous, utterly alien entities" (CF 3.406), Elder Things who were sealed away by the Great Race, are ineffably menacing in the story, with little description and no glimpse of their being at all; in Fritz Leiber's famous phrase in his seminal essay "A Literary Copernicus" (1949), Lovecraft "shows us horrors and then pulls back the curtain a little further, letting us glimpse the horrors of which even the horrors are afraid!" (57). Peaslee explores the ruins of the Great Race's library and thus makes his own literal nightmares recrudesce into reality, but his final terrified flight and unremembered plunge into the abyss are not seen at all by the reader for all the fears and excitement they create as they read it.

"The Haunter of the Dark" (1935) draws this all to a natural conclusion, with the titular creature given no more description than (possibly) black wings and the artful yet somewhat insane "three-lobed burning eye" (CF 3.477), yet being terrifying enough to have killed Robert Blake by its mere appearance. In truth, given that the tale starts with consideration of Blake's fear-distorted corpse, there is nothing that could have been described at the end that would have sufficiently accounted for such to the majority of readers. Again, as we have seen constantly with Lovecraft's writings, he delivers the information in the story via a medium that removes the reader a step from the information, such as in this case reporter Edwin M. Lillibridge's memoranda, the newspaper accounts of which the reader gain only a summary, or Father Merluzzo's or the telephone exchange's account of the precise time. All this ultimately creates a perfect horror tale out of the most basic and antiquated of premises: a fear of the dark and an unseen monster.

In managing to create both individual stories and a wider mythopoeia that has both sufficient information to be filled with verisimilitude and creates an instantly distinctive sense of itself, Lovecraft's work manages to remain vibrant and sustained a century after he began composing it. The artful obscurement of his monsters while simultaneously depicting them in a manner in which readers will paradoxically see them clearly for themselves remains a cornerstone in the power of his work. By utilizing deeper levels of both thought and engagement Lovecraft's design of the monstrous as a construction of the universe, rather than as a focus upon the monster itself, has created something that is truly a working paradox, something that ultimately is not dead and which can last and lie eternal, yet constantly awaken.

Works Cited

In the Mouth of Madness. John Carpenter, dir. New Line Cinema, 1994.

Joshi, S. T. *The Rise, Fall, and Rise of the Cthulhu Mythos.* New York: Hippocampus Press, 2015.

Leiber, Fritz. "A Literary Copernicus." In S. T. Joshi, ed. *H. P. Lovecraft: Four Decades of Criticism.* Athens: Ohio University Press, 1980. 50–62.

Lovecraft, H. P. *Letters to C. L. Moore and Others.* Ed. David E. Schultz and S. T. Joshi. New York: Hippocampus Press, 2017.

———, and Clark Ashton Smith. *Dawnward Spire, Lonely Hill: The Letters of H. P. Lovecraft and Clark Ashton Smith.* Ed. David E. Schultz and S. T. Joshi. New York: Hippocampus Press, 2017.

Murray, Margaret. *My First Hundred Years.* London: William Kimber & Co., 1963.

"What Has Sunk May Rise": How H. P. Lovecraft Re-emerged

Steven J. Mariconda

S. T. JOSHI. The Recognition of H. P. Lovecraft: His Rise from Obscurity to World Renown. New York: Hippocampus Press, 2012. 339 pp. $25.00 tpb.
S. T. JOSHI. Journals, 1974–1987. Seattle: Sarnath Press, 2021. 3 vols. $14.95 tpb each.

Truth has been stranger than fiction since at least 1823, when Lord Byron wrote the line in *Don Juan*. Given Lovecraft's recent rise to prominence, this cliché must officially be amended to "truth is weirder than weird fiction." When the author died eighty-five or so years ago, the proposition that he would be ubiquitous in 2021 was an outside chance. A wager with even worse odds would have been: a teenage polymath from India will become the agent by which Lovecraft ascends into the literary canon. Collectively, the four books at hand—*The Recognition of H. P. Lovecraft: His Rise from Obscurity to World Renown* by S. T. Joshi, plus three volumes of the latter's *Journals* (1974–87)—constitute a basis for future historiographers. Scholars will look back and consider how perceptions of Lovecraft and his fiction changed over time, and these books will be foundational. For this generation, they document two remarkable "long shots" that not even a Damon Runyon gambler would take.

Circumstances collude such that the person who made some of this history—S. T. Joshi—is the sole person presently able and willing to write it. There is an unavoidable self-referential element here: Joshi's perspective is from within the bubble he himself largely created. The inherent bias is mitigated, in part, because his career has not been solely devoted to Lovecraft: he

218

has credentials as a genuine scholar with extensive contributions addressing the genre as a whole, other subject areas, and dozens of other writers.[1] Once we acknowledge the inevitable pitfall there is much to enjoy and learn here. It remains for commentators of the twenty-second century to sort it all out. For now, there are facets of interest to contemporary readers following Lovecraft's contemporary progress.

In the preface to *The Recognition of H. P. Lovecraft*, Joshi lays out this project: the book "seeks to chart both the dissemination of H. P. Lovecraft's work during and after his lifetime and to identify and assess the discussions of his life, work, and thought among academicians, critics, reviewers, and (where possible) general readers in that same period." Never one to shy away from controversy, he immediately dispatches the elephant in the room:

> There is good reason to question whether I am the right person to write a book of this sort, given my own intimate involvement in the propagation of Lovecraft's texts and in the critical analysis of his life and work over the past four decades. . . . [I]t could well be asked (a) whether I have anything new to say on this subject, and (b) whether I can gauge my own contributions with the objectivity that I seek to bring to other sections of this work.

The *Journals* recount Joshi's experiences from age sixteen to twenty-nine and are a (three-ton) literary pendant to *The Recognition of H. P. Lovecraft*. Some will ask, how could this be interesting? The *Journals* help understand how Joshi (nominally an emigrant adolescent domiciled in backwater Indiana) pulled off the daunting task of making Lovecraft (nominally a bad hack writer for cheap pulp magazines) respectable. They show the nitty-gritty detail that the average person could never otherwise see.

Against all odds, Lovecraft and Joshi were each the right person in the right place at the right time.

---

1. It is difficult not to rehearse Joshi's accomplishments in the context of this piece; but even more encyclopedic detail can be found on the Internet: www.stjoshi.org.

Questions of Recognition

The Recognition of H. P. Lovecraft discusses the diverse issues
around literary respect: what makes a text "a classic"; what
makes it art; what are the aspects of acceptance; what tangible
circumstances drive recognition; and the effects that a changing
readership has on a writer's status. These are difficult questions:
there are elements of awareness, persistence, and respect. Most
concretely, there are external markers that show that a particular book resonates with a specific generation—for example, distinguished editions such as the Library of America. If a book
keeps its place as a classic, it does so by a series of changing appeals or causes over time. It gains reputation when it has a favorable relation to a particular period; it may lose reputation
when external variables make that relation unfavorable. An
ephemeral work is one that enriches one particular set of readers, but bores or puzzles another. An enduring work is reaffirmed
by later generations, even if for wholly different reasons. A classic, then, is something that attains a permanent—though not a
fixed—position of prominence. It has enough depth to appeal to
the differing sensibilities of successive periods.

A work's aesthetic appeal need not by tempered by a reader's
ideological dissent with its creator; its value lies in the emotional
and cognitive effect on the reader moving through the text line
by line, an effect evoked by the amalgam of style and substance
that abides in the work itself. My logical break with Milton's
unique theology, for instance, need not diminish my engagement with *Paradise Lost*. Each individual will make associations
with the words on the page, and these associations will vary as
widely as the number of individuals. Over time, as each experiences the world and hones his understanding, the words of true
literature can take on power and deeper shades of meaning. On
revisiting a certain item with an augmented perspective, the familiar elements of the narrative give us a foothold to slowly ap-
prehend and assimilate things we did not previously recognize or
experience (Wellek and Warren 253). Enduring literature must
thus possess *multivalence*—ambiguity, alternate meanings, multiple types of emotional value. This may manifest in subordinate
features like diction, syntax, prosody, and more importantly at

higher levels such as imagery, theme, or tone. Books of lasting value are complex at both lower and upper levels.

English philosopher Bernard Bosanquet distinguishes "easy beauty" from "difficult beauty." The latter may confound enjoyment when some aspect of the artwork (for example, its intricacy) is mismatched with some aspect of the observer (imagination, experience, or effort). This mismatch will cause, at least temporarily, inability to appreciate the artwork. Wellek and Warren extend the notion of difficult beauty, proposing that the "unorthodox" elements of literature are pivotal to its enduring achievement. Readers, they propose,

> "realize" the words and what they symbolize only when [the words] are freshly and startlingly put together. Language must be "deformed," i.e., stylized . . . before readers attend to it. . . . So [Russian structuralist] Viktor Shklovsky speaks of poetry as "making it new," "making it strange." . . . There is no aesthetic norm, says [Czech linguist Jan] Mukařovský, for it is the essence of the aesthetic norm to be broken. (Wellek and Warren 252)

But no style stays strange; the effect wears off, so to speak. As literary history moves on and audiences evolve, a particular text may lose and perhaps regain its strangeness. The Lovecraftian approach—diluted by re-reading and by the glut of inferior imitations—can lose its tang. But the astute can later return to it and see fresh aspects, not more things of the same kind but "new levels of meaning, new patterns of association."

Literary recognition is not one-dimensional. There are numerous factors: book sales; inclusion in anthologies, curricula, and textbooks; approval by popular commentators, academics, book reviewers (and in Lovecraft's case, by cultists).[2] Likewise,

---

2. The ultra-loyal "cultist" mentality regarding Lovecraft goes all the way back to the 1930s, and is the inverse phenomenon to the ultra-hostile anti-Lovecraft faction. As early as 1945, W. Paul Cook, who knew HPL as a close friend and amateur colleague, tried to conduct a cultist intervention: "As one of the idolaters writes me: 'Lovecraft is almost a god to me.' Irreparable harm is being done to Lovecraft by indiscriminate and even unintelligent praise, by lack of unbiased and intelligent criticism, and by a warped sense of what is due him in the way of publication of his works." "A Plea for Lovecraft," *Ghost* No. 3 (May 1945); rpt. in Joshi, *A Weird Writer in Our Midst* 148.

authors may succeed or fail on various measures: meaningful findings from critical exegesis, judgment of pure formal value, broad awareness, and so on.

A book may be said to rise and fall based upon two external sets of factors. The first is the circumstances of its creation and dissemination. This includes the conditions of the creator's life, his community of advocates, and his publication history. The second is the readership—its characteristics and culture. These two sets of factors interact to drive a book's reception, which waxes or wanes based upon their confluence.

To achieve lasting awareness, a writer must have advocates; he may also benefit from having antagonists. (At times it seems that Lovecraft's foes have done as much to keep his name alive as his friends.)[3] Jane Tompkins and others have documented how the contingencies of an author's life and literary environment conspire to help or hinder his fiction's success during his career and after. Tompkins uses Nathaniel Hawthorne as a case study. Hawthorne had several prominent advocates—Poe, Longfellow, and Melville all made favorable public comment—and by sheer luck, other less prominent advocates with publishing connections. Also vital to his reputation were the predicates surrounding the genesis of *The Scarlet Letter* (1850). Hawthorne's prospective publisher wanted a novel and advised him to take something—anything—and expand it to book length. Hawthorne retrieved his jottings about a former place of employment (the Custom-House) and used them as a framing device for the rest; the resulting novel was an immense boost to his academic and popular ascent.

Lovecraft found little commercial demand for his unique brand of fiction; *Weird Tales* turned out to be almost his sole outlet. *Weird Tales* (and pulp magazines in general) commanded

---

3. Some devotees of Wallace Stevens (1897–1955) run a website called "The Friends & Enemies of Wallace Stevens," which sheepishly explains that the poet's "demeanor at times could rub people the wrong way . . . [S]ome of his co-workers [at the Hartford Accident and Indemnity Company, where he spent forty years as a surety bond attorney and executive] were terrified of entering his office if he was in a bad mood." (www.stevenspoetry.org/stevensabout.htm). Lovecraft, who evidently also rubs a lot of people the wrong way, has benefited by an outstanding semi-official website created and maintained by Donovan K. Loucks, "The H. P. Lovecraft Archive" (www.hplovecraft.com).

little respect, not only for its physical aspect (paper stock with a built-in sell-by date, garish covers) but for the notion that its devotees were socially and economically marginal—young, working-class, uneducated. This audience was considered to be, in Erin A. Smith's phrase, the people who move their lips when they read. According to Smith:

> Many of the "high-class" readers of pulp magazines whom [mystery author] Erle Stanley Gardner occasionally ran across were ashamed of their tastes. They confessed to being readers of *Black Mask* and admitted that they were often so embarrassed about asking for it at the newsstand that they whispered their request. (Smith 23)

The other format in which pulp stories sold well was the paperback, which appeared on the scene at the end of the 1930s with the ascent of Pocket Books. The paperback cost twenty-five cents, about as much as a pulp magazine; it targeted a similar demographic, and went on to largely replace the pulps after World War II. The pulp magazine business and the nascent paperback business had much in common. Paperbacks were looked down upon in the same manner as pulp magazines, did not get reviewed, and were distributed using the same supply chain (newsstands, drugstores, train stations, bus depots, and the like). But over time the dynamic changed for the better, as the physical process of getting a book in front of the public evolved. By the 1970s, the paperback format had repositioned itself to address the mainstream; and a torrent of softcovers from Panther, Ballantine, and others surged out to consumers.

The state of copyright is likewise an external variant that can stifle a book's dissemination and thus its level of acceptance. Until recently, Lovecraft copyright has been notoriously convoluted.[4] Arkham House, for all the benefit it provided by bridging

---

4. There seems to be no up-to-date and definitive status of copyright information related to Lovecraft, but there is unverified information on the Internet. One extensive item is Chis Karr, "The Black Seas of Copyright: The Arkham House Copyright Hypothesis" (www.aetherial.net/lovecraft/arkham-hypothesis.html). Elsewhere Chaosium is said to have somehow trademarked the phrase "The Call of Cthulhu."

the fiction's visibility from the *Weird Tales* era to legitimate book publication, also acted as a drag on widespread availability. Founder August Derleth adopted a proprietary (and spurious) attitude regarding who could play in the Lovecraft sandbox. One especially heinous instance is a letter from Derleth to an aspiring writer, Thomas R. Smith (aged fifteen—apparently a real threat to the franchise). Smith had submitted a Mythos pastiche entitled "The Forest of the Ravens." Like the big bully he was, Derleth smugly admonished the youth:

> . . . I should point out that the Mythos and its pantheon of Gods etc. are under copyright and may not be used in fiction without the express permission of Arkham House. We are not niggardly [sic] with such permission, but we do require that stories reach certain standards of excellence; I fear that this story does not.[5]

Largely due to the passage of time, the copyright logjam has been broken. The negative effect is the print-on-demand and digital editions using corrupted texts. The positive effect is that the tales are free to anyone who might be curious as to the provenance of Cthulhu plushie slippers.

The Role of the Readership

Books exist not as a static artifact of the author, but as a collaboration between author and reader. This collaboration has phases. When a book is released it has a certain interest by virtue of being new; but this appeal fades; it may go up or down as popular attitudes and values change or other circumstances (e.g., a film adaptation) dictate. Prior to the World Wars, fans of Rudyard Kipling or Edgar Rice Burroughs were certainly not searching for deeper meaning. John Steinbeck and Sinclair Lewis, conversely, reflect an interest in more than a cracking good yarn. With the global conflicts at least temporarily behind them, consumers as a group grew reflective, or perhaps more sophisticated. Munchausen adventures, Horatio Alger rags-to-riches bromides, and hairbreadth escapes receded in the face of irony,

---

5. "What Is the Cthulhu Mythos? A Panel Discussion," *Lovecraft Studies* No. 14 (Spring 1987), 17.

existentialism, disjunctive narration, and other increasingly subtle approaches.

Tompkins illustrates the phenomenon of a changing readership in her case study of Hawthorne. Nineteenth-century admirers liked his stories for the "repose" and "wistful tranquility" found in vignettes such as "A Rill from the Town Pump" or "Little Annie's Ramble," and seemed indifferent to the conundrums of "Wakefield" and "My Kinsman, Major Molineux." Hawthorne survived the cultural changes, and later generations picked up on these deeper levels of meaning. Similarly, Mark Twain was progressively repositioned from a cracker-barrel humorist like Artemus Ward to a cynical dialectician asking "What Is Man?" and expostulating on free will and psychological egoism. Herman Melville went from a purveyor of risqué South Sea adventures to a metaphysical inquirer on the nature of illusion.

E. E. Kellett draws an analogy between physical taste (how the palate reacts to flavors such as bitter, savory, sweet) and literary taste (how a person does or does not enjoy a work of art). Of literary taste, he writes: "[T]he pleasures and pains are registered and recalled in memory, compared, and analyzed . . . True [literary] taste . . . is thus [Wordsworth's] "emotion recollected in tranquility." . . . The moment you begin to *realize* your enjoyment, but not before, you are exercising taste." But literary taste, like the physical palate, need not seek out only the sweet, or even the pleasant. The appeal may

> contain an element of pungency and the pleasure involve[d] arises from a slight irritation. Such tastes are the saline, the alkaline, the sour, the astringent, the fiery, the acrid.. . . Often, they are "acquired" tastes: they demand considerable use before the initial repulsion is first overcome and then transformed into liking. . . . Many will recall . . . the repulsion they felt on first approaching the style of Sterne, Carlyle, Meredith, or any other astringent, difficult, or eccentric author. (Kellett 11)

But the taste is worth the trouble of acquisition for those who can manage a period of discomfort, or perhaps exasperation.

The Famous and the Forgotten:
"Sinister, and Possibly Disastrous"

Around 1870 advances in public education, combined with improved methods of printing and distribution, had broadened the audience for books and magazines. However, as Jay Hubble remarks, "the increase was unfortunately chiefly on the lower intellectual level." In the late nineteenth century good taste reached its nadir. Hubble assays the impact on the fortunes of writers. In 1887, New York literary weekly magazine *The Critic* examined "The Comparative Popularity of Authors" based on regional book sales. Ranked at number one—by a large margin—was the writer E. P. Roe. No, not E. A. Poe: Edward Payson Roe (1838–1888) was a Presbyterian minister and novelist, enjoying the remarkable success of his recent novel *He Fell in Love with His Wife* (1886) (Hubble 80–82).

Similar aberrations show in other surveys in the period of transition from one cohort of readers to another around the turn of the century. Initially the reputation of current stalwarts such as Thoreau, Twain, and Whitman is shaded by the dire fare of James Whitcomb Riley and the "Fireside Poets" (the very same Holmes, Lowell, and Longfellow whose remains, literary and otherwise, were consumed by ghouls in Lovecraft's "Pickman's Model" [1926]). The *Critic* took another temperature in 1893, polling subscribers to select "The Best Ten American Books." The top three books, each garnering over 400 votes, were revealed in June: Emersons *Essays*, Hawthorne's *The Scarlet Letter*, and Longfellow's *Poems*. Frances Burnett's *Little Lord Fauntleroy* and similar tours de force crowded out Melville and even Poe. The latter did not show, even in the bottom ranks of "Miscellaneous Other." Edmund Gosse (an English literary man who supported Ibsen, Yeats, and Joyce) stated in the *Critic's* letter column that the absence of Poe was "extraordinary and sinister. If I were an American, I should be inclined to call it disastrous" (Hubble 88–89).

Eventually the lesser stars of earlier times (such as James Fenimore Cooper and William Cullen Bryant) finally began to fade. Yet, even after 1900, figures considered non-negotiable today still did not have a stable reputational foothold in such surveys and related contexts. As late as 1919, Melville was absent from *A History of American Literature* by Percy H. Boynton.[6] Eventually the "modern literature" of the 1920s ushered out the old guard altogether, making space for newcomers such as Sinclair Lewis and Sherwood Anderson.

The First World War turned the whole scheme completely upside down; by 1931, journalist William Allen White could lament in the *Bookman:* "When the popular fiction of the last quarter of the old century was written and published, I read it. I enjoyed it. It seemed . . . splendid and beautiful. . . . Now, as I reread those old books, I find their charm as vanished. The vividness, the truth and the glamour of the pages have gone dead and run drab and saddened" (229). White identified Ambrose Bierce and Stephen Crane as insurgents from the 1890s whose fiction had made it unscathed into the era of James Joyce.

Why Lovecraft Persists—at Least for the Moment

When examining how Lovecraft came out on top of the literary heap, it is illuminating to consider his progress to relative to possibly analogous authors who did not. There is no exact parallel, but a few names suggest themselves. Of figures once held in high esteem, James Branch Cabell was a non-realistic writer with a flamboyant style. Among those of humbler provenance, why not Clark Ashton Smith or Robert E. Howard? Could it be that Lovecraft's tales are somehow more accessible? Or is it due to Lovecraft's metaphysical foundation in a seemingly chaotic and indifferent universe?

An essential but little-cited Lovecraft item here is the set of essays called *In Defence of Dagon* (1921). To a skeptical group of amateur journalists, he explained that his approach was neither realistic nor romantic. He was a writer of a "third way," which he labels "imaginative literature."

6. Lovecraft commented favorably on *Moby-Dick* (1851) in a letter of January 1925; remarkably, by 1931 he would write: "Poe's main faults were simply those of his age . . . but he had, behind these, a solid genius shared by no other American then or since with the very possible exception of Whitman & Melville, & the less certain exception of Mark Twain." HPL to Elizabeth Toldridge (25 January 1931); *Letters to Elizabeth Toldridge* 172.

Fiction falls generally into three major divisions; romantic, realistic, and imaginative. The first is for those who value action and emotion for their own sake; who are interested in striking events which conform to a preconceived artificial pattern. ... Romanticists are persons who on the one hand scorn the realist who says that moonlight is only reflected wave-motion in aether; but who on the other hand sit stolid and unmoved when a *fantaisiste* tells them that the moon is a hideous nightmare eye—watching ... ever watching. ... [T]he realism which rules the public today is for those who are intellectual and analytical rather than poetical or emotional. ... It has the virtue of being close to life, but has the disadvantage of sinking into the commonplace ... Both romanticism and realism have the common quality of dealing almost wholly with the objective world—with *things* rather than with *what things suggest.* ... Romanticism calls on emotion, realism on pure reason; both ignore *the imagination,* which groups isolated impressions into gorgeous patterns and finds strange relations and associations among the objects of visible and invisible Nature. (CE 5.47)

He continues with a kind of aesthetic manifesto:

The imaginative writer devotes himself to art in its most essential sense. It is not his business to fashion a pretty trifle to please the children, to point a useful moral, to concoct superficial "uplift" stuff for the mid-Victorian hold-over, or to rehash insolvable human problems didactically. He is the painter of moods and mind-pictures—a capturer and amplifier of elusive dreams and fancies—a voyager into those unheard-of lands which are glimpsed through the veil of actuality but rarely, and only by the most sensitive. He is one who not only sees objects, but follows up all the bizarre trails of associated ideas which encompass and lead away from them. ... [H]e exists not for praise, nor thinks of his readers. His only goal is to paint the scenes that pass before his eyes. (CE 5.47–48)

This passages is, I think, key to understanding both Lovecraft's value and his appeal. He rejected realism, including recent developments in local color lead by Sarah Orne Jewett. He also rejected the romantic and post-romantic, including the kind of fantasy that Clark Ashton Smith later wrote. Lovecraft was left with his own especial technique of internal analysis. He found the instruments for probing and documenting his own consciousness using the language of symbolism. Leveraging the aestheticism of Poe and Wilde, he developed an art divorced from didacticism and ethical significance. He was devoted entirely to his vision, striving to embody it with perfection of form and complexity of technique. Over time he succeeded: his tales become progressively more intricate and layered. It is this complexity and ambiguity, rather than the hewing to realism or romanticism, that produced other outstanding American literature of the period, and, I believe, that distinguishes Lovecraft's work. His concerns are not transitory. They do not involve boy meets girl who meets other boy, strong-jawed heroes, pageantry, or battle scenes. They speak to two fundamental issues—the unknown of the external world, and the isolation of existing inside a human mind. Cabell was a topical satirist, Smith was a post-romantic, and Howard was an action writer.

Darwin's theory of evolution, Frazer's anthropological account of the religious sense, and Haeckel's notion of humanity as a trivial incident in a mechanistic cosmos—as well as the widespread advent of technology and the Great War—created the need for a new basis in art. Lovecraft early settled on the creation of what he called *non-supernatural cosmic art* (SL 3.295). He wished to present phenomena that were possible *supplements rather than contradictions* to the sciences—non-Euclidean geometry, quantum physics and atomic indeterminacy, multiple dimensions and alternate universes, curved space-time—in a new manner while exploring their implications for the human psyche.

Lovecraft's renascence indicates that in addition to his substance, there is something compelling—positive or negative—about his style. His language is (in the term used by Wellek and Warren) "deformed." His instantly identifiable idiom "makes it new." It lends the open-minded a sense of enlargement, a realization of an increase of power. For many, Lovecraft is evocative; but for others he merely provokes. As Kellett states:

> [T]he taste for the grotesque is a sophisticated taste. It postulates a knowledge of the conventional rules of the art in question and a determination to gain an effect by violating them . . .

The spectator, again, to appreciate the irony, must have formed a fair conception of the rules that are being laughed at. He will otherwise be simply bewildered and find none of the awkward pleasure which the artist means to give him. (221–22)

This lack of appreciation can even rise to the level of "repulsion." This must be what underlies the odd affect of *personal affront* conveyed by Edmund Wilson, Charles Baxter, and online chat room dwellers when experiencing Lovecraft. Kellett's description of our reaction to "the grotesque writer" could well have been written to describe this specific phenomenon: "We do not *quite* like him; and unless we feel that he is a man of genius, whose message is in itself worth hearing, we glance at his work for a moment, taste its peculiar flavor . . . and pass on" (*Fashion in Literature* 221–22). (I have noticed that at times the offended parties recover and go on to become Lovecraft supporters.)

The "split decision" regarding Lovecraft's worth began as early as the publication of "Dagon" in the amateur press (1919). For now, the group that "gets it" have an edge on the group that insists the writer was merely foolish and incompetent. The latter are impervious to any other conclusion, including the suggestion that Lovecraft was technically capable of playing it straight relative to his "purple prose" and "invisible whistling octopi."[7] If at age thirty-nine Lovecraft could expunge the eighteenth-century mannerisms of Alexander Pope from his verse and write *Fungi from Yuggoth* (1929–30), he surely could have written stories conventional enough for Edmund Wilson to endorse and the *Saturday Evening Post* to print. Happily, he could not be bothered to do so.

The *Recognition of H. P. Lovecraft* does a fine job of tracing these various circumstances around the author and his tales. Lovecraft was fortunate to have an encouraging community during much of his life. This started as a youth. Family and neighbors were the audience for his hectographed journals on science; in 1906 he had a weekly astronomy column in the *Pawtuxet Val-*

---

7. Paraphrasing Edmund Wilson, "Tales of the Marvellous and the Ridiculous," *New Yorker* (24 November 1945); rpt. *Classics and Commercials: A Literary Chronicle of the Forties* (1950).

ley Gleaner; he wrote columns for the Providence *Tribune* (1906–08), Providence *Evening News* (1914–18), and *Asheville* [NC] *Gazette-News* (1915). In 1913–14 he became a minor celebrity in the letter column of the Munsey magazines *Argosy* and *All-Story Weekly,* with a dozen appearances over a couple of years; beginning 1914 he was a prominent amateur journalist; and beginning 1924 he was lauded by the constituencies of *Weird Tales.*

Lovecraft's imaginary cosmogony (now called the Cthulhu Mythos) was extensible and equivocal rather than prescribed and defined, and it became a cooperative among a community of advocates. His immense correspondence served as a kind of clearing-house of ideas and cemented him as literary presence with this group. He had up to 100 correspondents concurrently, of whom a high proportion were young people; these sustained his presence during the low ebb of interest during the 1940s and 1950s until it flared up again in the 1960s. In the "Golden Age" science fiction pulps, for instance, Lovecraft's name was common coin in letter columns, the implication being that subscribers would be familiar with him.[8] In addition to the fans, Lovecraft inspired an emerging group of science fiction writers who grew up with *Weird Tales.* This took varied forms, from the subtle (Fritz Leiber) to the ridiculous (C. Hall Thompson and other pasticheurs).

One obscure instance of Lovecraft's hovering presence is the case of Richard S. Shaver (1907–1985), a welder from the Midwest who spent intermittent time in psychiatric facilities. Shaver achieved notoriety after the Second World War as the reporter of "true" adventures (printed primarily in *Amazing Stories*) involving an ancient civilization that filled earth's caverns with mind-control machines. Shaver's stories were promoted as "The Shaver Mystery," a kind of bargain-basement Cthulhu Mythos (if one can imagine such a thing). The audience was conversant enough with Lovecraft to pick up the influence: in the May 1948 *Fantastic Adventures,* a subscriber wrote in that "Shaver did come pretty close to matching H. P. Lovecraft in his 'Slaves Of

8. Much of this material is also collected in *A Weird Writer in Our Midst.*

The Worm' in the February issue." The editor replied: "Your comparison of Shaver's work to that of the master of mood, Lovecraft, is interesting. . . . We're inclined to agree with you." Five months later, Lovecraft's name popped up again when his Providence friend Muriel Eddy wrote in to endorse the comparison.[9]

Similarly, when interest in Lovecraft was somewhat fallow later in the century, he was boosted by the emergence of Chaosium's *Call of Cthulhu* role-paying game (RPG) and the enthusiastic community that resulted. Released in 1981, it saw seven updates over the next three decades. years. "Many [Lovecraft] fans," says Justin Mullis, "testify to being first introduced to the Mythos via . . . *Call of Cthulhu,* and . . . the game remains one of the primary channels for gaining new converts."[10] (Indeed, conventions of the period saw Lovecraft students outnumbered by Lovecraft gamers.) The advent of the RPG proved a tipping point, ushering in the present epoch in which Lovecraft is often known but not read. Much of the gamer community remains unfamiliar with the source material (so too with the bulk of online Lovecraft "authorities"). Even among book-buyers, there is an intractable contingent for whom the stories of Lovecraft and those of Nick Mamatas are pretty much (shall we say) fungible.

Mullis goes on to propose that gaming fandom, like religion, "generate[s] pockets of order . . . as well as spaces of joy and inspiration and a sense of identity for their devotees." He reviews the varied ways Lovecraft fans create "as-if" worlds by seeking out non-Lovecraft Mythos stories, composing pastiches, creating visual art, and performing "ritualistic acts" of play and joking.

---

9. There was little need to speculate: Shaver had already said he was well versed with the source material. In the brief note "Lovecraft and the Deros" (*Vampire,* June 1946) he advised others to "[r]ead Lovecraft's rewrite for a woman friend of his [Zealia Bishop]—'The Mound' in *Beyond the Wall of Sleep* [Arkham House, 1946], quite a long story and as good a picture of the underworld as I ever read." (Deros ["Detrimental Robots"] are diminutive subterraneans who use technology to inflict misfortune on surface-dwellers.)

10. Remarkably, a poll by *Arcane* magazine on the most popular RPGs of all time ranked *Call of Cthulhu* first ahead of *Dungeons & Dragons.* Paul Pettengale, "Arcane Presents the Top 50 Roleplaying Games 1996," *Arcane* 14 (Christmas 1996): 25–35.

He proposes that the Mythos is popular because it helps people "escape from reality while simultaneously not denying it." It is as reasonable a guess as any, for it is otherwise impossible to account for the range of Mythos toys, music, videos, memes, sporting goods, jewelry, home décor, drinkware, herbal tea, and India Pale Ale.

At minimum, all that swag further confirms that Lovecraft answers a need of the current moment. Roger Luckhurst, editor of Lovecraft in the Oxford World's Classics, ventured to say that the author is speaking anew to a world that feels on the brink of catastrophic change.[11] Cthulhu has become what cultural commentator Mark Dery calls a "Zeitgeist Mascot."[12] Today the polarization around Lovecraft is mostly about the man rather than his tales. People cannot seem to separate the two. Lovecraft's similarities to Poe are extended here. The work of the latter, for decades after his death, was banished because the writer was seen as a drunk and a reprobate. Eventually people realized that even if this was the case, it had no bearing on the experience of reading "The Fall of the House of Usher." Likewise, one may easily stipulate Lovecraft the man was racist; but this need not diminish the power of "The Colour out of Space."

"To Him Who Shal Come After": Enter Joshi

Literary critics can do nothing to rehabilitate the man, but can help us better appreciate the fiction. A critic is one who is sensitive to a variety of nuances in a text—cadence, sentence structure, vocabulary—and an ability to express clearly the elements that it uses to evoke experience. He or she merely facilitates receptiveness, so we can better sense the conveyance of the text. We may become aware of irony, or distinguish between the author and the narrative voice, or observe subtle connections that inform and edify. S. T. Joshi's efforts help enrich the interested

---

11. Roger Luckhurst, "Lovecraft Resurgent," *OUPblog.* www.blog.oup.com/2016/10/lovecraft-resurgent.

12. Mark Dery, "Kraken Rising: How the Cephalopod Became Our Zeitgeist Mascot," *H+ Magazine*, May 27, 2010. www.hplusmagazine. com/2010/05/24/kraken-rising-how-cephalopod-became-our-zeitgeist-mascot.

reader. They go beyond explicating a book, and make bold to offer a conclusion on its success. Such judgment is not just a blunt "rating," but follows from systematic appraisal and analytical comparison. It is not an unconsidered reflex, but a reasoned—one might, recalling Poe, even say *ratiocinative*—assessment.

At times, it appears that Joshi is almost as misunderstood as Lovecraft. The former is a polemicist in the manner Poe the critic, whose nickname was "the Tomahawk man."[13] This is not a bad thing, but requires fortitude to stay the course. As H. L. Mencken wrote in 1921 regarding the state of literary criticism in the United States:

> One of the most hopeful symptoms of the new Aufklärung [age of Enlightenment] in the Republic [i.e., the U.S.] is the revival of *acrimony* in criticism—the renaissance of the doctrine that aesthetic matters are important. . . . In the days when American literature was showing its first vigorous growth, the native criticism was extraordinarily violent and even vicious. . . . The typical critic of [this] era was Poe . . . [who] carried on his critical jihads with such ferocity that he often got into lawsuits, and sometimes ran no little risk of having his head cracked. He regarded literary questions as exigent and momentous. . . . When he encountered a book that seemed to him to be bad, he attacked it almost as sharply as a Chamber of Commerce would attack a fanatic preaching free speech. . . . His opponents replied in the same Berserker manner. Much of Poe's surviving ill-fame, as a drunkard and deadbeat, is due to their inordinate denunciations of him. They were not content to refute him; they constantly tried to dispose of him altogether. (Mencken 440)

Poe died under mysterious conditions, but not from being beaten and robbed by a writer he reviewed. Probably.

---

13. First depicted by writer Augustine J. H. Duganne (1823–1884) and illustrator Octavius C. Darley (1822–1888) in "Edgar Allan Poe," *Holden's Dollar Magazine* (3 January 1849): 22.

From a distance the critic Joshi sprang forth fully formed; but from the *Journals*, we learn that he is a combination of nature and nurture. He had talent and disposition, complemented by an environment that included parents who were academics (professors of mathematics and economics). These things conspired such that, from early on, Joshi was confident he could succeed with his Lovecraft project, and aware of the logistics involved. It was a unique blend of ability and alacrity.

Relative to the need or advisability of publishing the *Journals*, Joshi again addresses the potential questions up front: "I am not prepared to defend myself from the accusation that the publication of my journals is anything but an exercise in narcissism; but I hope that some other countervailing elements might be found in the hundreds of thousands of words I jotted down at odd moments at this time." They do illuminate the journey to recognition. As Joshi was collating the definitive text for Lovecraft fiction, pre-digital, he lugged around 1,000 pages typescript for years, finding and recording new variants, making emendations, and retyping each story multiple times. This was the merest fillip. Nowhere in the *Journals* does he even bother to mention the endless hours spent in library basements filling out request slips, scrolling through blurred microfilm of periodicals, and standing in front of copying machines accompanied by $20 in dimes. Though early on Joshi found resolute fellow-travelers in the form of David E. Schultz and a few others, there was no imprimatur of legitimacy in sight to affirm the broader worth of the effort.[14]

---

14. In may have been appropriate for Joshi in *Recognition* to provide more space to a couple of other people who have (as he has) made a financial as well as a personal commitment to Lovecraft—specifically during periods (e.g., 1970–80) where no one of any legitimacy wanted anything to do with HPL. It is easy to be a Lovecraft enthusiast, but few have been so enthusiastic (I might even say courageous) enough to "put their money where their mouth is." Of course, Derleth and Donald Wandrei funded the print run (1,268 copies) of the epoch-making *The Outsider and Others* (1939); it took them four years at $5.00 a copy to claw back their investment. Robert M. Price did outstanding work as the editor of *Crypt of Cthulhu: A Pulp Thriller and Theological Journal* (more than 100 issues, published as frequently as eight times a year, 1981–2001; relaunched in 2017), mostly funded with his personal income. But the unsung

Having rounded up the primary sources, Joshi's next challenge was to ingest and synthesize the content into coherent shape, so he could assess its merits and defects, consider it in literary context, and create a synthesis of his findings. And then, perhaps most difficult of all, the composition of the essays.

The *Journals* began as an assignment from a middle school English teacher in Muncie, Indiana. The first installment sees Joshi through high school graduation. The second encompasses his time at Brown University, where he secured a B.A. (1980) and M. A. (1982) in Classics. The third covers the years at Princeton University (1982–84) working toward a Ph.D. in Classical Philosophy, and the initial years of employment in New York City.

By seventeen, Joshi was already making serious efforts toward legitimate critical publication. In the summer of 1975 he wrote a 20,000-word treatise called *H. P. Lovecraft: A Critical Analysis*. Soon this initiative was joined by *A Collection of H. P. Criticism* (published in 1980 as *H. P. Lovecraft: Four Decades of Criticism*). The *Critical Analysis* was accepted for publication by a small press but never saw print, in part because Joshi was not of legal age to execute a contract. That fall, he undertook a letter-writing campaign to academic and amateur publishers. Among the latter was R. Alain Everts of Madison, Wis., in the vanguard of Lovecraft biography and publisher of the Strange Company. Everts was forming the Howard Phillips Lovecraft (yclept Necronomicon) Amateur Press Association, enlisting a select group with a mission to accumulate significant essays for publication in book form; he invited Joshi to join, and put him in touch with like-minded individuals. One was Dr. Dirk W. Mosig, a Lovecraft scholar who taught psychology at Georgia Southwestern College; he would become pivotal in supporting the young man's progress. Mosig in turn put the newcomer in touch Schultz, Peter Cannon, and others. Just prior to high school graduation Joshi received an offer from Kent State University Press to compile a new bibliography of Lovecraft.

---

hero of the 1970–80 era—with significant financial "skin in the game" relative to Lovecraft's appeal—was Marc A. Michaud, founder and publisher of Necronomicon Press. While a handful of the 50 or so books he published during 1977–87 were merely photocopied, much of the printing had to be paid for up front.

Every adolescent has difficult phases of adjustment, but Joshi's moments of self-doubt in *Journals,* Volume 1, are remarkably infrequent. In August 1977 he muses momentarily upon

> the precariousness of my position—what publisher would issue a book of high criticism by a 19-year-old undergraduate? I must hide the fact of my age to publishers, else I shall not be dealt with at all. Yet am I capable of high criticism? Do I really belong here? I don't yet—I'm too ignorant, and the knowledge is coming too slowly. I am forced into pretense—the collection of Lovecraft Criticism will create only the illusion that I'm a formidable scholar.

Mosig urged Joshi to apply to Brown University, where the Lovecraft papers were domiciled. This would be an intimidating idea for any prospective college student, but neither seemed to have any qualms as to the outcome.[15] The applicant was accepted and matriculated—not merely for the academic credential, but for the opportunity to make his project definitive.

Journals, Volume 2, encompasses the period in Providence at the University, 1977 to 1982. The freshman gets a running start, translating (from the French) Maurice Lévy's excellent *Lovecraft: A Study in the Fantastic* (published 1988 by Wayne State University Press), writing a Lovecraft radio script (forerunner of the podcast, apparently), and studying a wide variety of foundational matter in addition to his Classics textbooks. In a burst of audacity, Joshi and local aspiring publisher Marc A. Michaud seize on the idea of publishing Lovecraft's juvenile fiction and poetry. They blithely approach Robert Harrall, administrator of the Lovecraft estate, and ask him if they could do so. Harrall says yes. 1977 saw Joshi's debut between book covers: the forward to Necronomicon Press's *H. P. Lovecraft: Writings in* The Tryout.

Following Joshi as he obtains undergraduate and graduate degrees from an Ivy League school *as a sidelight to researching Lovecraft* is (to borrow an adjective from him) imperishable. From his advent to Providence until the acceptance of *H. P. Lovecraft: Four Decades of Criticism* by the Ohio University Press,

---

15. Acceptance proved to be no issue; Joshi even declined admission to one other Ivy League school.

he submits to publishers no fewer than thirty proposals for the book. Compiling the content, he fires off a request to Paul Buhle, eminent scholar of radicalism, for permission to reprint "Dystopia as Utopia: Howard Phillips Lovecraft and the Unknown Content of American Horror Literature" (*Minnesota Review*, Spring 1976). Buhle happened to be local; and he quickly agrees, phoning Joshi to suggest another item. Similarly, Joshi canvassed prominent Lovecraftians by mail asking for contributions and assistance. He was welcomed, and soon was soon at the center of a pre-Internet Lovecraft network.

A typical day of this period involves typing Lovecraft texts, Lovecraft research at the library, reading Greek, reading for pleasure, and then writing letters. Joshi barely alludes to those occasions that loom large for collegians—exams. By 1978 he has twelve books completed or in progress—put another way, twelve more books than other twenty-year-olds. In that year we see the first mention of *The Collected Works of H. P. Lovecraft.* He had mapped out an edition in thirteen volumes (three of original fiction, two of revisions, two of poetry, and six of essays). Never one to shoot low, all the items were to be annotated along with textual apparatus.[16]

He continues to be confident in both the merit of Lovecraft and his own abilities—usually. In a rare moment of hesitation (1978) he confesses: "I want to achieve certain very specific goals and am frantically trying to meet them; but I am haunted by the hideous possibility that my striving may be comically vain." A year later he entertains a concern that future scholars "will at once admire my multi-faceted talents and achievements and be repelled by my grievous flaws of character." But this time uncertainty evaporates, apparently of the instant and for good, as he adds laconically: "I wish I had bought a fine-point rather than a medium-point fountain pen."

---

16. Joshi shared his typewritten copy of the draft prospectus for the *Collected Works* with me in New York City, in November 1982. I was in my early 20s, and Joshi was only a couple of years older. I was impressed, of course, but had only a vague concept that the goal seemed daunting, and had no concept as to how anyone might make it happen. It has. I mention this because it is illustrative of how, from a very young age, Joshi was operating on a much different plane from that of the "average citizen."

Letter-writing was increasingly complemented by social time, and the local "Providence Pals" (Michaud, Cannon, Jason Eckhardt, Ken Neily, etc.) enjoyed visits from a regional contingent (Don and Mollie Burleson, Robert M. Price, etc.). A few of these were enlisted as scholars whom Joshi mentored; he was remarkably generous in sharing hard-won primary research such as unpublished letters. *Journals*, Volume 3, continues the saga with Joshi as New Yorker and employee of several literary-related firms.

As if anticipating that merely learning of this diligent activity might be exhausting, the narrative is punctuated by aphorisms from wits including Ben Hecht, Gore Vidal, Oscar Wilde; Lucan, Sallust, Seneca, Pascal, Emerson, Nietzsche, Carl Van Vechten, T. S. Eliot, Wyndham Lewis, Flaubert, Hermann Hesse, André Maurois, and others. One little-known aspect, Joshi's interest in classical music, is shown in detail—initially as listener and student, he eventually becomes a player and even a conductor. There are, too, amusing moments. In June 1976 Joshi recounts an anecdote that will evoke a smile from anyone who has been involved with pretty much any kind of hobby.

> Another most interesting day, though not as far as my Lovecraft books are concerned. I met John H. Stanley at the John Hay today. He was not at all as I had imagined him, proving to be youngish, bearded, and of keen mind, where I had pictured a portly, fiftyish, slow-witted chap. He seemed quite up on modern Lovecraft scholarship, though I was irritated when he expressed dubiety [*sic*] of Prof. Mosig's abilities. Surely Dirk is by far the world's greatest Lovecraftian.

In fandom, apparently the backbiting exceeds even the logrolling. Another entertaining episode is a month-long 1977 visit to Joshi's dorm room by another (less fastidious) Lovecraft scholar. This individual continually blasts *Die Walküre* on the stereo and then apparently damages Joshi's prized possession—his IBM Selectric. Joshi dryly observes that he is "decidedly the most obnoxious human that I've ever had the misfortune to meet." But the transgressor commits one final outrage: "He slurps his tea!!"

Recognition or Respect?

Moving from the *Journals* to *The Recognition of H. P. Lovecraft* feels like coming out the far end of a tunnel. By the conclusion of the *Recognition*, it is "mission accomplished." The narrative follows the twists and turns of Lovecraft's fiction from the amateur press to the pulp magazines and then, after the writer's death, to book form via Arkham House and other publishers, fanning out to translations in more than thirty languages. In parallel, we follow the development of criticism and scholarship on Lovecraft. This book is especially noteworthy in how it marks the inflection points, the highs and the lows, of the progression; the next edition might benefit from a chronology or even a visual timeline.

The watershed came in 2005 when the Library of America—"an independent nonprofit cultural organization founded . . . to preserve our nation's literary heritage by publishing, and keeping permanently in print, America's best and most significant writing"—issued Lovecraft's *Tales*. This prestigious occasion flushed out a number of prominent reviewers, some of whom appeared to want to stuff Lovecraft, as it were, back into his box. Luc Sante in the *New York Review of Books* started by reminding us that Edmund Wilson—whose "bad taste and bad art" pronouncement had seemed to be a stake in the literary heart—was the person who conceived the Library of America:[17]

> In a 1945 review [Wilson] dismissed Lovecraft's stories as hackwork, with a sneer at the magazines for which they were written, *Weird Tales* and *Amazing Stories*, "where . . . they ought to have been left." Lovecraft had been dead for eight years by then, and although his memory was kept alive, . . . his reputation was strictly marginal and did not seem likely to expand.

Sante, whose own (nonfictional) oeuvre reflects a real literary gift, at least admitted that Lovecraft had "unusual and idiosyncratic strengths." In the *New York Times*, Daniel Handler (whose pen name is Lemony Snicket) was not merely skeptical but apparently alarmed. While he notes (as we have seen) that

---

17. Luc Sante, "The Heroic Nerd," *New York Review of Books* (19 October 2006). www.nybooks.com/articles/2006/10/19/the-heroic-nerd.

Lovecraft "is not read as widely as he is regarded," he continues: "frankly it's not difficult to see why."[18]

Another waypoint came about a decade later with Leslie Klinger's *The New Annotated H. P. Lovecraft* (Liveright [an imprint of W. W. Norton], 2014). A review by English professor and novelist Charles Baxter (*NYRB* again) contained a volley of negative comments that is comedic in its crash and clang. He acknowledges that "[w]e don't read books in our late middle age or old age in the same way that we did when we were young." Unfortunately, the implication is that books we enjoy in youth are incapable of enlightening for different reasons at later dates. (What about Ray Bradbury?) Baxter's conclusion that Lovecraft appeals solely to "readers of a certain age" recalls the assessments of Poe by Henry James ("an enthusiasm for Poe is the mark of a decidedly primitive stage of reflection")[19] and Yvor Winters ("it is a matter for astonishment that mature men can be found to take this kind of thing seriously").[20] Baxter admits that Lovecraft's fiction has a powerful effect on "susceptible readers," but then says that this effect had "little to do with its purely literary qualities."[21] I'm not sure what other qualities might be causative, since all we have are words on a page. In a later interview, Baxter admits that he received "a lot of hate mail" regarding his review[22]—not least of which, no doubt, was a withering 18-page broadside by Joshi (published partially in *NYRB* and fully in the *Lovecraft Annual*) whose intensity evokes

---

18. Daniel Handler, "H. P. Lovecraft: Unnatural Selection," *New York Times* (17 April 2005), sec. 7, p. 7.
www.nytimes.com/2005/04/17/books/review/h-p-lovecraft-unnatural-selection.html
19. Henry James, "Baudelaire," in *French Poets and Novelists* (1878; rpt. Freeport, NY: Books for Libraries Press, 1972), 76.
20. Yvor A. Winters, "Edgar Allan Poe: A Crisis in the History of American Obscurantism," *American Literature* 8 (January 1937).
21. Charles Baxter, "The Hideous Unknown of H. P. Lovecraft," *New York Review of Books* (18 December 2014). www.nybooks.com/articles/2014/12/18/hideous-unknown-hp-lovecraft.
22. Jeremiah Chamberlin, "What We Owe Each Other: An Interview with Charles Baxter," *Michigan Quarterly Review* 54, No.4 (Fall 2015).

nothing less than an artillery bombardment.

A few may be surprised at the mild tone Joshi adopts for the bulk of the *Recognition*. A young adult biography of Lovecraft is not abysmal but "serviceable"; of a popular biography there is merely "very little to be said"; a book about Lovecraft and practical black magic is not absurd but "sober, straightforward, and engaging"; a quickie coffee-table book on Lovecraft is "appealing." A heterogeneous group of Internet pundits insist that Lovecraft was not merely a bad writer but also an evil person; instead of wielding the tomahawk, Joshi gently asserts that their case is "not very well argued." He remarks:

> The current obsession with Lovecraft's racial views is itself a product of our times—a result of a multitude of historical and cultural factors that has led some of us to focus single-mindedly on this one element of Lovecraft's life, work, and thought to the exclusion of nearly all others. I daresay it will pass when (or if) our society becomes a little less polarized. One can only hope that, at that time, the full range of Lovecraft's achievement will be appreciated without the current tunnel vision and with a proper understanding of the place of racism—as well as atheism, aesthetic integrity, political rumination, travel, and countless other facets of Lovecraft's personality—in the totality of his work. One does not wish to ascribe base motives for the level of indignation that certain individuals feel on the matter, but one cannot help feeling that there is a liberal dose of virtue signaling going on here, among other features even less flattering.

He even refrains from blasting certain current academic Lovecraft criticism—vague, jargon-filled, and detached from pertinent sources—which is manifestly inferior to many prior contributions, including his own. Specimens of this are type of analysis were collected in *The Age of Lovecraft* (ed. Carl H. Sederholm and Jeffrey Andrew Weinstock; University of Minnesota, 2016)[23] and *New Critical Essays on H. P. Lovecraft* (ed. David

---

23. Speaking of logrolling, a back-cover blurb for this book by Darryl Hattenhauer, Associate Professor of English, Arizona State University claims that "This anthology is the most significant book on Lovecraft ever written." I would insist that it most certainly is not, but the sheer illogic in the very nature

Simmons; Palgrave Macmillan, 2013). Of groundbreaking Love-craft scholars, only Joshi (who is non-negotiable in such set-tings) and Donald R. Burleson (still a professor) are represented in these collections; where are Schultz, Cannon, Price, or Ken-neth W. Faig? Too straightforward and pragmatic, apparently. Joshi just comments:

> Other publishers—including a number of academic presses—fostered the growth of Lovecraft criticism, although in many cases their products left much to be desired. Over the last several dec-ades, academic criticism had passed through a succession of fads that proved relatively short-lived: semiotics, structuralism, post-structuralism, deconstruction, and so on. The current fad seems to be a relentless focus on race, class, and gender—in spite of the fact that most academic literary critics are singularly ill-equipped to address these issues in any incisive or informed man-ner, leaving aside the broader issue of whether such work really constitutes literary criticism or is merely amateur sociology.

Publishers Weekly said *The Recognition of H. P. Lovecraft* "bogs down in laundry lists that read more like an annotated bibliog-raphy than a useful guide for the nonacademic."[24] This is (as Joshi himself warns) indeed the case, perhaps by necessity. The challenge is especially evident near the end, with slabs of sec-ondary material breaking off from the narrative, accompanied by an avalanche of unconsolidated items. Again, coming scholars will have to better "summarize the summary."

For Lovecraft, where to from here? Devotees once dreamed of a day that everyone would know who Lovecraft was, a day that "legitimate" scholars would help us understand him. This has largely happened, and regrettably the bar seems to be set both too low (cyber-pontificators) and too high (meaningless academicism). Cthulhu has joined Dracula, Frankenstein, the Wolfman, and the Mummy in the Monster Pantheon.[25] Will the

---

of this claim prevents me.

24. *Publishers Weekly* (31 January 2022). www.publishersweekly.com/9781614 983453.

25. This despite Lovecraft's best—and truly perverse—attempt to make the name "Cthulhu" impossible to pronounce, or even to spell.

future see Lovecraft included in standard textbooks such as *The Norton Anthology of World Literature,* or *The Longman Anthology of World Literature,* or *The Bedford Anthology of World Literature?* Would that we might be here to observe the progress. The vagaries of changing taste guarantee that Lovecraft ultimately will fade away. The virulent anti-Lovecraft contingent will be pleased. But, as usual, we can leave the coda to Lovecraft: "Who knows the end? What has risen may sink, and what has sunk may rise."

Works Cited

Bosanquet, Bernard. *Three Lectures on Aesthetic.* London: Macmillan, 1915.

Foerster, Norman, et al. *Literary Scholarship: Its Aims and Methods.* Chapel Hill: University of North Carolina Press, 1941.

Fulton, Joe B. *Mark Twain under Fire: Reception and Reputation, Criticism and Controversy, 1851–2015.* Rochester, NY: Camden House, 2016.

Hart, James D. *The Popular Book: A History of America's Literary Taste.* New York: Oxford University Press, 1950.

Harman, Graham. *Weird Realism: Lovecraft and Philosophy.* Winchester, UK: Zero Books, 2012.

Hubbell, Jay B. *Who Are the Major American Writers? A Study of the Changing Literary Canon.* Durham, NC: Duke University Press, 1972.

Hutcherson, Dudley R. "Poe's Reputation in England and America, 1850–1909." *American Literature* 14, No. 3 (November 1942): 211–33.

Joshi, S. T. "Charles Baxter on Lovecraft." *Lovecraft Annual* No. 9 (2015): 106–23.

———, ed. *A Weird Writer in Our Midst: Early Criticism of H. P. Lovecraft.* New York: Hippocampus Press, 2010.

Kellett, E. E. *Fashion in Literature: A Study of Changing Taste.* London: Routledge, 1931.

Landsberg, Melvin. "Edmund Wilson's Journals" (review article). *American Studies* 36, No. 2 (Fall 1995): 139–47.

Longfellow, Henry Wadsworth. [Unsigned review of *Twice-Told Tales* by Nathaniel Hawthorne.] *North American Review* 45 (July 1837): 59–73.

Lovecraft, H. P. *Letters to Elizabeth Toldridge and Anne Tillery Renshaw.* Ed. David E. Schultz and S. T. Joshi. New York: Hippocampus Press, 2014.

Lovecraft, H. P. *The New Annotated H. P. Lovecraft.* Ed. Leslie S Klinger. New York: Liveright, 2014.

Mailloux, Steven J. "Evaluation and Reader Response Criticism: Values Implicit in Affective Stylistics." *Style* 10, No. 3 (Summer 1976): 329–43.

Mencken, H. L. "The Critical Process." In *A Mencken Chrestomathy: His Own Selection of His Choicest Writing.* 1949. New York: Knopf, 2021.

Monk, Patricia. "The Shared Universe: An Experiment in Speculative Fiction." *Journal of the Fantastic in the Arts* 2, No. 4 (1990): 7–46.

Mott, Frank Luther. *Golden Multitudes: The Story of Best Sellers in the United States.* New York: Macmillan, 1947.

Mullis, Justin. "Playing Games with the Great Old Ones: Ritual, Play, and Joking within the Cthulhu Mythos Fandom." *Journal of the Fantastic in the Arts* 26, No. 3 (2015): 521–30.

Smith, Erin A. *The Hard-Boiled Writer and the Literary Marketplace.* Philadelphia: Temple University Press, 2000.

Spiller, Robert E. *The Third Dimension: Studies in Literary History.* New York: Macmillan, 1965.

Tompkins, Jane. "Masterpiece Theater: The Politics of Hawthorne's Literary Reputation." *American Quarterly* 36, No. 5 (Winter 1984): 617–42.

Wellek, René, and Austin Warren. *Theory of Literature.* New York: Harcourt, Brace & World, 1942.

White, William Allen. "A Reader in the Eighties and Nineties." *Bookman* 57, No. 3 (November 1930): 229–34.

Wilson, Edmund. *Notebooks and Diaries.* New York: Farrar, Straus & Giroux, 1975–93. 6 vols.

Wolfe, Gary K. "Malebolge, Or the Ordnance of Genre." *Conjunctions* No. 39 (2002): 405–19.

Reviews

ARTHUR S. KOKI. *H. P. Lovecraft: An Introduction to His Life and Writings.* New York: Hippocampus Press, 2022. 280 pp. $25.00 tpb. Reviewed by Ken Faig, Jr.

Arthur S. Koki (1937–1989) originally wrote his M.A. thesis on Lovecraft at Columbia University in 1962. It was one of the earliest academic theses written on Lovecraft, following James Warren Thomas's 1950 M.A. thesis at Brown University. Despite being sixty years old, Koki's thesis has stood the test of time well. To enhance this first published version of his thesis, editors S. T. Joshi and David E. Schultz have added notes to bring Koki's account up to date. (Their footnotes are distinguished from Koki's own by the use of square brackets.) Co-editor Joshi has also written an introduction, whose biographical portion is based largely on a series of accounts published by Marcos Legaria in the Esoteric Order of Dagon amateur press association.

Like Thomas, Koki relied heavily on Lovecraft's letters to his aunts as archived in the Lovecraft Collection at the John Hay Library, but Koki cast a wider net, interviewing and corresponding with many of Lovecraft's friends and relatives, including Sonia Lovecraft Davis and Ethel M. Phillips Morrish. He met in person with many of Lovecraft's New York City associates, including Frank Belknap Long, Samuel Loveman, and Kenneth Sterling, and even turned up lesser-known associates such as Margaret (Sylvester) Ronan. He paid particular attention to the assessment of Lovecraft's work by French scholars.

Even the diehard Lovecraftian will learn new things when reading Koki's thesis. Koki caught a mild case of the Lovecraft collecting bug and owned a number of mementos of the author, perhaps most notably the autograph manuscript of "The Terrible Old Man." Koki also owned Lovecraft's own copy of *Ollendorff's*

New Method of Learning to Read, Write and Speak the Spanish Language, which Lovecraft had purchased on 27 May 1911 and inscribed with his ownership signature. This is a work that editors Joshi and Schultz can probably add to future editions of *Lovecraft's Library.*

Then there is the matter of the cafeteria at the foot of Federal Hill with apple chevron doors which Koki states was frequented by Lovecraft when he resided at 66 College Street. Wilfred B. Talman had introduced Lovecraft to Jake's on Canal Street just north of Market Square, but this establishment was hardly at the foot of Federal Hill and had in any case closed in 1935. Just where Lovecraft transferred his patronage would be interesting to know. While he bought most of his food at downtown markets and at the Calef Market at the corner of North Main and Thomas Streets, he may have dined out more than we know, especially at inexpensive eateries which offered "much for little."

Koki takes a balanced approach to Lovecraft's shortcomings and prejudices. Not everyone admired Lovecraft or agreed with W. Paul Cook that the author emerged from his New York travails "pure as gold." Koki cites one person who knew Lovecraft as a young man who called him "crazy as a bedbug." One would like to know who this was. Some of Lovecraft's early school acquaintances did remark upon his nervous tics. A friend as close as Samuel Loveman posthumously repudiated Lovecraft based on passages in letters shown to him after the author's death. Koki takes all these divergent views into account, but emerges with a balanced view of the man and his work, and a hope that his work will be more widely read and appreciated in the future. While unfavorable opinions of Lovecraft and his work persist, Koki's hope has certainly been fulfilled. The publication of his thesis by Hippocampus Press is certainly one token of the growth of Lovecraft's literary reputation.

Koki's thesis is not really a "reading" of Lovecraft's oeuvre. He highlights works he considers noteworthy or innovative, but neglects others. There are only a few sparse mentions of a story as important as "The Dunwich Horror." The reader looking for a more balanced reading of Lovecraft's works will have to turn to other sources such as Donald R. Burleson's *H. P. Lovecraft: A Critical Study* (Greenwood Press, 1983) or Peter Cannon's *H. P. Lovecraft* (Twayne, 1989). A half-dozen or more other titles could probably be cited, such is the richness of the criticism that has emerged since Koki's writing. While Koki's coverage of the Lovecraft oeuvre is uneven, many of his critical insights are perceptive—e.g., his characterization of *The Dream Quest of Unknown Kadath* as a surrealist work.

I was encouraged to discover that many of Koki's enthusiasms match my own. He pays due respect to Lovecraft's masterpieces of science fiction *At the Mountains of Madness* and "The Shadow out of Time," but is also enthusiastic about "The Shadow over Innsmouth," "The Dreams in the Witch House," and "The Haunter of the Dark" among Lovecraft's later works. Koki and I concur that "The Colour out of Space" was Lovecraft's single most masterful work. However, Koki and I also like *The Case of Charles Dexter Ward* and *The Dream-Quest of Unknown Kadath* among the output of his great creative surge following his return to Providence in 1926. Among Lovecraft's early works, "The Outsider" and "The Rats in the Walls" probably deserve their favor; personally, I also particularly esteem "The Music of Erich Zann" and "He."

Most of Koki's cited influences are sound, although the editors do catch him in a number of anachronisms. Koki believed that Robert W. Chambers's *The King in Yellow* influenced Lovecraft's story "The Festival" (1923), but Lovecraft did not read Chambers's work until 1927. Similarly, Lovecraft wrote "The Tomb" (1917) long before he first read Walter de la Mare's *The Return* (1910; revised editions 1922 and 1945), which Koki detected as an influence. Not every reading of a Lovecraft story by Koki seems wholly sound; for example, he writes of a nonhuman possessing Asenath Waite, but was the possessor not actually her father Ephraim? Koki makes note of Lovecraft's propensity for graphic description of his "monsters," but takes Edmund Wilson to task for suspending disbelief regarding the Great Race while scorning the shoggoths. Both Koki and Wilson agree that "The Colour out of Space" is a masterful story, which according to Wilson prefigured the effects of the atomic bomb.

I think that Koki hits the nail on the head when he attributes Lovecraft's lack of productivity in his final years to the dispiriting effect of rejections. He was willing to accept low pay for revision work because it did not involve the economic or the psychological impact of rejections. Yet Lovecraft remained true to his artistic integrity and refused to write down to pulp standards. When the editor at *Astounding Stories* chopped up *At the Mountains of Madness* to make it more palatable for his readers, Lovecraft protested that he considered his novel unpublished. Nevertheless, he did not refuse his check, which helped to stave off economic disaster in 1936.

I will close with a few random notes evoked by my reading of Koki's thesis.

Koki cites the 1827 date usually claimed by Lovecraft for the arrival of his paternal ancestors in America, although subsequently developed evidence points toward 1831. Of course, it is always possible that some unknown family member arrived earlier as a "first venturer."

Louise Imogen Guiney probably met Susie Phillips through their mutual acquaintance with her neighbors the Banigan sisters, who met Guiney when she and they were students at the Sacred Heart Academy on Smith Hill in Providence in the 1870s.

The diminutive schoolteacher friend of Mrs. Lovecraft who was enjoined by her to stoop down when walking with her young son was in fact Ella L. Sweeney (1870–1945).

As for Lovecraft's sequester following his failure to obtain his high school diploma in 1908, I think that the degree of his isolation has probably been somewhat exaggerated. He took an extended interstate excursion via interurban trolley to celebrate his twenty-first birthday in 1911. He wrote that he spent with relative extravagance until 1915 when the death of Dr. Clark may have first raised the prospect of financial ruin. I suspect he was much in evidence in the bookstores and the movie theatres of downtown Providence during the 1910–15 era. Koki's copy of Heinrich Gottfried Ollendorff's Spanish text is one physical evidence of Lovecraft's spending during this time. During the prior decade, his family bought many newly published astronomy books for their young scion. Of course, the lack of a high school diploma and only a modest aptitude for mathematics probably dispelled any thought of a career as a professional astronomer. In an earlier era, Lovecraft might have found a slot as an observational astronomer or an observatory assistant.

As for the Lovecraft's emergence from his 1908–14 "sequester," Koki mentions that Lovecraft came to the attention of UAPA recruiter Edward F. Daas as a result of a contest. Perhaps this is simply a misrecollection of the "contest" between Lovecraft and Fred Jackson's supporters in the letter columns of *All-Story*. However, it deserves to be mentioned that Lovecraft's first known mention in print in 1905 resulted from his participation in a weather prediction contest.[1] It is likely that the *All-Story* letter column controversy was the principal factor in Lovecraft's discovery by Daas, but it is not impossible that a contest in which Lovecraft participated may have also attracted Daas" interest.

As for Lovecraft's "long and delightful" letters written to his mother when she was confined at Butler Hospital in 1919–21, only one survives. Given the problematical nature of their relationship, it is possible that Susie Lovecraft's doctors advised that meetings with her son be limited. Given the length of Providence winters, I must admit that I am skeptical of the recollection recorded by Winfield Townley Scott that Lovecraft only visited his mother on the hospital grounds, and never within its buildings.

In some cases, I think Koki might have dug a little deeper for sources. The quotation on p. 88 concerns Lovecraft's visit to the Captain Samuel Fowler house in Danvers, Massachusetts. The two old lady curators were lineal descendants of the captain. Also, regarding Jonathan Curwen of *The Case of Charles Dexter Ward*, the notable Curwen family of Salem might have been mentioned.

The stories that Lovecraft married suddenly are worthy of notice. In fact, I think that Lovecraft and his bride-to-be spent several months planning the details of their marriage. One wonders if they were physically intimate when they sat out the 1922

1. See Richard Bleiler, "H. P. Lovecraft's First Appearance in Print," *Lovecraft Annual* No. 14 (2020): 26–36.

New York City NAPA convention in Rockport, Massachusetts. On balance, I believe that the conservative mores of both were such that the probable answer is no.

I would like to know the origin of Koki's assertion that Whipple Phillips's home at Angell and Elmgrove had four negro servants in its heyday. The household was in financial decline by the time of Lovecraft's birth in 1890 and had just one live-in servant (an Irish-born maid) when the 1900 U.S. census was enumerated. Granted that Delilah Townsend was probably serving table for the Phillipses in the 1890s,[2] if there were ever as many as four "inside" servants in the Phillips household, I think it must have been in the 1880s.

Koki remarks upon Susie Lovecraft's "steady disintegration." However, her condition did take several severe downward jogs—at the institutionalization of her husband Winfield Scott Lovecraft in 1893, at the death of her brother-in-law Franklin C. Clark in 1915, and at the death of her brother Edwin E. Phillips in 1918. She was herself institutionalized within four months of the death of her brother in November 1918.

Two Lovecraftian achievements that Koki dreamed of have not yet been realized (to my knowledge). He dreamed of a deluxe illustrated edition of *The Dream-Quest of Unknown Kadath*.[3] Perhaps Kenneth J. Krueger's poorly produced Shroud Press edition (1955) made Koki long all the more for something better. Koki also shared Guillermo del Toro's belief that *At the Mountains of Madness* could be adapted as a film.

Regarding Lovecraft's 1929 divorce petition, I doubt that the judge failed to sign the final decree. It has always been my understanding that Lovecraft himself was the party who failed to sign the return, thereby leaving the matter open. I do not know whether the papers relating to Lovecraft's 1929 divorce petition are public records. If they are, they should certainly be published before too many more years elapse. The editors' note 106 on p. 177 cites the case number.

---

2. She was probably not a "live-in" servant, but lived with her husband William and their young son in their own home on Thayer Street.

3. I believe there have been comic book and animated film adaptations of the novel.

In 1932, Lovecraft did get home from his southern travels before Mrs. Clark expired, although she was unconscious by the time he returned. As for Clark family burials from 1711, they would have been removals from earlier burial grounds, since Swan Point Cemetery was only founded in 1846.

That Lovecraft found Charles Fort's work as exciting as he did is perhaps somewhat problematic, given his rigid adherence to the scientific method. Lovecraft is not known to have explored Fort's work beyond *The Book of the Damned* (1919). Perhaps the sheer weirdness of many of the phenomena reported by Fort—whether true or false—was what appealed to Lovecraft.

The editors doubt that Lovecraft ever encountered Soame Jenyns's *Free Inquiry into the Origin and Nature of Evil* (1757). Nevertheless, Jenyns's speculation that superior beings might be as indifferent to our fortunes as we are to the fortunes of lesser creatures would probably have interested Lovecraft. Given his specialist's knowledge of eighteenth-century literature, it is possible that Lovecraft knew by repute of Jenyns's work. Soame Jenyns (1704–1787) was a Member of Parliament and advocated for the ethical treatment of animals. There was a collected edition of his works in 1790. In 2021, an online reproduction of the 1761 fourth edition of *Free Inquiry* was available at ccel.org/ccel/jenyns/evil/evil.i.html.

Koki notwithstanding, Robert Ervin Howard did not drive into the desert to commit suicide. He shot himself in the driveway of his own home in Cross Plains, Texas.

Out of respect for the author's achievement, editors Joshi and Schultz have limited their notes to only the most significant advances in our understanding since the time Koki wrote. It's only fair that I as a reviewer halt my nit-picking.

Koki wrote one gem of a master's thesis. It extends to some 350 pages in its original typed version on bordered thesis paper. I think that Koki's master thesis was of doctoral dissertation caliber. Its parsimony regarding academic jargon may be more of an advantage than a disadvantage, at least for the general reader. Editors Joshi and Schultz and their publisher Hippocampus Press have finally given Koki's work the presentation it deserves. Hopefully, the influence of Koki's balanced, evidence-based approach to Lovecraft will continue to grow now that it is finally available in published form. I wish I might have been a fly on the wall when Arthur S. Koki was interviewing Frank Belknap Long. It would probably have been a fascinating conversation. But now that his thesis has at last been published, we can all, to a degree, share the fruits of that discussion.

KEN FAIG, JR. *Lovecraftian People and Places*. New York: Hippocampus Press, 2022. 254 pp. $25.00 tpb. Reviewed by Bobby Derie.

In the development of Lovecraft studies as a scholarly pursuit above and beyond the level of fandom, Ken Faig holds a pivotal place. While Dirk W. Mosig is often acknowledged as raising the standard of literary criticism of H. P. Lovecraft and his work during the 1970s, it was Ken Faig who set the standard for research into the facts of Lovecraft's life and ancestry. From *Lovecraftian Voyages* (1973) to the mammoth genealogical project that was *Some of the Descendants of Asaph Phillips and Esther Whipple* (1993) to the current volume, Faig's half-century career has been marked with meticulous research—and his hard work, not always acknowledged but influential on every biography published on Lovecraft since 1975, has deepened our understanding of Lovecraft, his family, life, and fiction.

Lovecraftian People and Places is a collection of Faig's latest essays, focused on the finer details of Lovecraft's life: his genealogy, the places he lived and his neighbors there, some possible inspirations for his fiction, and his amateur journalism career. In Faig's own words, "It is really a matter of adding bits and pieces at this point"—but that does not really do this book justice. These essays represent Advanced Lovecraft Studies, of a kind that very few scholars are capable of, and shine a penetrating light on some of the murkier corners of Lovecraft's life and work.

To appreciate the importance of Faig's work, it is necessary to understand that there while interest in Lovecraft's life and personality have been entwined with interest in his fiction almost from the first, there has been very little hard data. Most of the information about Lovecraft's life came from himself, through his letters or brief essays such as "Some Notes on a Nonentity" (1933). Early biographical pieces on Lovecraft, including Winfield Townley Scott's "His Own Most Fantastic Creation: Howard Phillips Lovecraft" (1944) and August Derleth's *H. P. L.: A Memoir* (1945), focused on Lovecraft's immediate life and upbringing, based largely on his letters or memories of those still living who knew him. They were not scouring city directories and vital records, scrutinizing names and dates on gravestones and in family Bibles. Consequently, they repeated many "facts" without verification. Even Lovecraft erred in some aspects of his own genealogy, copying errors from his paternal great-aunt's chart.

Bonus dormitat, H.P.L.? Nothing to fear: Ken Faig is here.

The first four essays in this book cover issues of genealogy. "Devonshire Ancestry of Howard Phillips Lovecraft" examines Lovecraft's assertions about the origin of the name Lovecraft or Lovecroft from his letters and traces them back to England; "Edward Francis Gamwell and His Family" examines the husband of his surviving aunt Annie Emeline Phillips Gamwell; "George Elliott Lovecraft: Lost Scion of the House of Lovecraft" attempts to trace Lovecraft's paternal cousin; and "Lovecraft Was Our Neighbor: The People of The Arsdale" surveys the neighbors who occupied the boarding-house next door to 66 College Street, Lovecraft's final residence—who included Marion F. Bonner, one of Lovecraft's last correspondents, whose letters have lately been republished in *Letters to Family and Family Friends* (2020).

Genealogy is often more of an exercise in frustration than facts. Good researchers such as Faig have taken advantage of multiple sources of data: family records, census, city directories, tombstones, newspaper obituaries, etc., but the mass of accumulated names and dates do not often agree. Even today, when so many records are online through databases such as Ancestry.com and the Church of Latter-Day Saints' Family History Library, a potential researcher is struck with spelling errors and vague ages in census forms and obituaries, name changes and variations, gaps from records that are lost, destroyed, or undigitized. Building a

Lovecraft family tree is not as simple as filling in some names and birth, death, and marriage dates, especially when you get into the cousins like George Elliott Lovecraft: these people had complicated, messy lives, and we have incomplete data with which to try and trace them. To be able to put together even a sketch of their lives is the result of considerable diligence and keen insight. Finding out where all Lovecraft and his family lived and who his neighbors were might seem, by comparison, a bit of black magic—but that is all part of what Faig has been doing for the last fifty years, scouring records and putting the pieces of the puzzle together to get a better picture of Lovecraft's life, family, and ancestry.

The second group of essays is focused on Lovecraft's homes in Providence: "The Story of 454 Angell Street: The Birthplace of Howard Phillips Lovecraft" deals with Lovecraft's childhood home; "The People of 598–600 Angell Street" examines the house where Lovecraft and his mother lived after the death of his grandfather forced the breakup of that home; and "Can You Direct Me to Ely Court? Some Notes on 66 College Street" takes a look at Lovecraft's final residence atop the "antient hill." These are best understood as addenda to standard works such as *I Am Providence:* they are individual essays that expand on these individual localities rather than an effort to systematically examine every house or apartment Lovecraft stayed at.

If readers are left wondering how this applies to Lovecraft's fiction, they need look no further than two of Faig's best essays in this volume: "The Site of Joseph Curwen's Home in *The Case of Charles Dexter Ward*" and "Ethnic Names in Lovecraft's 'The Dreams in the Witch House.'" Here, Faig opens the genealogist's toolbox to answer literary questions. While many critics have read autobiographical elements into Lovecraft's fiction, or appreciated the depth of his research into the settings and details of his story in terms of geography, astronomy, etc., very few have thought to check census data and city directories to gauge why Lovecraft might have placed a certain house at a particular address, or peopled Arkham with Polish immigrants with particular names. As with filling in the gaps of the Lovecraft family tree, the results are not usually definitive, but present interesting and insightful probabilities—the revelation at the end is who really lived at 6 Olney Court in Providence during 1927–28 is one that may well surprise even serious students of Lovecraft.

Another fascinating essay is "John Osborne Austin's Seven Club Tales: Did They Inspire Lovecraft?," which examines in depth two very obscure works from Lovecraft's library: *The Journal of William Jefferay, Gentleman* (1899) and *More Seven Club Tales* (1900). These hoary volumes of turn-of-the-century weird fiction cast back to the days of Colonial Rhode Island, and Faig's survey of the contents shows how in some ways Lovecraft was part of a traditional of weird fiction set in Rhode Island and inspired by its rich history.

The final essays in the book deal with Lovecraft's efforts in amateur journalism. "The Providence Amateur Press Club: 1914–16" is mostly remembered today for its two most famous members, H. P. Lovecraft and John Dunn—and the latter mostly for what he had to say about Lovecraft. Lovecraft's letters to Dunn were recently reprinted in *Letters to Alfred Galpin and Others* (2020), and this essay gives additional context and background to how Lovecraft and Dunn came to meet and their final falling out.

"The Lovecraft–Gidlow Centenary" examines another often-overlooked episode in Lovecraft's life, and one of the few points where he intersects LGBTQ+ history. Elsie Alice Gidlow was an amateur journalist and poet contemporary with Lovecraft, but she was also a lesbian, author of *On a Grey Thread* (1923), the first book of lesbian poetry in the United States, and co-editor/publisher of *Les Mouches Fantastiques* (1918–20), an amateur journal that included works on homosexuality—which Lovecraft and other amateurs commented on. By chance, Lovecraft and Gidlow ended up as presidents of rival branches of the United Amateur Press Association in 1917, and this piece written a hundred years later revisits how both of them came to that position, and what they accomplished.

Lovecraftian People and Places is a book in keeping with the best of Faig's scholarship, meticulous in its research and cogent in its presentation. Those who study the life and work of H. P.

Lovecraft would do well to appreciate how Faig handles the sometimes conflicting evidence uncovered, how he balances Lovecraft's letters and stories with other records, and how he evaluates the whole within the historical context. There is solid detective work here, and if readers take away nothing else from this book, it should be one thing:

There is more about H. P. Lovecraft to be considered. Keep digging.

H. P. LOVECRAFT. *Miscellaneous Letters*. Edited by David E. Schultz and S. T. Joshi. New York: Hippocampus Press, 2022. 597 pp. $30 tpb.
H. P. LOVECRAFT. *Letters to Woodburn Harris and Others*. Edited by S. T. Joshi and David E. Schultz. New York: Hippocampus Press, 2022. 514 pp. $30 tpb. Reviewed by Martin Andersson.

As the huge (and hugely important) project of bringing the entirety of H. P. Lovecraft's extant letters into print is slowly approaching its goal, these two latest installments serve as a reminder of how lucky *and* unlucky we, the readers and scholars, are. Lovecraft's correspondence can, as is well known, best be characterized as staggeringly voluminous, with the most reliable estimates of the total number of letters ranging from 60,000 to 80,000. Of this vast mass of paper, only a fraction has survived—but what a fraction!

The first volume here reviewed is the reminder of what is lost (or, in the best of worlds, at least unavailable). For most of the correspondents in this book, only a handful of letters, or one letter, or even a fragment of a letter, has survived, hinting at the extent of what once was. It is frustrating to see that what we have of Lovecraft's letters to Houdini is a P.S. scribbled on an envelope. And of his vast correspondence with his wife Sonia (described by her as amounting to "a trunkful" before she burned it), only a single postcard and a few scraps embedded in "[Nietzscheism and Realism]" and "[Lovecraft on Love]" have come down to us. The sources of the text are as varied as the letters themselves; in some cases, the editors have had to decipher images from bookdealers" websites. (Putting this book together has clearly been a herculean task—more demanding than ever before in this series—and Messrs. Schultz and Joshi deserve the greatest accolades for their efforts.)

But there is still an abundance of riches in this book: not only are there many letters, but they are occasionally quite lengthy and their recipients are a mixed and varied bunch, to say the least. The letters to the Kleicomolo and the Gallomo—two round-robin correspondence cycles involving Lovecraft, Rheinhart Kleiner, Ira A. Cole, and Maurice W. Moe, and Lovecraft, Moe, and Alfred Galpin, respectively—while few in number, make up almost one fifth of the book. There are postcards to the aged amateur journalist Jonathan E. Hoag, for whose birthdays Lovecraft used to write congratulatory poems; one letter to the African-American literary critic William Stanley Braithwaite; the odd letter to pulp writers H. Warner Munn, Seabury Quinn, and Carl Jacobi; and letters to fans such as Charles D. Hornig, Julius Schwartz, and Forrest J Ackerman, to mention but a few. In all, the table of contents lists more than fifty correspondents (counting a few stray letters addressed to people covered earlier in the series), and in addition to these there is a large section of letters previously published in various newspapers and journals, such as the *Scientific American* and the *Providence Sunday Journal*, including both sides of Lovecraft's feud-by-correspondence with the hapless astrologer J. F. Hartmann.

As a direct consequence of this great variation, more aspects of Lovecraft's personality than usual in these letter collections are on display: the weird fiction connoisseur, the philosopher, the antiquarian, the traveler, the commentator on his times—as always presented in his inimitable style, frequently sprinkled with a healthy dose of his sharp wit. Old readers of the series will know what to expect.

The book also contains a few letters by others. There is a brief versified New Year's greeting by Hoag, and one fairly long (and interesting) letter by the future Mrs. Lovecraft. The greatest number of non-Lovecraft letters appear in the chapter on Harold S. Farnese—not because Farnese was a tremendously important or even interesting correspondent, but because his misinterpretation of what Lovecraft actually wrote to him lead to the (no doubt inadvertent) fabrication of the infamous "Black Magic Quote" later used by August Derleth in support of the erroneous view of Lovecraft's work and thought that hampered serious Lovecraft criticism for decades.

The by now customary appendix of related material is very brief in this volume: it is limited to the score for the elegy that Farnese (a composer) wrote for Lovecraft.

Then we have the other volume reviewed here, containing the letters to J. C. Henneberger, Edwin Baird, Farnsworth Wright, Walter John Coates, Woodburn Harris, Zealia Brown Reed Bishop, and William Lumley—and it is the other side of the coin: a reminder of what has been rescued from oblivion. The letter to Henneberger (owner of *Weird Tales*) surfaced at the Harry Ransom Center only a few years ago. Only a few letters to Harris survive—but one of them is the longest known letter by Lovecraft: "[I]t comes to just *70 pages*—being, so far as I recall, the longest letter I have ever written in a lifetime now numbering 39 years, 2 months, and 26 days." And a cache of letters addressed to Zealia Bishop was fortuitously discovered by her relatives and purely by accident came to the attention of the H. P. Lovecraft Historical Society.

As might be expected, Lovecraft's wide range of learning and interests is once more on display. That long letter to Harris (a farmer and former teacher of English and drama, living in Vermont) may serve as an example: it starts with a discussion of American civilization, moves on to the background of the Greek and Elizabethan dramas, then the reader is hit with lamentations of the approaching machine-culture age, followed by a discussion of the psychology of sex (!), and later the importance of precision in language—and *we are only a little more than halfway through the letter!*

The letters to Bishop are worth singling out. For all his (primarily posthumous) fame as a master of weird fiction, Lovecraft himself considered his profession to be that of the revisionist and ghostwriter, so that it is unfortunate that so little of his interactions with his clients has been preserved. As far as I know, the only revision clients to whom there are letters still extant are Adolphe de Castro and Zealia Bishop. In his letters to her, we see Lovecraft not only as her revisionist, but as her mentor and advisor in matters of writing and literature.

The customary appendix is stuffed to the gills with goodies: a poem by Farnsworth Wright, a letter from Woodburn Harris to Vrest Orton asking about Lovecraft's death, Zealia Bishop's story "One-Man Girl" that Lovecraft revised (reprinted here for the first time, as far as I can tell—it is not particularly good, but it definitely must be more Bishop than Lovecraft and thus forms a good indicator of how little Bishop there is in, e.g., "The Mound"), and a few poems by Lumley (one of which, "The Ferryman", is not likely to have been revised by Lovecraft).

As the series winds down (only about three additional volumes are forthcoming), I doff my hat to S. T. Joshi, David E. Schultz and Derrick M. Hussey for pulling off this mind-blowing project, which I dared not even *imagine* a quarter-century ago. My most heartfelt thanks!

www.ingramcontent.com/pod-product-compliance
Lightning Source LLC
Chambersburg PA
CBHW051817090426
42736CB00011B/1529